The Anatomy of Insults in Shakespeare's World

RELATED TITLES

The Merchant of Venice: A Critical Reader
Edited by Sarah Hatchuel and Nathalie Vienne-Guerrin
978-1-3500-8229-8

Shakespeare's Insults: A Pragmatic Dictionary
Nathalie Vienne-Guerrin
978-0-8264-9833-5

Shakespeare and London: A Dictionary
Sarah Dustagheer
978-1-3500-0682-9

The Anatomy of Insults in Shakespeare's World

Nathalie Vienne-Guerrin

THE ARDEN SHAKESPEARE
LONDON • NEW YORK • OXFORD • NEW DELHI • SYDNEY

THE ARDEN SHAKESPEARE
Bloomsbury Publishing Plc
50 Bedford Square, London, WC1B 3DP, UK
1385 Broadway, New York, NY 10018, USA
29 Earlsfort Terrace, Dublin 2, Ireland

BLOOMSBURY, THE ARDEN SHAKESPEARE and the Arden Shakespeare logo are trademarks of Bloomsbury Publishing Plc

First published in Great Britain 2022
This paperback edition published 2023

Copyright © Nathalie Vienne-Guerrin, 2022

Nathalie Vienne-Guerrin has asserted her right under the Copyright, Designs and Patents Act, 1988, to be identified as the author of this work.

For legal purposes the Acknowledgements on pp. viii–x constitute an extension of this copyright page.

Cover design by Charlotte Daniels
Cover images: Taken from *The Historie of Foure-Footed Beastes* by Edward Topsell (© Folger Shakespeare Library)

All rights reserved. No part of this publication may be reproduced or transmitted in any form or by any means, electronic or mechanical, including photocopying, recording, or any information storage or retrieval system, without prior permission in writing from the publishers.

Bloomsbury Publishing Plc does not have any control over, or responsibility for, any third-party websites referred to or in this book. All internet addresses given in this book were correct at the time of going to press. The author and publisher regret any inconvenience caused if addresses have changed or sites have ceased to exist, but can accept no responsibility for any such changes.

A catalogue record for this book is available from the British Library.

Library of Congress Control Number: 2022933409

ISBN:	HB:	978-1-3500-5549-0
	PB:	978-1-3503-2861-7
	ePDF:	978-1-3500-5551-3
	eBook:	978-1-3500-5550-6

Typeset by Integra Software Services Pvt. Ltd.

To find out more about our authors and books visit www.bloomsbury.com and sign up for our newsletters.

To my other self, Sarah Hatchuel;
to my dear friend, Victoria Bladen;
to my wonderful family;
and to the healing power of words

CONTENTS

Acknowledgements viii
List of abbreviations xi

Introduction: 'No abuse?' 1

1   The spectacular rhetoric of insult 19
2   The 'merry war': Insult as a love game 49
3   'Quarrelling by the book': Insult and duelling codes 81
4   Insults as actionable words 111
5   Insult and the taming of the tongue 143
6   The trauma of insult 173
7   Insult beyond words 207

Epilogue: Shakespeare's theatre of insult 241

Notes 249
Bibliography of work cited 285
Detailed outline 304
Index 307

ACKNOWLEDGEMENTS

My first thanks go to The Arden Shakespeare, especially to Lara Bateman and Mark Dudgeon, for their trust, generous help, constant support and benevolent patience.

Like the *Dictionary* that preceded it, this book is the fruit of more than twenty-five years of work on Shakespeare's insults. This work started under the supervision of Pierre Iselin when I was a PhD student. I remain grateful to him for accompanying me during so many joyful years of research.

The idea of this book emerged when I was a lecturer at the University of Rouen, and I wish to warmly thank my faithful friends Michèle Willems and Raymond Willems for encouraging me from the beginning to the end of this project.

Finishing this book at the Université Paul-Valéry Montpellier 3, I also wish to thank my Montpellier friends and colleagues. My deep gratitude goes to the members of the Institut de Recherche sur la Renaissance, l'âge Classique et les Lumières (IRCL, UMR5186 CNRS/Université Paul-Valéry Montpellier 3) for the help and support they have constantly brought me. I warmly thank Jean-Pierre Schandeler, Brigitte Belin and Vanessa Kuhner-Blaha for their invaluable human and logistic support, without which I could not have put the finishing touch to this book. My deep gratitude also goes to my Montpellier friends and daily research companions, Janice Valls-Russell, Florence March, Jean-Christophe Mayer and Pierre Kapitaniak, with all of whom it is a pleasure to work, for their understanding support and friendship. It is a great privilege to work with such a team, in such a stimulating research environment, with the invaluable support of the Université Paul-Valéry Montpellier 3 and the CNRS, the latter of which I wish to warmly thank for generously granting me a research leave from September 2018 to February 2019. I also wish to thank my colleagues from the English department for allowing me to put my teaching and administrative tasks aside during my research leave and I am very grateful to my students for the stimulating discussions I regularly have with them, not exclusively but especially on the topic of Shakespearean insults.

I also wish to thank other colleagues who have encouraged and helped me in one way or another on this long journey: Leo Carruthers, Évelyne Larguèche, François Laroque, Ann Lecercle, Jean-Marie Maguin, Marie-Madeleine Martinet, Patricia Parker, Christopher R. Wilson. I am grateful to Dominique Goy-Blanquet and the members of the Société Française Shakespeare for giving me the opportunity to discuss my methods and ideas on several occasions. I am very grateful to my friend Andrew Hiscock with whom it has been a privilege and a pleasure to work for many years now.

I wholeheartedly thank my dear friend and colleague Victoria Bladen for her so generous help in correcting this book.

My deepest gratitude goes to my friend – the best friend in the world – and now Montpellier colleague, Sarah Hatchuel, for the unfailing support she has brought me since 1998. It is a real treat to work with her, and her friendship is invaluable.

I finally owe loads of gratitude to my family for their unfailing patience, love and support: my dear mother, Geneviève Vienne, my dear brothers, Jean-Paul Vienne and Frédéric Vienne, and my dear sisters, Catherine Fortin and Fanette Devin.

I again wholeheartedly thank my children, Pierre, François, Clément, Nicolas and Sophie, for their incredible patience, and my husband, Serge Guerrin, for his constant love and patient understanding.

This book being the fruit of a long-term research, I have used some of the material that appeared in earlier publications, mostly in French: 'L'anatomie de l'insulte dans *1 Henry IV*', *Bulletin de la Société de Stylistique Anglaise* 17 (1996): 21–35; 'Des mauvaises langues dans *Richard III*', XVII–XVIII. *Revue de la Société d'études anglo-américaines des* XVIIe *et*

*XVIII*ᵉ *siècles* 49 (November 1999): 55–76; 'La réécriture de la Mégère dans le théâtre de Shakespeare', in *Réécritures*, ed. Jean-Pierre Maquerlot, Publications de l'Université de Rouen, 2000, 77–92 ; 'La réécriture des codes de duel dans l'injure Shakespearienne', in *Réécritures*, ed. Jean-Pierre Maquerlot, Publications de l'Université de Rouen, 2000, 37–53; 'L'injure et la guerre dans *Troilus and Cressida*', *Bulletin de la Société de Stylistique Anglaise* 22 (2001): 21–36; '"Killing courtesy": *Le Songe* ou la courtoisie mise en pièce(s)', *XVII–XVIII. Revue de la Société d'études anglo-américaines des XVII*ᵉ *et XVIII*ᵉ *siècles* 55 (2002): 27–49; 'Les jeux de l'injure dans *Henry IV*', in *Shakespeare et le Jeu*, Proceedings of the Société Française Shakespeare Conference, ed. Pierre Kapitaniak, 2005, 185–99; 'Le miel et le fiel: des excès de bouche dans *Timon of Athens*', in *Shakespeare et l'excès*, Proceedings of the Société Française Shakespeare Conference, ed. Pierre Kapitaniak and Jean-Michel Déprats, 2007, 206–22; '"He'll rail in his rope/robe tricks": l'injure comme feu d'artifices dans *The Taming of the Shrew*', in *L'artifice*, ed. Élisabeth Angel-Perez and Pierre Iselin, *Sillages Critiques* 10 (2009); '"'tis worse than murder": *King Lear* ou les derniers outrages', in *'The true blank of thine eye', Approches Critiques de* King Lear, ed. Pascale Drouet and Pierre Iselin, Presses Universitaires de la Sorbonne, 2009, 265–78 ; '"His meanest Garment": la mémoire du mot dans *Cymbeline*', Proceedings of the 2013 Société Française Shakespeare Conference, 2013, 167–81.

An earlier version of part of Chapter 6 was published in English in '"You Have Rated Me": The Insults of *The Merchant of Venice*', *Literaria Pragensia* 23, no. 45 (September 2013), *Memory, Conflict & Commerce in Early Modern Europe*, ed. Martin Procházka, Paola Spinozzi and Rui Carvalho Homem, 82–97. It is with the journal's kind permission that I have included a sub-section of this article in this book.

LIST OF ABBREVIATIONS

AC	*Antony and Cleopatra*
AW	*All's Well That Ends Well*
AYL	*As You Like It*
CE	*The Comedy of Errors*
Cor	*Coriolanus*
Cym	*Cymbeline*
Ham	*Hamlet*
1H4	*King Henry IV, Part 1*
2H4	*King Henry IV, Part 2*
H5	*King Henry V*
1H6	*King Henry VI, Part 1*
2H6	*King Henry VI, Part 2*
3H6	*King Henry VI, Part 3*
H8	*King Henry VIII*
JC	*Julius Caesar*
KJ	*King John*
KL	*King Lear*
LLL	*Love's Labour's Lost*
Luc	*The Rape of Lucrece*
MA	*Much Ado About Nothing*
Mac	*Macbeth*
MM	*Measure for Measure*
MND	*A Midsummer Night's Dream*
MV	*The Merchant of Venice*
MW	*The Merry Wives of Windsor*
Oth	*Othello*
Per	*Pericles*
R2	*King Richard II*
R3	*King Richard III*

RJ	*Romeo and Juliet*
Son	*Sonnets*
TC	*Troilus and Cressida*
Tem	*The Tempest*
TGV	*The Two Gentlemen of Verona*
Tim	*Timon of Athens*
Tit	*Titus Andronicus*
TN	*Twelfth Night*
TNK	*The Two Noble Kinsmen*
TS	*The Taming of the Shrew*
VA	*Venus and Adonis*
WT	*The Winter's Tale*

The edition of reference for the Shakespeare quotations is, for each play, the Arden Shakespeare, Third Series.

In the quotations from early printed texts, I have just restored 'v' into 'u' and reversely, and 'i' into 'j'.

Introduction: 'No abuse?'

'No abuse?' (*2H4*, 2.4.321): after years of exploration of Shakespeare's insults, I think that this phrase best illustrates the complexities of the insulting speech act, the issue of intentionality it raises, the instability that characterizes it, the volatile effect of words that it reveals, the pragmatic approach that it demands, the theatrical liveliness it contains, the critical moment it often represents and the questioning of the limits that it entails. The word 'abuse' is as polysemic now as it was in Shakespeare's days: it could mean to 'misuse', to 'deceive', to 'to use yll, dishonestly, uncomely, contrary to that it serveth for: to use out of order, or in vaine: also to weare out'.[1] Catachresis, the improper use of a word, was defined by George Puttenham as 'the figure of abuse';[2] abuse could refer to violation but it was also associated with offense, for example, in John Florio's definitions of *Ingiuria* as 'injurie, wrong, abuse, misusage, trespasse, offence, hurt, displeasure' or of *Malfare* glossed as 'to misdoe, to do ill, to do wrong, to abuse.'[3] If one considers the *Oxford English Dictionary*,[4] it seems that the Elizabethan period saw the emergence and consolidation of the word in its meaning of 'verbal insult' or 'contemptuous or insulting language; reviling, scurrility'[5] and 'injury, wrong, insult'.[6]

'No abuse?': for Poins, who has just heard Falstaff disparaging Hal and then heard Old John claim that he did not intend to 'abuse' the prince, the question means 'No offence?' 'No insult?' and it answers Falstaff's denial of any kind of abuse: according to the old Knight, in the festive context of *Henry IV*, words of dispraise cannot possibly hurt or be outrageous:

> No abuse, Ned, i'th' world! Honest Ned, none. I dispraised him before the wicked, [*to Prince*] that the wicked might not fall in love with thee – in which doing, I have done the part of a careful friend and a true subject, and thy father is to give me thanks for it. No abuse, Hal; none, Ned, none. No, faith, boys, none.
>
> (*2H4*, 2.4.322–8)

Falstaff's 'palpable' (*1H4*, 2.4.219) lying self-justification expresses the paradox that is at the heart of the play: 'abuse' can be 'the part of a careful friend and a true subject' indeed. As McLaverty notes on the tavern scenes in *Henry IV*:

> Paradoxically, it is when the Prince and Falstaff are most in conflict, when they are exchanging abuse, that they are most aware of how close they are and how much they share. In their efforts to cap insults they reveal their familiarity with and dependence on, one another.[7]

Yet Falstaff's defence in this 'No abuse' sequence, which is evidently part of his art of comic improvisation, also reveals that what went without saying in the festive world of Part 1 – that there was no abuse between the two verbal sparring partners – no longer goes without saying in the darker world of Part 2, where, as McLaverty notes, the two characters lose 'the intimacy which makes abuse innocuous'.[8]

This 'No abuse?' reveals the unpredictability and variability of the effect words can have on an addressee, an aspect that Évelyne Larguèche has theorized as *l'effet injure* (the insulting effect), showing that the impact of words can only be assessed and explained from a 'pragmatic' perspective, that is, in a specific context of enunciation.[9] According to Larguèche, insult does not exist per se but what matters is the insulting *effect*, that is, etymologically, what it does or make, effect deriving from *ex-facere*. The fiction that Falstaff spins to defuse the insulting impact – a word deriving from *impingere*, meaning to 'strike against', to 'drive into' – that his words may have had on Prince Hal, the verbal shield that he tries to erect, shows that the same words may lead to different interpretations, different receptions, that they can be emitted in one way and received in another, and can be 'abuse' to one while they are 'no abuse' to another.

The question 'No abuse?' suggests that the art of insult that characterizes the festive world of the first part of *Henry IV* is put into question in the second part but it also expresses the ambivalence of the tongue that delivers words whose effects can be unexpected. 'Quò tendis?',[10] 'Whether goest thou?',[11] 'No Heart can thinke, to what strange ends, / The Tongues unruely Motion tends':[12] the mottoes accompanying Claude Paradin's and George Wither's emblems of the tongue seem to find their reflection in Poins' comic incredulous interrogation: 'No abuse?' The question reveals that the same words of abuse can point in different directions and reach different aims. They can be ludic and serious, benevolent and malevolent, benign and lethal, and they can find their place in comic as well as tragic agendas and often both at the same time. Insults are indeed emblematic of the ambivalence that, according to Mikhail Bakhtin, characterizes the world of carnival, where insults, while 'humiliating and mortifying', are 'at the same time revived and re-newed'. According to Bakhtin, 'It was precisely this ambivalent abuse which determined the genre of speech in carnival intercourse'.[13]

The insulting effect: To do or not to do things with words

The ambivalence of insults is inscribed in the definition and etymology of the words that most often refer to this speech act: insult, abuse and injury, three words in which the verbal merges with the physical.

The etymology of the word 'insult' is interesting. It derives from the Latin word *insultus*, related to *saltus*: a leap (*sauter sur* in French). In his *Dictionarium Linguae Latinae et Anglicanae* published in 1587, Thomas Thomas defines the term as follows:

> Insulto, as, ex In & Salto. To leape up, to rebound, to leape up for joy: to scorne, to delude, to speake or doe in reproch of one: to insult, triumph in words, or vaunt over: to rejoyce at: to thump or beat at.[14]

In *A World of Words,* John Florio defines *Insultare* as 'to insult, to injurie, to delude, to scorne, to offer wrong, to reproch. Also to leape, to rebound or leape up for joy'.[15] In his *Dictionary in Spanish and English* (1599), Richard Perceval, defines *Insultár* as 'to insult or leape on, to triumph or vaunt over in disdainfull manner'.[16] Randle Cotgrave's *A Dictionary of the French and English Tongues* (1611) reads: 'Insulter. To insult, crow, vaunt, or triumph over; to wrong, reproach, affront; contemne; also, to rebound, rejoice at, leape for joy.'[17] The link between insult and triumph is articulated in Shakespeare's plays, where the word, which is relatively rarely used, conveys a triumphant, exulting reaction.

In *King Lear*, Oswald describes the way he has been mistreated by Kent by using the word. When Cornwall asks him 'What was th' offence you gave him [Kent]?', Oswald answers:

> I never gave him any.
> It pleas'd the King his master very late
> To strike at me upon his misconstruction,
> When he [Kent], conjunct, and flattering his displeasure,
> Tripped me behind; being down, *insulted*, rail'd
> And put upon him such a deal of man
> That worthied him, got praises of the King
> For him attempting who was self-subdued;
> And, in the fleshment of this dread exploit,
> Drew on me here again.
>
> (KL, 2.2.112–22)

'No offence', says Oswald, 'I never gave him any'. The word 'insult' is here literally associated with a physical assault ('tripp'd me behind') and the leap of triumph is suggested by the reference to the 'dread exploit'. In *As You Like It*, Rosalind uses the word when she chides Phoebe for scorning Silvius: 'Who might be your mother, / That you insult, exult, and all at once, / Over the wretched?' (*AYL*, 3.5.36–8). In the two cases the insult is associated with a position of superiority, and yet Phoebe previously claimed she did not want to hurt Silvius: 'I would not be thy executioner / I fly thee for I would not injure thee' (*AYL*, 3.5.8–9). The word 'injure' here has a physical meaning, but in the context of this scene, it can also be in resonance with the word 'insult', the two terms combining the physical and the verbal.

No injury? The meaning of the word 'injury', which appears more regularly than the word 'insult' in Shakespeare's plays, also invites exploration. Claude Hollyband, in his *Dictionary French and English* (1593), briefly defines the French word 'injure' as 'wrong, injurie' and 'Tort & dommage' as 'injurie, wrong, hurt'.[18] Cotgrave defines 'S'Entr'injurier' as 'To revile, or abuse, one another' and 'Injurier' as 'To wrong, injure, misuse, abuse; hurt, offend; outrage; miscall, reproach, revile, rayle on'.[19] These definitions give an idea of the cloud of words referring to Shakespeare's insults that this book aims to anatomize.

What emerges from the Elizabethan lexicons is that the term 'injury' is related to the legal field of *jus, juris*. It is this meaning of the word 'injury' that is at the heart of *Romeo and Juliet* (3.1.65; 67) when Tybalt challenges Romeo. The word refers to an injury in deed, a form of transgression, an infringement of the law that Romeo's presence at the ball meant for Tybalt:

TYBALT
  Boy, this shall not excuse the *injuries*
  That thou hast done me; therefore turn and draw.
ROMEO
  I do protest I never injuried thee, […]
                                         (*RJ*, 3.1.65–7)

'No injury', says Romeo, while, from Tybalt's perspective, there has been an injury indeed and *in deed*. The question of 'the law' that is or is not on one's 'side' is present from the opening scene of the play through the questions raised about the thumb-biting provocation in a sequence that can be seen as a variation on the 'No abuse?' motif.[20]

Thus, the three terms 'abuse', 'insult' and 'injury' can refer to both the verbal and physical fields, and their uses all point to the articulation of saying and doing. The roots of the philosophy of language that J. L. Austin famously formulated in his *How to Do Things with Words*[21] are obviously present in Shakespeare's metalinguistic comments on insults.

Scholars such as Évelyne Larguèche or Pierre Guiraud have stressed the link between insult and the body. For them, insults have to do with the body, and when you insult someone, you *do* more than you *say*. In a book on bad language – *gros mots* in French –, Pierre Guiraud refers to the 'vocal and physical expressivity of insults' and notes that an insult is a 'speech act, a speech that is a deed through which the insulter physically faces the insulted'.[22] For Guiraud, the insulting speech act is similar to and often accompanied by spitting,[23] an idea that Shakespeare spectacularly dramatizes when Lady Anne spits at Richard (*R3*, 1.2.147),[24] thus revealing how, with insults, saying may dissolve into doing. Larguèche describes insults as 'screams that are disguised as words',[25] or 'a speech in which words constitute verbal gestures even more than a language'.[26] She compares insults to an 'infant's cries' that are a vocal expression and at the same time 'a desperate effort you make to avoid stifling'.[27] She explains that the bodily dimension of what she calls 'non-specific insults' – insults whose meaning seems to be disconnected from any aspect that would be specific to the insulted[28] – can be described as being sexualized, in so far as words are treated like projectiles, objects. These revivify or 'as it were, reincarnate [...] the oral cavity of the mouth, [giving] the mouth a sensorial dimension which the usual speech activity as a means of transmission using words for their meaning, tends to make us forget'.[29] Thus for her, with insult, the voice becomes re-sexualized as it no longer is a means of transmitting words and meanings, but it is an extension of the body.[30]

Insults stimulate reflections on the power of words. In *Language and Symbolic Power*, Pierre Bourdieu considers the relationships between words and deeds from another perspective. Bourdieu notes that insults are one way, among others ('gossip, slander, lies, [...], commendations, criticisms, arguments and praises') with which the 'social agent' has 'the power to name and to create the world through naming'.[31]

For Bourdieu,

> [T]he 'qualifying nouns' ('idiot', 'bastard') which feature in insult have a very limited symbolic efficacy as *idios logos*, and involve only the person who offers them. But what both [i.e. insults and common nouns] have in common is what may be called a performative or magical intention. Insults, like naming, belong to a class of more or less socially based acts of institution and destitution through which an individual, acting in his own name or in the name of a group that is more or less important in terms of its size and social significance indicates to someone that he possesses such and such property, and indicates to him at the time that he must conduct himself in accordance with the social essence which is thereby assigned to him.[32]

The insulter creates the other by insulting him or her. Stressing the limits of J. L. Austin's approach, Bourdieu notes that it is a mistake to '[look] within words for the power of words, that is, looking for it where it is not to be found'.[33] To him, it amounts to forgetting that 'authority comes to language from outside, a fact concretely exemplified by the *skeptron* that, in Homer, is passed to the orator who is about to speak'.[34] Bourdieu notes that:

> The symbolic efficacy of words is exercised only in so far as the person subjected to it recognizes the person who

exercises it as authorized to do so, or, what amounts to the same thing, only in so far as he fails to realize that, in submitting to it, he himself has contributed, through his recognition, to its establishment.[35]

Bourdieu further explains that:

> Symbolic imposition – that kind of magical efficacy which not only the command and the password, but also ritual discourse or a simple injunction, or even threats or insults, purport to exercise – can function only if there is a convergence of social conditions which are altogether distinct from the strictly linguistic logic of discourse.[36]

Thus, Bourdieu revisits Austin's theory to develop his vision of pragmatic sociology. The aborted marriage sequence in *Much Ado* may be seen in the light of Bourdieu's view as it seems that Don Pedro's position of authority has a crucial impact on the way words institute things in the church scene:

LEONATO [*To Don Pedro*]
  Sweet Prince, why speak not you?
DON PEDRO
            What should I speak?
  I stand dishonoured, that have gone about
  To link my dear friend to a common stale.
LEONATO
  Are these things spoken, or do I but dream?
DON JOHN
  Sir, they are spoken, and these things are true.
                    (*MA*, 4.1.62–6)

Don Pedro's testimony gives Claudio's words their destructive efficacy and allows Don John the villain to transform things 'spoken' into things 'true'. Once Don Pedro, the voice of authority, has been heard, Hero becomes the whore, the 'common stale' that she is wrongly accused of being and insult turns into a transformational act of naming. Accusation becomes truth. Coming from an authority, 'these things are spoken' *so* 'these things are true'. Relying on Don Pedro's position of authority, saying amounts to doing in a sequence that leads to Hero's symbolic death through words.

In *Excitable speech, A Politics of the Performative*, Judith Butler theorizes about the connection between the verbal and the physical when she stresses the physical impact that words can have. She notes that the only words we have to refer to verbal injury are borrowed from the field of physical injury:

> it appears that there is no language specific to the problem of linguistic injury, which is, as it were, forced to draw its vocabulary from physical injury. In this sense, it appears that the metaphorical connection between physical and linguistic vulnerability is essential to the description of linguistic vulnerability itself. On the one hand, that there appears to be no description that is 'proper' to linguistic injury makes it more difficult to identify the specificity of linguistic vulnerability over and against physical vulnerability. On the other hand, that physical metaphors seize upon every occasion to describe linguistic injury suggests that this somatic dimension may be important to the understanding of linguistic pain.[37]

In *The Force of Language*, Denise Riley also explores the overlapping of words and deeds when she notes that:

> Verbal attacks, in the moment they happen, resemble stoning. Then is it not too laboured to ask how they do damage: isn't the answer plain, that they hurt just as stones hurt? At the instant of their impact, so they do. Yet the peculiarity of violent words, as distinct from lumps of rock, is their power to resonate within their target for decades after the occasion on which they were weapons.[38]

Riley refers to the trauma of verbal assault in terms of 'anamnesia' or in terms of 'unforgetting': some words of insult are unforgettable.

In *A Slap in the Face*, William B. Irvine notes that the words 'humiliate', 'mortify' and 'sarcasm' express the physicality and materiality of insults and 'tell us something about how intense the pain caused by insults can be'. 'Humiliate', he notes, derives from the Latin *humus*, meaning 'ground' and it suggests that when you are humiliated, 'It feels like someone has pushed you to the ground and treated you like dirt'. The word 'mortify' is related to *mortificare*, meaning to kill while sarcasm derives from the Greek *sarkazein* and means 'to tear flesh'.[39]

'Foul wind' and 'poniards'

Shakespeare's plays oscillate between two contradictory and complementary visions of insults, two perspectives that are probably best illustrated in *Much Ado About Nothing*, a title which in itself shows the tension between opposite notions, 'much' and 'nothing'. Insults are both much and nothing, as two major metalinguistic comments show. On the one hand, the play dramatizes Benedick's outraged reaction to Beatrice's 'Lady Tongue' that he cannot 'endure' (*MA*, 2.1.251–2):

> I stood like a man at a mark, with a whole army shooting at me. She speaks poniards, and every word stabs. If her breath were as terrible as her terminations there were no living near her, she would infect to the North Star.
> (*MA*, 2.1.225–9)

Benedick here comments on the insults he has had to swallow in silence during the ball scene and that have apparently hurt him. Yet the play offers a counterpoint to this apprehension of insults, when Beatrice refers to Benedick's challenge to Claudio:

> Foul words is but foul wind, and foul wind is but foul breath, and foul breath is noisome, therefore I will depart unkissed.
> (*MA*, 5.2.49–51)

Here words are denounced as being inefficient ('wind'), compared with the materiality of the deed Beatrice has asked for, through the 'Kill Claudio' injunction (4.1.288). Yet, the word 'noisome' that is used to characterize 'foul breath' is justly glossed as 'offensive' by Claire McEachern.[40] 'Wind' can be a source of 'noise', that is of conflict, if we consider that *noise* in French means 'conflict' (hence the expression '*chercher des noises*'), as Kenneth Gross points out in *Shakespeare's Noise*.[41] *Much Ado* dramatizes this double side of 'foul breath', both the vanity and efficiency of insults. In *Much Ado*, Beatrice claims that 'foul word is but foul wind', while earlier on she denounces the way Claudio had undone her cousin with words: 'Sweet Hero! She is wronged, she is slandered, she is undone' (*MA*, 4.1.310–11).

Shakespeare's plays more generally convey this ambivalent conception of language. Words are approached in their efficient materiality on numerous occasions in metalinguistic comments. Saying amounts to doing when, at the beginning of *Richard II*, Mowbray refers to 'Slander's venomed spear' (*R2*, 1.1.171) or when, in *Antony and Cleopatra*, Antony declares to Pompey that 'We'll *speak* with thee at sea' (*AC*, 2.6.25), a line that suggests that speaking and fighting are one and the same thing. Shakespeare's plays are full of metaphors that describe tongues as weapons: 'you are *keen* my lord', says Ophelia to Hamlet (*Ham*, 3.2.241). In *Love's Labour's Lost*, Boyet declares that 'The tongues of mocking wenches are as keen/As is the razor's edge invisible' (*LLL*, 5.2.256–7), while Berowne asks Rosaline to punish him for his perjury as follows:

> Here stand I, lady; dart thy skill at me.
>   Bruise me with scorn, confound me with a flout;
> Thrust thy sharp wit quite through my ignorance,
>   Cut me to pieces with thy keen conceit, [...]
>   (*LLL*, 5.2.396–9)

The etymological meaning of the word 'sarcasm' ('tear flesh') is not far. Shakespeare's scripts tell us that tongues do hurt, through a series of tropes that are inherited from a biblical tradition and especially from the Proverbs: 'Life and death are in the power of the tongue' (Prov. 18–21), and James' Epistle 3 ('Of the Tongue'), according to which 'the tongue can no man tame; *it is* an unruly evil, full of deadly poison' (James 3: 7–8).[42]

In Shakespeare's plays, to insult means to act, but it also means *not to* act. Characters curse and abuse *because* they cannot act. The vanity of insults that may dissolve into thin air is recurrently thrown into relief. 'Talkers are no good doers', says one of the murderers in *Richard III* (*R3*, 1.3.350), thus opposing doing and saying. The war of tongues can be a ghostly war in which only air and wind circulate and that can in no way compete with deeds. Insults then may appear as a mere 'Abundance of superfluous breath' (*KJ*, 2.1.148), as is the case in *Richard III*, where they seem to be the weapons of the feeble, conveying the idea that 'calamity' is 'full of words' (*R3*, 4.4.126). In *Richard III*, women insult to act but also because they cannot act and their curses are reduced by Richard to the status of a mere din to which he opposes the noise of his trumpets so that the 'clamorous report of war' may 'drown [their] exclamations' (*R3*, 4.4.149–54). In the opening scene of *Richard II*, the war of tongues is described by Mowbray as 'a woman's war' (*R2*, 1.1.48–9), which is nothing compared to the duel that the two parties, himself and Bolingbroke, are asking for. All the insults that Mowbray and Bolingbroke exchange aim at triggering off the duel that they hope Richard will grant them. Thus, when Richard prevents them from switching from words to deeds, it is the very manliness of the two characters that he puts into question and denies, by forcing them to go no further than 'The bitter clamour of two eager tongues' (*R2*, 1.1.49). In *Timon of Athens*, Timon curses when he can no longer act and the flow of abuse and maledictions that he delivers may be heard as dissolving into a mere noise, be it nihilistic, a kind of babbling that cannot be efficient, except as a process through which the character evacuates his gall.[43] In *The Taming of the Shrew*, Petruccio debunks the power of words and expresses the vanity of insults when he ridicules Kate's noisy exclamations in a bombastic tirade starting with the question: 'Think you a little din can daunt mine ears?' (*TS*, 1.2.198).

Shakespeare thus dramatizes both the inefficiency of the tongue and its deadly efficacy, what Russ McDonald has termed 'Words effectual, Speech Unable' and it is in this context that the insults of the plays should be understood.[44]

The Shakespearean flyting or the phony war

What a few critics have identified as Shakespeare's flyting[45] can be seen as epitomizing the complexities of the tongue that are mapped by the Elizabethan 'tongue culture' or what I have called elsewhere the Elizabethan 'tonguescape'.[46] With flyting, the spectator is given access to the core of a tongue that is described by Erasmus, in his treatise *Lingua*, as an 'ambivalent organ'[47] or later by Thomas Adams, in his sermon 'The Taming of the Tongue' as an 'insubjectible subject'.[48]

The *OED* defines *flyting* as 'the action of flite, contention, wrangling; scolding, rebuking; a reproach' and as 'Poetical invective; chiefly, a kind of contest practised by the Scottish poets of the sixteenth century, in which two persons assailed each other alternately with tirades of abusive verse'. Priscilla Bawcutt notes that the words *flyting, flyte, flyter* were used before the sixteenth century to refer to non-literary practices, the old English word *flytan* meaning 'strive, dispute', an equivalent of the word 'scold'.[49] Yet it is also more specifically used to refer to a Scottish literary form of verbal fight, the most famous of which was *The Flyting of Dunbar and Kennedy*.[50] This was an exchange of insults in verse opposing two poets who, it is generally thought, had no real animosity towards each other. This flyting, that Tom Scott described in 1966 as 'the most repellent poem known to me in any language – a penance to read and write about',[51] is supposed to have been a game and constitutes a linguistic *tour de force* or verbal feat that is offered to readers who may decide who the winner is. This flyting is both a real-life practice and a literary form, both an expression of violence and a ritual.

Since Margaret Galway's 1935 article, that exclusively focused on the comedies,[52] few critics have explored the characteristics of this potentially highly theatrical speech act. But the term has led to several theoretical uses and constructions that articulate a distinction between 'ludic flyting', an expression which sounds a little redundant, and 'heroic flyting'.[53]

A few examples may illustrate the characteristics of what Johan Huizinga called 'slanging matches'.[54] In *The Dyer's Hand and other Essays*, W. H. Auden notes that the comic dimension of this verbal form of duelling derives from the fact that it associates two incompatible ingredients: anger and play.

> Flyting seems to have vanished as a studied literary art and only to survive in the impromptu exchanges of truckdrivers and cabdrivers. The comic effect arises from the contradiction between the insulting nature of what is said which appears to indicate a passionate relation of hostility and aggression, and the calculated skill of verbal invention which indicates that the protagonists are not thinking about each other but about language and their pleasure in employing it inventively. A man who is really passionately angry is speechless and can only express his anger by physical violence. Playful anger is intrinsically comic because, of all emotions, anger is the least compatible with play.[55]

In real everyday life, insulters usually have a limited stock of terms, always the same, to inveigh against their adversaries and to vent their anger. These words seem to burst out straight from the heart to the tongue, raw, unprocessed, without any form of art. Sounding like cries, insults seem to be the infancy of language in their inarticulation and their lack of syntax. Exclamations are hurled like 'sticks or stones',[56] all disordered. They are often uncontrolled verbal gestures[57] rather than mastered articulated speech. An angry person lacks imagination and always harps on the same terms. So that when, occasionally, a new term of abuse crops up in everyday exchanges, it seems to inevitably become a source of surprise and comedy and an object of comment. According to Auden, the artificiality of the new-coined insult contradicts the natural feeling of anger from which insults mainly derive. His analysis is an invitation to interrogate the complex interactions between anger and insults, between emotional excess and verbal excess, in an artistic, theatrical context. Real-life insults are obviously different from insults that are part of a theatrical fiction, but both find their main fuel in passion and anger. In *Emotional Excess on the Shakespearean Stage*, Bridget Escolme suggests that anger or choler is usually the cause or the effect of injuries. Considering that *Coriolanus* is a play about anger, she notes that 'anger is Martius' personal problem. When he is angry, then he "speaks / What's in his heart" '[58] (*Cor*, 3.3.28-9). What Auden throws into relief is the tension between emotion and game.

In *Shakespeare's Universe of Discourse*, Keir Elam defines flyting as a 'ritual exchange of abuse' and confirms Auden's vision of flyting, noting that 'that which makes the contest a worthy spectacle, is that the insults should be wittily and inventively varied. It is this witty inventiveness, and not the vilification that is on show.'[59] In *Forbidden Words: Taboo and the Censuring of Language*, the linguists Keith Allan and Kate Burridge relate this flyting tradition to its American contemporary version known as 'playing the dozens':

> Essentially, flyting and the dozens are (at best) a confrontation of wit, insight and upmanship, in which people try to outdo each other in the richness of their rhetorical scorn by taunting another person with insults about them and their family in front of an audience. [...] Ritual insult is a competitive game, a kind of teasing; it is not an attack

on an enemy or someone who is an outsider, despised or disparaged; it is an expression of group solidarity.[60]

Geoffrey Hughes, in *An Encyclopedia of Swearing*, also emphasizes the innocuous nature of flyting:

> language that would normally be taboo and extremely provocative does not lead to hostilities, but is tolerated in this particular conventional use [...] Flyting [...] has an essential element of license, of wordplay, since otherwise the grievous insults would lead to duels and other extreme modes of exacting satisfaction.[61]

It seems that there is no gall in this type of flyting, and that the term refers to a verbal exchange of abuse that is supposed to be harmless, 'benign insults' or '*un-sults*', as Irvine calls them.[62]

The term '*un-sult*' may illuminate many Shakespearean episodes, from the verbal jousting or 'excellent sport' (*1H4*, 2.4.380) opposing Hal and Falstaff, to the 'merry war' (*MA*, 1.1.58) that is mentioned by Leonato in *Much Ado About Nothing*, to refer to the 'skirmish[es] of wit' (*MA*, 1.1.61) between Benedick and Beatrice. Considered from this perspective, words are not expected to hurt, but appear to be what Frank Warnke called 'amorous Agon' or 'erotic flyting'[63] based on a non-aggression pact and rather on an intimate knowledge of one another. The flyting of Hal and Falstaff is a spectacle based on verbal acrobatics and a linguistic competition that is meant to feed a sense of admiration in the audience on- and off-stage. Thus, flyting epitomizes the paradoxes of a tongue that insults without insulting, of an amorously abusive speech act, of a cooperative form of fighting, of a war waged without hostility. That is why the frontier becomes blurred between insults and terms of endearment.

But the concept of flyting has been used in other contexts and with other meanings. Ward Parks has explored what he calls 'heroic flyting'. For him, if ludic flyting is a substitute for war that rests on a pact of non-physical-aggression, heroic flyting, on the other hand, is a prelude to war through which one seals a pact of aggression. He defines heroic flyting as '[t]he public exchange of personal insults and boasts between warriors contracting on a martial test'.[64] One can find traces of this other kind of flyting in such plays as *Troilus and Cressida* or *Henry IV*. On the battlefield, Hal and Hotspur may be seen as performing an episode of heroic flyting (*1H4*, 5.4.68–73) in a battle of words, a '*joute de jactance*'[65] that precedes and frames physical confrontation. In *Troilus and Cressida*, the 'most despiteful'st gentle greeting' between Aeneas and Diomedes (4.1.34-35) and then the challenging exchanges between Achilles and Hector (4.5.231–70) fail to mask the absence of heroic warriors in a play where the war of tongues most often replaces war. In this play, Shakespeare dramatizes the codes of heroic flyting to better emphasize their transgression.

Whether it be ludic or serious, flyting rests on codes and thus both paradoxically epitomizes the excesses and the limits of the tongue. Shakespeare's plays constantly show how porous the boundary is between abuse and no abuse and how one may easily mistake a merry war for a true hostility. This is what Leonato suggests at the beginning of *Much Ado*, when he gives the spectators of Beatrice and Benedick's tiffs the codes to decipher them: 'You must not, sir, mistake my niece' (*MA*, 1.1.58): there is always a danger that words may be mis-taken, or not taken as they were meant to be. This simple warning opens the door of interpretation and reception and displays a key aspect of the way words of insult are to be apprehended and comprehended.

The seven chapters that follow aim to show that Shakespearean insults constitute a rich dramatic material. The first two chapters will suggest that verbal fighting is a spectacular, metadramatic device that provides a counterpoint to military conflict and allows the playwright to stage the battle of the sexes. The rhetoric of insult will be analysed in *Henry IV*, *Troilus and Cressida* and *Timon of Athens*, plays that illustrate the spectacular festive but also the acerbic and nihilistic practices of abusive mouths. The 'merry war' in *Much Ado About Nothing* and *A Midsummer Night's Dream* will be the object of the second chapter that will show how a comic mode of insult may easily slip into a darker mood. Chapters 3 and 4 will provide a reading of the plays' insults at the light of two Elizabethan concomitant cultural phenomena: the duelling vogue and the proliferation of defamation cases. Chapter 3 will focus on insult and duelling codes as they appear in *Romeo and Juliet*, *As You Like It* and *Twelfth Night*. Chapter 4 will examine how *Much Ado About Nothing* and *Measure for Measure* dramatize the complex relationships between slander and insult, two speech acts that fuel the plots of the plays. Chapter 5 will inscribe insult in a complex dialectics of tongue-taming. The analysis of *Richard III* and *The Taming of the Shrew* will show that insult is the symptom of a rebellious tongue but also a paradoxical way of taming this tongue. Chapter 6 will explore insults as a source of trauma in *Othello*, *The Merchant of Venice* and *Cymbeline*. Chapter 7 will analyse *Henry V* and *King Lear* as plays in which insults go beyond words and often act without words. The whole book will show to what extent Shakespeare's drama can be seen as a theatre of insult.

1

The spectacular rhetoric of insult

Shakespeare's plays convey the banality of certain raw insulting words yet also cultivate artistic forms of abuse that rest on a spectacular rhetoric, reminiscent of the tradition of flyting.[1] They combine excess and creativity. Key insulting terms emerge from the whole corpus, the three most recurrent of which are 'villain', 'rogue' and 'knave'. These constitute the 'triple pillar' of Shakespeare's world of insults, illustrating what C. S. Lewis called the 'moralisation of status words'.[2] When combined with other words to form strings of abuse and being shaped into theatrical material, these common terms become a source of originality. The three plays on which this chapter will focus, *Henry IV Part 1*, *Troilus and Cressida*, and *Timon of Athens*, are emblematic of the ways in which insults articulate profusion and invention to make insults a spectacular speech act.

1 Henry IV or 'gormandizing' abuse

One of the plays that most memorably illustrate the art of excess is *Henry IV Part 1* in which the flyting scenes between Falstaff and Hal are most spectacularly festive. In this play, anger is fake and insults are a sign of friendship rather than a symptom of enmity. It is probably in this play that the title of this book, 'the anatomy of insults', takes on its most extensive meaning, as appears when the spectators hear the strings of abuse that are at the heart of the central scene:

HAL

[...] Why, thou clay-brained guts, thou knotty-pated fool, thou whoreson, obscene, greasy tallow-catch.

(2.4.219–21)

HAL

[...] This sanguine coward, this bed-presser, this horse-back-breaker, this huge hill of flesh –

(2.4.235–7)

FALSTAFF

'Sblood, you starveling, you eel-skin, you dried neat's tongue, you bull's pizzle, you stockfish! O, for breath to utter what is like thee! You tailor's yard, you sheath, you bow-case, you vile standing tuck –

(2.4.238–41)

HAL

Why dost thou converse with that trunk of humours, that bolting-hutch of beastliness, that swollen parcel of dropsies, that huge bombard of sack, that stuffed cloak-bag of guts, that roasted Manningtree ox with the pudding in his belly, that reverend Vice, that grey Iniquity, that father Ruffian, that Vanity in years?

(2.4.436–42)

The battle between Carnival and Lent, in which our contemporaries could now hear a form of 'sizeism', has clearly been identified in *1 Henry IV*.[3] It takes the form of sequences of flyting that Keir Elam defined as '[a] ritual dispute between two opponents, consisting in an exchange of invective and abuse'.[4] The dialogues between Hal and Falstaff in the tavern scenes, contrary to Hotspur's mostly solitary angry expostulations, epitomize insult as a ritualized festive spectacular speech act.

The tavern where these scenes take place represents both abundance of drink and food and abundance of words.

In Shakespeare's period, the tavern was considered as a world of excess, a place of disorder where unruly tongues and foul mouths reigned supreme. The *Homyly against gluttonie and dronkennes* warns that 'Wyne dronken with excesse, maketh bytternesse of mynde, and causeth brawlyng and stryfe' but also that 'many fonde, foolyshe, and fylthy wordes are spoken when men are at theyr bankettes'.[5] To tame one's tongue, one needs to tame one's life and avoid drunkenness. It is precisely what the newly crowned King Henry V means in *2 Henry IV* when he rejects Falstaff and asks him to 'leave gormandizing' (*2H4*, 5.5.52), meaning he must say adieu to all sins of the tongue. The exchanges of abuse that Hal and Falstaff indulge in are an expression of a life of 'gormandizing' that rests on pleasure and seems to be a perpetual 'feast of words'.[6] They constitute a spectacle within the spectacle, a 'play extempore' (*1H4*, 2.4.271), an expression that theorizes the exchanges between Hal and Falstaff, to better display their metatheatrical nature. In the world of the tavern, words of insult are spectacular objects of collective delight, eatables to share and relish that feed some key metastylistic comments.

'Unsavoury similes'

'Thou hast the most unsavoury similes and art indeed the most comparative, rascalliest, sweet young prince' (*1H4*, 1.2.76–8): this is how Falstaff reacts when Hal compares him to 'the melancholy of Moorditch', a comparison that suggests Falstaff should be evacuated as some kind of filth, and anticipates what happens to him in *The Merry Wives*.[7] It is not surprising that the greasy old man should stylistically define that speech act by using food imagery ('unsavoury'), thus signifying that offensive words can be considered as food that is hard to swallow and digest. This idea is memorably dramatized in *Henry V* when the Welsh Fluellen forces Pistol to eat a leek,[8] thus countering the verbal abuse he has received through physical abuse (5.1.14–68), literally transforming a speakable into an eatable. What Michel Jeanneret[9] calls 'les mets et les mots', eatables and speakables, words and food, have much in common. Falstaff's metalinguistic comment stresses the analogical dimension of abusive language, which is again emphasized when, gasping for breath or for inspiration, he exclaims: 'O, for breath to utter what is *like* thee!' (2.4.239–40). The assaulting words he hurls at Hal are based on what Puttenham calls 'resemblance' or 'similitude',[10] or what Hal calls 'base comparisons' (*1H4*, 2.4.243). When Henry IV blames his son for being like Richard, the 'skipping king' who became a sort of Carnival figure who '[stood] the push of every beardless vain comparative' (*1H4*, 3.2.66–7), Henry too equates insult with comparison, as the term 'comparative' may be glossed as 'dealer in insults'.[11] By insulting, you translate the target you have chosen, by means of 'base comparisons' and 'unsavoury similes'. The art of insult is an art of translation and in *1 Henry IV*, it is the body that is transformed or deformed by means of tropes such as metaphors or synecdoches.

Most of the insults in this play have to do with the physical aspect, notably with corpulence or thinness. The body contaminates the intellect when Hal verbally assaults Falstaff, as the old man wakes up, saying: 'thou art so fat-witted with drinking of old sack [...]' (1.2.2) or when he calls him a little later 'thou clay-brained guts' (2.4.219–20). The body is the mirror of the mind and a deformed body cannot but be the sign of a sinful soul, as appears when Hal tells Falstaff that he is all body and no spirit: 'there's no room for faith, truth, nor honesty in this bosom of thine; it is all filled up with guts and midriff' (3.3.150–4). There is no room for soul or virtue in Falstaff and his body is a book in which one can read all the vices that dominate his life: laziness, gluttony and lust. Shakespeare draws the portrait of Falstaff mainly through insults that show that he embodies all the Vices of the Medieval Morality plays. Behind adjectives such as 'fat', 'round', 'greasy', 'oily', one may hear 'lazy', 'greedy', 'drunkard' or 'vicious', as is confirmed in Georges Vigarello's study of obesity which argues that this negative vision of fatness emerged during the Renaissance.[12] The whole world of vice lies in Falstaff's corpulence which leads the Prince to call him: 'that reverend Vice, that grey Iniquity, that father Ruffian,[13] that Vanity in years' (2.4.441–2), words that refer to abstractions that Medieval plays transformed into characters and to which Falstaff is compared. He becomes a sort of Satan, 'That villainous, abominable misleader of youth, Falstaff, that old white-bearded Satan' (2.4.450–1).[14]

Falstaff's huge body undergoes metamorphoses and is dislocated by means of synecdoche. He is reduced to guts and becomes a paunch: 'ye fat guts' (2.2.31), 'Sir John Paunch' (2.2.64), 'ye fat paunch' (2.4.138). Through exaggeration, insults build up a deformed, disproportioned and thus grotesque 'bodyscape' that is also shaped by oaths,[15] verbal excesses *par excellence*, by which the speaker tears God's body limb by limb. Those who swear by God's body, blood or wounds, tear Him to pieces, crucifying him again.[16] It is in this play that one finds the most numerous occurrences of "Sblood'.[17] What Hotspur would term 'good mouth-filling oaths' (3.1.250) are part of the 'soundscape'[18] of the tavern.

Food and its excesses nourish the language of insults in *1 Henry IV*: Falstaff is '[a]s fat as butter' (2.4.498); he is called 'Ribs' (2.4.108), 'Tallow' (2.4.108), 'that damned brawn' (2.4.107), names that are both metonymical and metaphorical as Falstaff both resembles and is assimilated to what he eats. He ironically reverses roles when he calls the travellers he is robbing 'bacon-fed knaves' (2.2.82), 'gorbellied knaves' (2.2.86) and 'bacons' (2.2.88) in a passage that sounds like a self-portrait and will inevitably make the audience laugh.

Reifying metaphors add to the food imagery as Falstaff is transformed into pots and pans, objects that Bakhtin identifies as carnivalesque.[19] Such insults as 'tallow-catch' (2.4.221), 'that huge bombard of sack' (2.4.439), 'that bolting-hutch of beastliness' (2.4.437–8), 'that trunk of humours' (2.4.437), 'a tun of man' (2.4.436) or even 'Jack' (1.2.108) all refer to containers. Reversely, Falstaff transforms Hal into objects that convey the Prince's thinness, which goes together with a primarily sexual form of impotence.[20] When Hal is associated with food, he is compared to fish, that is, the food that characterizes Lent, thus standing in sharp contrast to the meat with which Falstaff and Carnival are associated and foreshadowing the days when Falstaff will be required to 'leave gormandizing'.

'Breathe a while and then to it again'

When Hal interrupts Falstaff's string of abuse, telling him to 'breathe awhile' (*1H4*, 2.4.242), this ironical advice shows that insulting is a tiring physical activity for the fat old man. Behind this 'breathe awhile', one can find all the excesses that are characteristic of insults in this play where words of abuse are so abundant that they lead to physical exhaustion. The *copia verborum* (abundance of words)[21] that Falstaff indulges in leads to breathlessness, a symptom that is emblematic of his character and goes together with his corpulence. Sir John's insulting language reflects his anatomy: it is bombastic, unbounded, overflowing. Such phrases as 'my sweet creature of bombast' (2.4.318) or 'blown Jack' (4.2.48) convey this correspondence between the old man's language and his body. Falstaff's language is as 'blown' and gigantic as his body. By adopting the language of insult and its rhetoric of excess, Prince Hal makes himself as big as Falstaff. From this perspective, the old man's abusive sentence 'The Prince is a jack' (3.3.85) may take on a new meaning. In the play, Hal verbally becomes a Jack Falstaff, as one can hear 'The Prince is a jack', i.e. a knave, as well as 'The Prince is a *Jack*'. Using the rhetoric of excess, Lent becomes as big as Carnival.

In *1 Henry IV*, hyperbole goes together with lies, an idea that is present in Puttenham's *The Arte of English Poesie* where the rhetorician describes the figure as the 'over reacher' or the 'loud lyer'.[22] Hyperbolic insults are everywhere: 'starveling' (2.4.238) answers 'huge hill of flesh' (2.4.237) or 'horse-back-breaker'

(2.4.236). They can sometimes be ironical, as when Hal calls Falstaff 'bare-bone' (2.4.318). The lexical proliferation that appears in the enumeration or accumulation of insults is part of an inflationary art. Shakespeare cultivates strings of insults that are often made of a succession of mini-strings of words, compounds such as 'woolsack' (2.4.129), 'clay-brained-guts' (2.4.219–20), 'knotty-pated fool' (2.4.220), 'bed-presser' (2.4.236), 'horse-back-breaker' (2.4.236), 'eel-skin' (2.4.238), 'stock-fish' (2.4.239), 'tailor's yard' (2.4.240), 'bow-case' (2.4.240), 'pint-pot' (2.4.387), 'tickle-brain' (2.4.387), 'bolting-hutch of beastliness' (2.4.437–8) and 'cloak-bag of guts' (2.4.439). The main and smallest insulting unit is often a 'compound', a term that is associated with Falstaff and Hal (2.4.117). Insults are delivered in the form of accumulations that are only interrupted by the opponent's reaction or when the abuser is short of breath.

Breathlessness is the symptom of verbal competition. In *1 Henry IV*, to insult means to play at inventing. As far as insults are concerned, it seems that the more varied they are, the better. Repetition is a fault and abusers should be verbal creators. The rhetoric of inflation is not enough; Hal and Falstaff also coin insults. There is an erosion of the insulting potential of such traditional words as 'rogue', 'villain', 'knave' or 'rascal' which are so often used that they become common, compared with the verbal coinages the play teams with. Many insults that are exchanged by the two main abusers, but also by other characters, are *hapax legomena* in Shakespeare's plays: 'popinjay' (1.3.50), 'bacons' (2.2.88), 'chuffs' (2.2.87), 'paraquito' (2.3.82), 'trifler' (2.3.86), 'salamander' (3.3.46), 'otter' (3.3.124), 'quilt' (4.2.48), 'chewet' (5.1.29) and most of the compounds quoted above only appear once in the dramatist's work. Creative abuse is an art based on combination, composition. It consists in gluing or sewing words together. Insult is here the art of variation on a major theme: the battle of the fat and the lean. The anaphorical repetition of 'you' and 'thou' corresponds to the pause the contestants give themselves to create insults. Variety is the key to the abusive art, and it is not surprising that Hal should mock Francis for his limited use of language. The poor 'anon, anon's he utters (2.4.43–84) contrast with the wealth of Hal's and Falstaff's vocabulary. It is tempting to hear in that 'anon' a multilingual pun on the French '*ânon*' (that is a 'young ass'). Francis' favourite word would then mirror his poor intellect.

It is Falstaff who lays down the rules of the insulting game, notably when he solemnly declares 'an I do not [i.e. take a purse tomorrow], call me villain and baffle me' (1.2.96–97), or 'If I tell thee a lie, spit in my face, call me horse' (2.4.186–7). Insults are the comic punishment Falstaff proposes to impose upon the liar. When Hal starts abusing the old man, he ironically applies one of the rules that have been decreed by him. When Falstaff declares that he contemplates having 'ballads' (2.2.44) written on Hal and Poins, he again throws into relief the punitive – and artistic – dimension that may characterize insult when it is part of the Elizabethan folklore.

The insulting game is also based on imitation. Even if they underline a contrast between the two main protagonists, the strings of abuse they deliver echo one another. Hal echoes Falstaff from the start with the stichomythia: 'What a plague have I to do / What a pox have I to do' (1.2.43–6). The Prince goes as far as to adopt one of Falstaff's stylistic features when he says 'if there were anything in thy pocket but tavern reckonings [...] I am a villain' (3.3.156–60). Falstaff keeps using this structure ('if..., then I am...') which is a kind of hypothetical self-insult. Sometimes Hal echoes Falstaff's words to coin his insults. The term 'woolsack' is inspired by Falstaff's image 'I would I were a weaver; I could sing psalms or anything' (2.4.126–7), which creates a semantic echo between 'weaver' and 'woolsack'. Hal here draws his insults from his opponent's mouth. The same cannibalistic mechanism appears when Falstaff uses Hostess Quickly's words ('There's neither faith, truth nor womanhood in me else', 3.3.110–11) to make his attack on her: 'There's no more faith in thee than in a stewed prune, nor no more truth in thee than in a drawn fox; and, for womanhood Maid Marian may be the deputy's wife of the ward to thee' (3.3.112–15). Then Hal utilizes the same words to insult Falstaff: 'There's no room for faith, truth nor honesty in this bosom of thine' (3.3.152–3). These multiple layers of echo give insults an ironic twist. Hal feeds on Falstaff's words, who had himself fed on the Hostess' words.

The game of insult is based on complicity rather than hostility. That is why in this play, probably more than in any other, the frontier disappears between abuse and praise. Calling someone names often amounts to calling him or her *pet*-names. According to Bakhtin, this blurred tone of words is characteristic of the festive verbal world. *1 Henry IV* is pregnant with what Bakhtin calls the 'ambivalent abuse' or the combination or fusion of 'praise and abuse'.[23] 'My old Lad of the castle' (1.2.40), 'the latter spring' (1.2.150), 'All-hallown summer' (1.2.150), 'my sweet creature of bombast' (2.4.318), 'good pint-pot', 'good tickle-brain' (2.4.387), 'Thou art the Knight of the Burning Lamp' (3.3.26–7), 'Dame Partlet the hen' (3.3.51), 'My sweet beef' (3.3.176): all these expressions, be they addressed to Falstaff, Hostess Quickly or Bardolph, waver between insults and endearments. The use of the possessive adjective 'my' within what sounds like an insult is characteristic of this in-betweenness. If insults and endearments overlap, it is because insult goes hand in hand with friendship in this play. If Hal and Falstaff hurl so many insults at each other, it is because they do not hurt. This double tone of words may be heard in Falstaff's tirade on Bardolph's nose which is emblematic of this ambivalent mixture of praise and abuse.

Bardolph's ambivalent nose

Bardolph is anatomized and reified when Falstaff presents him as a lantern, due to his conspicuous nose:[24]

FALSTAFF
    Do thou amend thy face, and I'll amend my life. Thou art our admiral, thou bearest the lantern in the poop, but 'tis in the nose of thee. Thou art the Knight of the Burning Lamp.

BARDOLPH

Why, Sir John, my face does you no harm.

FALSTAFF

No, I'll be sworn, I make as good use of it as many a man doth of a death's head, or a *memento mori*. I never see thy face but I think upon hell-fire and Dives that lived in purple: for there he is in his robes, burning, burning. If thou wert any way given to virtue, I would swear by thy face; my oath should be 'By this fire that is God's angel.' But thou art altogether given over and wert indeed, but for the light in thy face, the son of utter darkness. [...] O, thou art a perpetual triumph, an everlasting bonfire-light! Thou hast saved me a thousand marks in links and torches walking with thee in the night betwixt tavern and tavern, but the sack that thou hast drunk me would have bought me lights as good cheap at the dearest chandler's in Europe. I have maintained that salamander of yours with fire any time this two-and-thirty years, God reward me for it!

BARDOLPH

'Sblood, I would my face were in your belly!

FALSTAFF

God-a-mercy! So should I be sure to be heart-burnt.

(3.3.24–50)

This paradoxical encomium illustrates the mechanisms on which what Larguèche identifies as 'specific insults' are based.[25] One feature (the nose) dominates the whole picture and erases all the other features. Bardolph is reduced to a nose, a red nose that betrays his love of alcoholic drinks, in the same way as Falstaff is reduced to a 'paunch'. One detail dominating the whole picture is what makes the language of abuse so monstrous. With insults, the body is 'emblazoned'.[26] This paradoxical praise is also emblematic of the carnivalesque 'duality of tone'[27] that is a combination of compliment and abuse. Abuse has a transforming effect and as such it feeds the grotesque in the play. This idea is developed by Neil Rhodes in *Elizabethan Grotesque*, when he writes that 'the stylistic feature which best epitomises the grotesque in Renaissance literature is the "base comparison" ' and that '(...) elaborate base comparisons are the grotesque inversion of Euphuistic embellishments by similitude'.[28] This praiseful dispraise of the nose is emblematic of the gormandizing abuse that reigns supreme in the world of *1 Henry IV*. If insult is tasteful in *1 Henry IV*, it is mainly rank in *Troilus and Cressida*.

Troilus and Cressida or rank abuse

Insult in *Troilus and Cressida* has a main loudspeaker: Thersites, the railing satirist who vents his cynical words on the world that surrounds him, and mainly on three characters: Ajax, Achilles and Patroclus. If we consider the etymology that relates the word to *satura*, short for *lanx satura*, literally meaning 'full dish', satire is evocative of food, more precisely of 'a dish containing various kinds of fruit' or 'food composed of many different ingredients' (*OED*). The two functions of the tongue, eating and speaking, are again connected through this word, as well as through the word 'rank', the verbal and the material merging with one another. Chiefly uttered 'from the margins'[29] by a malcontent, insult could be considered as a peripheral or marginal phenomenon. Yet, considered in the context of the play, the exchanges of abuse appear as verbal substitutes for martial feats that reflect, comment on, debunk and are integrated into a world of war where the grotesque constantly seems to contradict and merge with the sublime.

'Come in and rail'

By the spectacular rhetoric that characterizes them, insults seem to provide the play with the only martial exploits and the only action scenes in a world where logorrhoea reigns supreme.

In *Troilus and Cressida*, idleness is the mother of insult. The scenes of insult seem to fill in the blanks in the war and 'factious feasts' (1.3.191) replace martial feats that remain dramatically absent. Insult is not the only form of verbal warfare that can be found in the play – as *disputatio* is also dramatized – but the warlike rhetoric that characterizes it makes it the most spectacular verbal confrontation. In a world that seems to be overwhelmed by apathy, flyting scenes are entertaining episodes. Ulysses denounces the bitter scorn that endangers order and hierarchy and describes what can be considered as scenes of insult:

> With him [Achilles] Patroclus,
> Upon a lazy bed, the livelong day
> Breaks scurril jests
> And with ridiculous and awkward action –
> Which, slanderer, he imitation calls –
> He pageants us.
>
> (1.3.146–51)

The image of Patroclus, lying upon a 'lazy bed' and making a show of himself to the great applause of Achilles, is emblematic of the entertaining function of insult in this play. Insulters give a 'pageant' in a world where nothing else happens and where the only martial *gestes* or feats are 'scurril *jests*'. Insult is a show business. The clan of insulters (Patroclus, Achilles, Ajax and Thersites) is already present in Ulysses' speech, before being present on stage. From the very beginning of the play, the margin is at the heart of the central discourse. Agamemnon presents Thersites as 'rank Thersites' (1.3.73) and the reference to his 'mastic jaws' (1.3.73) paves the way for the cynical/canine metaphor that is applied to him throughout the play.[30] Then it is old Nestor who describes him as 'a slave whose gall coins slanders like a mint' (1.3.193), an insulting machine activated ('set', 1.3.192) by another character (here Ajax) and whose favourite rhetorical weapon is humiliating comparison ('To match us in comparisons with dirt', 1.3.194). Thersites thus appears as a verbal war engine or as an instrument that mass-produces insults in what may be considered as a 'closet war' (1.3.205).

The entertaining dimension of insults crops up again in Act 2, Scene 3, when Patroclus invites Thersites to give himself over to the insulting art: 'Good Thersites, come in and rail' (2.3.21–2). It is in *Troilus and Cressida* that the word 'rail' (rail, railing, railest, rail'd, rails) is the most recurrent (eight occurrences). The word 'rail' derives from Middle French *railler, reillier*, meaning to brag, boast, to bark, growl and later to tease, mock and is probably related to post-classical Latin *ragulare*, a derivative of *ragere*, meaning to bellow, howl.[31] With this injunction, Patroclus gives the cynical Thersites[32] the official and 'privileged' (2.3.55) status of the insulter who, like the Fool – he is several times called 'fool'[33] – is supposed to amuse and divert an idle audience by providing 'factious feasts' (1.3.191). This impression is confirmed when Achilles greets him as follows: 'Why my cheese, my digestion, why hast thou not served thyself in to my table so many meals? Come, what's Agamemnon?' (2.3.39–41). The audience here attend a kind of dining show in which Thersites functions as an entertaining source both of indigestion and of digestion.

The theatrical force of abuse also comes from the fact that it is often accompanied by physical aggression. The confrontation between Thersites and Ajax illustrates the mechanism that leads from words to deeds. Thersites is beaten by a warrior who apparently has nothing else to beat or bite:[34] 'canst thou not hear? Feel, then!' (2.1.10). The stage directions[35] indicate that insulting words go together with blows and constitute the only scenes that can take the world of *Troilus and Cressida* out of its torpor. In this verbal duel that degenerates into a *bastinado*, Achilles plays the part of the witness and referee who counts the points ('there's for you, Patroclus', 2.1.113) and who, trying to interpose himself in the quarrel, gets beaten in his turn: 'What, with me too, Thersites?' (2.1.100). Thersites calls Achilles to witness, transforming Ajax into a fun fair monster:

THERSITES
 You see him there, do you?
ACHILLES
 Ay, what's the matter?

THERSITES
Nay, look upon him.
ACHILLES
So I do. What's the matter?
THERSITES
Nay, but regard him well.
ACHILLES
Well, why, I do so.
THERSITES
But yet you look not well upon him; for, whosomever you take him to be, he is Ajax.

(2.1.55–62)

As a skilful man of theatre, Thersites takes great trouble over his effects and creates what Irvine identifies as an 'ambush insult'.[36] This demonstration of the target increases the suspense and guarantees the *coup de théâtre* that consists in utilizing the very name of Ajax as a climactic word of abuse. The satirist again displays his art as a show man, an ass leader, when he underlines Ajax's poverty of intellect: 'Lo, lo, lo, lo, what modicums of wit he utters! His evasions have ears thus long' (2.1.66–7). When it is part of a show, insult is uttered in the third person.

Telling 'what thou art by inches'

In *Troilus and Cressida*, the exclamatory mode contributes to making words of abuse spectacular, as appears in the following selective catalogue:

Dog! (2.1.7), Thou bitch-wolf's son (2.1.10), thou mongrel beef-witted lord (2.1.11–12), thou vinewed'st leaven (2.1.13), Toadstool (2.1.19), porcupine (2.1.24), Mistress Thersites! (2.1.34), Cobloaf! (2.1.36), You whoreson cur! (2.1.39), Thou stool for a witch! (2.1.41), Thou sodden-witted lord (2.1.42), Thou scurvy-valiant ass (2.1.44), thou thing of no bowels, thou! (2.1.48), You dog! (2.1.49), You scurvy lord! (2.1.50), You cur! (2.1.51), Mars his idiot! (2.1.52), rudeness (2.1.52), camel (2.1.52), O thou damned cur (2.1.83), You rascal! (2.3.53), thou core of envy (5.1.4), Thou crusty batch of nature (5.1.5), thou picture of what thou seemest and idol of idiot-worshippers (5.1.6–7), fragment (5.1.8), thou full dish of fool (5.1.9), adversity (5.1.11), you rogue (5.1.16), thou damnable box of envy (5.124), you ruinous butt, you whoreson indistinguishable cur (5.1.27–8), thou idle immaterial skein of sleave-silk, thou green sarcenet flap for a sore eye, thou tassel of a prodigal's purse, thou (5.1.29–31), gall! (5.1.34), Finch egg! (5.1.35), All incontinent varlets! (5.1.95–6), Thou coward Troilus! (5.6.1), O traitor Diomed! (5.6.7), Hence, broker-lackey! (5.11.33)

The list, which could be much longer, gives an idea of the labelling process that insults constitute and of the exclamative syntax they rest on. In *Troilus and Cressida*, insults are the 'tempest of exclamation' that the Lord Chief Justice refers to in *2 Henry IV* (2.1.79). Insults are like blows dealt to the opponent, Ajax epitomizing this logic when he answers words with blows. In this spectacular verbal warfare, the insulters have favourite rhetorical ammunition that tends to generate monstrosity. An art of exaggeration based on hyperbole (1.3.161), redundancy and catalogue, an art of transformation conveyed through animal and food metaphors and an art of combination that appears in the recurrence of composed words, the insults of *Troilus and Cressida* produce monsters. A number of critics have noticed the importance of physical images in this play, and it is true that Shakespeare draws his insults from the bodily field, notably by cultivating disease imagery.[37] The targets are bodies that are torn to pieces. Most of the insults emitted by Thersites rob their targets of whatever intellectual substance they could have.[38] The war of words turns into an act of dissection. This is what Thersites stresses when he tells Ajax: 'If thou use to beat me, I will begin at thy heel, and tell what thou art by inches, thou thing of no bowels, thou' (2.1.46–8). This provides an interesting metalinguistic comment. To insult means to 'tell what thou art by inches', that is, to anatomize, in the same way as the Renaissance anatomists described by Jonathan Sawday dissected bodies in order to better know them.[39] The war of words merges with the war, the word ('tell') answering the deed ('beat'). One can catch a glimpse of this equivalence between words and deeds when Thersites tries to impress Ajax by brandishing the image of the great warrior Achilles: 'He would pun thee into shivers'[40] (2.1.37). It is not fortuitous that Shakespeare should use the word 'pun' for 'pound': this choice is emblematic of the marriage of doing and saying.

If insult is crucial in *Troilus and Cressida*, it is not only because it is spectacular, but also because it plays a part in the debunking enterprise dramatized by Shakespeare. The destructive impact of words is all the stronger since, here, insults feed on a world of myth and legend. The disruptive role of the insulter appears in Homer's *Iliad* where Thersites is described as the embodiment of imprecation. But if, in the *Iliad*, Thersites is quickly dismissed by Ulysses,[41] things are different in *Troilus and Cressida* where his railing voice produces insults that infect the heroic world that is presented.

'I'll decline the whole question'

In this play, to insult means to *de-base*. Insults demythify a world of so-called heroes. Thersites, described by McAlindon[42] as the embodiment of *tapinosis* (called 'abbaser' by Puttenham)[43] is, of course, the most conspicuous deflating voice in this play, a feature that Patroclus attributes to his 'gall' (5.1.34). To debunk his targets, he uses negation ('thou hast no more brain than I have in my elbows', 2.1.42–3), or reduction, a device that finds its most spectacular expression in the string of abuse that Thersites inflicts on Patroclus:

THERSITES
> Why art thou then exasperate, thou idle immaterial skein of sleave-silk, thou green sarcenet flap for a sore eye, thou tassel of a prodigal's purse, thou? Ah, how the poor world is pestered with such waterflies, diminutives of nature!

PATROCLUS
> Out, gall!

THERSITES
> Finch egg!

(5.1.29–35)

Deflation is paradoxically based on the inflationary rhetoric that characterizes the string of insults. The numerous echoing or mirroring effects between the speeches of the margin and the centre feed this demythification. As early as the confrontation between Ajax and Thersites, the spectator hears an ironic distortion of the message of war:

AJAX
> Toadstool, learn me the proclamation.

THERSITES
> Dost thou think I have no sense, thou strik'st me thus?

AJAX
> The proclamation!

THERSITES
> Thou art proclaimed a fool, I think.

(2.1.19–23)

Here appears the fusion of the martial discourse (the term 'proclamation' refers to the challenge Hector has sent to the Greeks) and the abusive discourse. This merging is confirmed when, interrupting the insulting exchange between Ajax and Thersites, Achilles asks them, 'What's the quarrel?' (2.1.87). The already potentially satirical phrase through which the Prologue uncovers the roots of the Trojan War ('And that's the quarrel', Prologue 10) finds its ironic counterpart. With this play on echoes Shakespeare blurs the boundary between war and squabble, between a war of words and a martial conflict.

Another ironic echo can be heard when Thersites reconstitutes by means of insults a burlesque hierarchy that strangely reminds the spectator of the society described by Ulysses in his famous speech on 'degree' (1.3.75–137):

> THERSITES
> I'll decline the whole question. Agamemnon commands Achilles, Achilles is my lord, I am Patroclus' knower, and Patroclus is a fool.
>
> PATROCLUS
> You rascal!
>
> THERSITES
> Peace, fool, I have not done.
>
> ACHILLES
> He is a privileged man. – Proceed, Thersites.
>
> THERSITES
> Agamemnon is a fool, Achilles is a fool, Thersites is a fool, and, as aforesaid, Patroclus is a fool.
>
> ACHILLES
> Derive this, come.
>
> THERSITES
> Agamemnon is a fool to offer to command Achilles, Achilles is a fool to be commanded of Agamemnon, Thersites is a fool to serve such a fool, and Patroclus is a fool positive.
>
> PATROCLUS
> Why am I a fool?
>
> THERSITES
> Make that demand of the creator; it suffices me thou art.
>
> (2.3.50–65)

This all-out attack takes the form of a rational demonstration that sounds like a burlesque rewriting of the bombastic speech in which Ulysses draws a panorama of Greek society and of the hierarchy that rules it. This speech is here reduced to its minimal expression. Although, by its enumerative form, Thersites' speech seems to reconstitute a ladder of 'degrees', it in fact tears to pieces Ulysses' hierarchy as all the characters, whatever their function, are eventually reduced to one basic status: they are all fools. The hierarchy drawn by Ulysses is here flattened, shattered. The word 'decline' suggests that Thersites' part consists in debunking heroic figures, having them sink to the status of universal foolishness.

The catalogue rhetoric that is so characteristic of abuse can also be considered as a burlesque version of the Homeric catalogue that already finds its ironic expression in the so numerous parades that punctuate the play.[44] The expression 'name-calling' reflects the possible parallel between the catalogue of abuse and the heroic catalogue.

The ambivalent use of the word 'Greek' also contributes to blurring the limit between the sublime and the grotesque. The word 'Greek', that is supposed to plunge the auditor into a world of legendary heroes, loses its evocative dimension in one of its first occurrences in the play. The adjective 'merry' to which it is associated empties the word of its mythical content. The phrase 'merry Greek' (1.2.105), here applied by Cressida to Helen, conveys an image of wantonness. Moreover, the pun that one can hear in 'the Trojans' trumpet/the Trojans' strumpet' (4.5.65) debunks the image of a noble martial world that the expression could have contained.

But it is probably the name 'Ajax' that best illustrates how the heroic and the grotesque overlap in this play. First the emblem of war heroism, the name becomes insulting *per se* in the Elizabethan world. Its well-known homophony with 'a jakes' associated the name with the lavatory. Thersites' pun had been explored earlier by John Harington in *The Metamorphosis of Ajax* (1596)[45] and finds an echo notably when Thersites describes Ajax pacing up and down the battlefield 'asking for himself' (3.3.246–7). One can decipher another debasing pun on the name at the beginning of the play when Alexander, describing Ajax to Cressida, starts his ambiguous portrait with: 'he is a very man *per se*' (1.2.15). Even if no editor seems to take this hypothesis into account, a French ear is tempted to hear 'percé' in this Latin *'per se'*, Ajax thus becoming a *chaise percée*, a commode. The multilingual homophony seems all the more convincing if we consider that Ajax is probably the character who has to bear the most numerous insults, insults that are described by Nestor as 'comparisons with dirt' (1.3.194).[46]

As is often the case in Shakespeare's plays, the relationships between words and deeds are ambivalent. If, as we have seen, word and deed seem to meet, this idea is contradicted by Thersites when he starts meditating on the powerlessness of his words:

> How now, Thersites? What, lost in the labyrinth of thy fury? Shall the elephant Ajax carry it thus? He beats me, and I rail at him. O worthy satisfaction! Would it were otherwise – that I could beat him whilst he railed at me. 'Sfoot, I'll learn to conjure and raise devils but I'll see some issue of my spiteful execrations.
>
> (2.3.1–7)

The rancour voiced by Thersites points to the gap between the vanity of words and the efficiency of deeds. Yet the 'Amen' that concludes his flow of imprecations ('I have said my prayers, and devil Envy say "Amen"', 2.3.19–20) also conveys a belief in the magical power of words. However inefficient insults seem to be for Thersites, they have a great impact on the spectator as they largely contribute to the 'declining' or waning of *Troilus and Cressida*'s heroic world. But faced with the vanity of insults, Thersites resorts to malediction, which may express his faith in the potency of words. This tension between the creative and destructive forces of 'abusive mouths'[47] is also at the heart of another play: *Timon of Athens*.

Timon of Athens and execration

'O you gods, what a number of men eats Timon, and he sees 'em not!' (1.2.39–40): the first part of *Timon of Athens* repeatedly conjures up the image of Timon being devoured by the flatterers around him, like Actaeon by his dogs.[48] In Shakespeare's time, flattery was considered as one of the worst sins of the tongue.[49] In *Timon of Athens*, it is presented as a sinful sort of table talk. The 'great flood of visitors' (1.1.43) who parade at Timon's are 'riotous feeders' (2.2.159), cannibalistic and 'gluttonous maws' (3.4.50), parasites who feed on and 'englut' (2.2.166) the substance of their host, 'tast[ing] Lord Timon's bounty' (1.1.281) and 'feed[ing] / Most hungrily on [his] sight' (1.1.258–9). Apemantus reminds us that the flattered is no better than the flatterer: 'He that loves to be flattered is worthy o'th' flatterer' (1.1.230–1). The ear that absorbs sweet words is just as guilty and greedy as the mouth that delivers them. Apemantus' formulation 'what a number of men eats Timon', with its verb in the singular, could well invert, or at least blur, the relationship between the eater and the eaten.[50] What Timon eats in the first part of the play is the honey of flattery.[51] What Timon ingests first, he vomits it in the second part.

'He pours it out'

From the beginning of the play, Timon is described in terms of excess: 'He passes' (1.1.12), 'He outgoes the very heart of kindness' (1.1.282), 'He pours it out' (1.1.275). When Apemantus joins him in the no man's land where he has taken refuge, he draws the portrait of an extraordinary man: 'The middle of humanity thou never knewest, but the extremity of both ends' (4.3.300–1). According to Apemantus, Timon does not know measure, he ignores the limits and explores the extremes. 'He is a man of excess', notes Robert C. Elliott in *The Power of Satire*,[52] describing a character whose excesses place him on the fringe of the sublime and the grotesque.[53] Richard Fly talks about 'The unmediated world of *Timon of Athens*',[54] while Frank Kermode writes that 'The play was evidently designed to consist of two halves illustrating contrasting modes of excess'.[55]

The common root of these excesses lies in the tongue, and the play stages a disorder of the mouth. In *Timon of Athens*, we go from one excess of the tongue to another and from ingestion to expulsion. What is often presented as a journey that leads from philanthropy to misanthropy, from an overflow of generosity ('bounty') to an overflow of hatred,[56] is also the chronicle of an indigestion, the story of the metamorphosis of honey into gall. Perhaps as much as angry or hateful, Timon is nauseous, 'sick' (4.3.371), as he says himself. The verbal outbursts, invectives, curses, imprecations, insults poured out in the second part of the play can be considered as waste thrown out by an organism that abhors and excretes the world it once relished. Before disgust, Timon enjoyed the taste of society. *Timon of Athens* offers a reflection on what Claude Gaignebet and Marie-Claude Périer study in terms of 'excretum',[57] the play featuring a gargoyle character. Timon is the throat evoked by Éric Beaumatin and Michel Garcia in a work devoted to invective in the Middle Ages; he is the mouth which 'chases outwards [...] a matter that the inside refuses'.[58]

Flattery, one of the sins in the catalogue of abuses of the tongue that are drawn up by the Elizabethans, is most often represented in terms of food and taste. It is a vice of the palate and the palace. What is at the heart of the representation of flattery is the ambivalent relationship that is established between the flatterer and the flattered: the flatterer eats the one he flatters; he feeds on him, before abandoning a carcass emptied of its substance. In the iconography of the time, flatterers are represented as parasites, rats or crows that abandon their prey once it is hollowed out.[59] But the flatterer also feeds the flattered with a honey that only reveals its bitter aftertaste too late. In Elizabethan culture, the flatterer is presented as a chameleon that changes colours according to situations and interlocutors, like a mirror that reflects the one who speaks to it,[60] an idea that is present in *Timon of Athens* when the Poet refers to the 'glass-faced flatterer' (1.1.60). But the flatterer is also the one who serves a poisoned honey to the other.

The beginning of the play shows that Timon suffers from a taste disorder. He does not know the difference between a friend and a flatterer;[61] he does not perceive the poison behind the sugar he is served. As Whitney reminds us in one of his emblems entitled 'fel in melle' ('poison in honey'), there is gall in honey.[62] *Timon of Athens* tells the story of this discovery, the story of a taste shock. 'But myself – / Who had the world as my confectionary' (4.3.267): the world was his 'confectionary', his sweet shop. But when you eat too much sugar, you get sick at heart. Apemantus had warned him:

> We make ourselves fools to disport ourselves,
> And spend our flatteries to drink those men
> Upon whose age we void it up again
> With poisonous spite and envy.
> (1.2.135–8)

From the beginning of the play the cynic offers us the premonitory image of the metamorphosis of honey into gall ('spite and envy'). After drinking at the source of flattery, he must regurgitate. The curses that Timon 'pours out' on the world are part of this execration and excretion. 'Would thou wert clean enough to spit upon!' (4.3.358), Timon hurls at Apemantus. 'A plague on thee, thou art too bad to curse' (4.3.359), answers Apemantus. At the turning point of this scene of flyting, where Elliott sees a switch from the sublime to the grotesque, 'past rage and into the ridiculous',[63] the equivalence of spitting and cursing is explicitly formulated. The image of Timon being a prey to the excesses of the mouth is evoked a little earlier by Apemantus:

> Will the cold brook,
> Candied with ice, caudle thy morning taste
> To cure thy o'ernight's surfeit?
> (4.3.224–6)

By ironically asking Timon if the cool stream will cure his hangover ('o'ernight's surfeit'), Apemantus conjures up the image of a man who has indulged in overeating and overdrinking and now tries to relieve his belly by vomiting, 'voiding' his guts on a world that has become indigestible.

A little later, Apemantus announces to Timon the arrival of the thieves: 'More things like men. Eat, Timon, and abhor them' (4.3.393). Although one is tempted to think that 'eat' refers to the poor 'root' Timon has just dug up to eat it, the two injunctions 'eat' and 'abhor them' seem to be connected and one is not far from hearing 'eat them and abhor them'. Apemantus asks him to eat these men, echoing Timon himself who said earlier: 'That the whole life of Athens were in this (the root)! / Thus would I eat it' (4.3.281–2). If Timon dreams of absorbing the world, it is to better vomit it.

'Multiplying bans'

The banquet scene in 3.7 dramatizes an allegorical act of spitting:

> May you a better feast never behold,
> You knot of mouth-friends! Smoke and lukewarm water
> Is your perfection. This is Timon's last;
> Who, stuck and spangled with your flatteries,
> Washes it off, and sprinkles in your faces
> Your reeking villainy. [*Throws water in their faces*]
>   Live loathed and long,
> Most smiling, smooth, detested parasites,
> Courteous destroyers, affable wolves, meek bears –
> You fools of fortune, trencher-friends, time's flies,
> Cap-and-knee slaves, vapours and minute-jacks!
> Of man and beast the infinite malady
> Crust you quite o'er!
>   [*as one is trying to leave*] What, dost thou go?

Soft! take thy physic first [*throwing things at him and others*]; thou too, and thou!
Stay, I will lend thee money, borrow none.
                              [*Exeunt lords in disarray*]
What, all in motion? Henceforth be no feast
Whereat a villain's not a welcome guest.
Burn house, sink Athens, henceforth hated be
Of Timon man and all humanity! [*Exit*]
                                                              (3.7.87–104)

The text offers a literalization of the image of the flatterer, when, uncovering the food, Timon shouts the spectacular 'Uncover, dogs, and lap' (3.6.84). But as he serves this mixture of lukewarm water and insults, he literally spits in his guests' faces.

The second part of the play, punctuated by the entrances and exits of the characters who visit Timon, duplicates this original rejection, this initial expulsion. The root that Timon digs up and devours is like the purgative food that helps him to evacuate what is in his heart and belly. It is with words that he evacuates what he can no longer swallow or digest. These successive dejections transform the world around him into 'general excrement' (4.3.437). The holes that he digs in the soiled earth are like the places in which he vents his execration and excretion. If in the first part of the play Timon's palace and palate could absorb a 'flood of visitors', in the second part he spits them out, one by one. Harold Fisch notes that the gesture of throwing stones or mud at visitors – what he calls the 'gesture of throwing' – is at the heart of the play.[64] This gesture seems to be the concrete expression of the speech act of cursing.

Seen from this angle, the 'cave' in which Timon takes refuge resembles a throat, an open mouth, a cavity, which can no longer swallow anything and pours its waste onto the world. Timon becomes a mouth; and from this open mouth, without any barrier, open to all winds, emanate the streams of imprecations that are so characteristic of the play.

Once alone, Timon indeed pours a garbage of words all over the world. From that moment on, all the action of the play is in his curses. The first of his imprecations begins with the image of a falling wall, a collapsing barrier:

> O thou wall
> That girdles in those wolves, dive in the earth
> And fence not Athens! Matrons turn incontinent.
> (4.1.1–3)

By becoming what the Elizabethans call 'a cursitor', a vagabond, Timon becomes 'a curser' at the same time. In his chapter on the curse in *King Lear*, Kenneth Gross suggests that the pun on 'curse' and 'cursitor' was probably perceived by Shakespeare's contemporaries.[65] The barriers that fall in Act 4 are in fact those of his mouth, which is no longer contained by anything. It is probably not fortuitous that the flood of imprecations that follows, for more than forty lines, opens with the image of 'incontinence' a term that refers to unchaste behaviour and more generally to a lack of restraint.

In *Timon of Athens*, as in *Richard III*, calamity is 'full of words [...] / Poor breathing orators of miseries' (*R3*, 4.4.126; 129). Insults are embedded in a string of curses that are pregnant with ever more curses, 'multiplying bans' (4.1.34). The long string of imprecations (4.1.1–41) is reminiscent of the ancient curse poems known as *arae*, based on the logic of 'exemplum', of enumeration, of accumulation. In his *Arte of English Poesie*, Puttenham describes 'arae' as 'great easment to the boiling stomacke'.[66] The text itself formulates the potential endless dimension of curses and an 'et caetera' logic: 'Take thou that too, with multiplying bans'. With this call to multiplying curses, Timon leaves the doors of the text, and of his mouth, open and seems to prevent closure. The ironic 'Amen' (4.1.41) that concludes this flow of words is not enough to bring it to a close; neither are the epitaphs in Act 5.

'Let... language end'

'Lips, let sour words go by, and language end' (5.2.210), says Timon, a few lines before becoming silent.[67] At the end of his course, this line, which again merges the two functions of the tongue through the word 'sour', seems to show that after having eased his boiling stomach on the world, Timon is now empty of words, as if he had exhausted all his vital and verbal resources, all the words in the world, and all in vain. John Jowett, in the Oxford edition, reports that in a 1978 production, Timon tore his tongue out at the end of the scene.[68] This physical excretion of language can be interpreted as a sign of disgust for language and its perversions. After being disgusted with the world, Timon is disgusted with language itself.

Timon has indeed become this evil tongue who curses and subverts language by mixing sweet and bitter, honey and gall. This subversion of the tongue is staged in three main sequences. During the dialogue with Alcibiades' prostitutes (4.3.1–174) and the exchange with the thieves (4.3.394–452), Timon curses and blesses with the same breath: 'Be a whore still, they love thee not that use thee' (4.3.83), he tells Timandra; 'Do villainy, do', he encourages the thieves. Praising and blessing the whores and the thieves, he curses humanity. During the senators' scene (5.2), Timon introduces his visitors to the taste shock he himself suffered in the third act. He covers the gall of his words with honey by practicing the delayed curse. To the senators who come to ask him to save Athens from Alcibiades, he says 'yes' to better say 'no', alternating the sweet and the bitter. Like the traveller in Aesop's fable,[69] he blows hot to better exhale the cold.

In *Timon of Athens*, language seems to be 'unremoveably' (5.2.109) bad and the good Flavius alone cannot redeem it. Like the evil rich man who, in the Bible (Luke 16:24), begged Abraham to appease his tongue, a tongue that had been so sinful that it was condemned to suffer the fires of hell,

Timon seems to want to stop the fire that consumes him. The evocation of the sinful tongue condemned to the punishment of fire appears when Timon greets the senators:

> Thou sun that comforts, burn! Speak and be hanged!
> For each true word, a blister, and each false
> Be as a cantherizing to the root o'th' tongue,
> Consuming it with speaking.
>
> (5.2.16–19)

These lines recall the punishments that were inflicted on bad tongues, especially on blasphemers who, under Louis IX, for example, were condemned to corporal punishment, and to have their tongues pierced with red-hot irons. Timon has become the embodiment of all the sins of the tongue, and his mouth is as corrupt as the 'medlar' (small fruit that is partially rotten) that Apemantus would like to make him eat (4.3.304). Ironically it is Timon who becomes the judge of language, discovering that there is no such thing as a good tongue. Therefore, it is not surprising that he should condemn language to death: 'and language end'. Language has been consumed by excess ('consuming it with speaking'). So one could say of language what the Poet says about the world at the very beginning of the play. When the painter asks him: 'How goes the world?', he answers: 'It wears, sir, as it grows' (1.1.3).

But beyond death, the epitaphs written by Timon, like the ancient curse tables or 'defixiones', described by Lindsay Watson in *Arae. The Curse Poetry of Antiquity*,[70] appeal to the magical power of the word. Yet they also freeze language that has become overflowing. Their brevity is like the manifestation of the establishment of a new linguistic economy. After flowing, the words are frozen in the wax that the soldier brings to Alcibiades. However, the text of *Timon of Athens* denies this closure in at least two ways. The textual mystery that constitutes the doubling of epitaphs forbids any stability of words and meaning. This overflow of epitaphs makes the text unstable, slippery. Moreover, the words of the second epitaph resound, beyond death:

> [*Here lies a wretched Corsican, of wretched soul bereft;*
> *Seek not my name; a plague consumes you, wicked caitiffs left.*] *(F)*
> *Here lie I, Timon, who alive all living men did hate;*
> *Pass by and curse thy fill, but pass and stay not here thy gait.*
> (5.5.70–1)

Even when frozen in wax, these words spill over, contradict each other, repeat themselves. The text opens at the very moment it closes. What turns the text back to the logic of excess is the 'pass by and curse thy fill': a text that curses its readers by enjoining them to curse, that condemns them to condemn, can never end cursing. What remains at the end of *Timon* is certainly silence, but this silence sounds like a deafening 'et caetera'. Language is dead, long live language!

2

The 'merry war': Insult as a love game

'You must not, sir, mistake my niece; there is a kind of merry war betwixt Signor Benedick and her. They never meet but there's a skirmish of wit between them' (1.1.58–61). At the beginning of *Much Ado About Nothing*, Leonato contextualizes the exchanges between Beatrice and Benedick to give the spectators both on- and off-stage the key to decipher them. Leonato embodies an informed audience who warns the uninitiated messenger, and, through him, the spectators, that this is going to be a show based on a playful contract. This comment presents insults as objects to be interpreted, as words that should be properly understood. Through Leonato, Shakespeare warns us from the very beginning: words of abuse are to be considered in context. Leonato's comment expresses an eminently 'pragmatic' approach to insults. With this metalinguistic comment the playwright also expresses one of the mechanisms that are at work in his plays, especially his comedies, a verbal mode that F. J. Warnke[1] has termed 'amorous Agon'. The object of this chapter is to analyze two examples of 'erotic flyting' and to show how the amorous duets or quartets that inhabit Shakespeare's *Much Ado About Nothing* and *A Midsummer Night's Dream* practise what can be termed verbal cannibalism, taking their verbal ammunition from the other's mouth, creating a form of 'musical discord' that often tumbles into a less ludic mode and amounts to 'killing courtesy', that is transgressing the codes of courtesy.

The 'skirmishes of wit' in *Much Ado About Nothing*

In *The Courtyer*, Castiglione describes what has been translated by Hoby as 'jests that are nipping'[2] as follows:

> But emong other meerie saiynges, they have a verie good grace that arryse whan a man at the nippynge talke of his felowe taketh the verye same woordes in the self same sence, and retourneth then backe agayne pryckynge hym wyth hys owne weapon. As an attourney in the lawe, unto whom in the presence of the judge his adversarye saide, what barkeste thou? furthwyth he answered: Bycause I see a thief. And of this sorte was also, whan Galeotto of Narni passyng throughe Siena stayed in a streete to enquire for an ynn, and a Senese seeinge hym so corpulente as he was, saide laughinge: Other menne carye their bougettes beehynde them, and this good felowe caryeth his beefore him. Galeotto answered immediatlye: So must menne do in the Countery of theeves.[3]

These merry injurious anecdotes can be related to Shakespeare's comedies in which insult is often conveyed by these jests in scenes that dramatize boomerang effects and reversals.

An art of repartee

The merry war that we witness at the beginning of *Much Ado About Nothing* reveals a series of insults that bounce off each other, in cascades and constitute an art of 'repartee':[4]

> BEATRICE
> I wonder that you will still be talking, Signor Benedick; nobody marks you.

BENEDICK
What, my dear Lady Disdain! Are you yet living?

BEATRICE
Is it possible Disdain should die, while she hath such meet food to feed it as Signor Benedick? Courtesy itself must convert to Disdain if you come in her presence.

BENEDICK
Then is Courtesy a turncoat. But it is certain I am loved of all ladies, only you excepted; and I would I could find in my heart that I had not a hard heart, for truly I love none.

BEATRICE
A dear happiness to women – they would else have been troubled with a pernicious suitor. I thank God and my cold blood, I am of your humour for that: I had rather hear my dog bark at a crow, than a man swear he loves me.

BENEDICK
God keep your ladyship still in that mind, so some gentleman or other shall scape a predestinate scratched face.

BEATRICE
Scratching could not make it worse an 'twere such a face as yours were.

BENEDICK
Well, you are a rare parrot-teacher.

BEATRICE
A bird of my tongue is better than a beast of yours.

BENEDICK
I would my horse had the speed of your tongue, and so good a continuer. But keep your way, o'God's name; I have done.

BEATRICE
You always end with a jade's trick; I know you of old.
(1.1.110–39)

In this witty battle of insults, each of the contestants uses the other's words to defend himself or herself, to counter-attack, hoist the other with his or her own petard and, as is formulated in *The Courtyer*, to 'nick [the other] with his owne wordes'.[5] Ironically, those who claim their independence and freedom throughout the play are inseparable in the art of insult. The sexual meaning of the word 'wit' suggests that these oratory matches are part of an erotic process. Sources of pleasure for the verbal sparring partners and the audience, these exchanges constitute a preliminary stage leading to the love declaration. During the ball scene, Beatrice unwittingly reveals a potential desire by saying to Benedick about Benedick himself 'I would he had boarded me' (2.1.130), which has a sexual meaning. It is not fortuitous that she should call him 'Signior Montanto' (1.1.29), which also contains a bawdy innuendo. The two contestants feed on each other's words and the roots of one's insult are in the other's words. What C. L. Barber called the 'festive comedy' is a privileged terrain for this amorous kind of insult that consists of a competition in which 'suitors' are 'shooters' who 'hit' the opponent.[6] It is the one who runs short of verbal ammunition who loses. By saying to Beatrice 'But keep your way, o'God's name. I have done' (1.1.136–7), Benedick abandons the game. Beatrice's 'You always end with a Jade's trick: I know you of old' (1.1.138–9) suggests Benedick is a bad player who spoils the game when he is in danger of being defeated. Throughout the play, the spectator has the impression that in this competition, Beatrice has the upper hand. The kiss Benedick gives her at the end, whether it be on his own initiative or to answer Leonato's order to 'stop [her] mouth' (5.4.97), is another way of leaving the game by shutting her up. According to C. L. Barber:

> the flyting match of Benedick and Beatrice, while appropriate to their special characters, suggests the customs of Easter Smacks and Hocktide abuse between the sexes. Much of the poetry and wit, however it may be occasioned by events,

works in the economy of the whole play to promote the effect of a merry occasion where Nature reigns.[7]

Insults create and belong to a festive atmosphere. Barber relates these exchanges of insults to ancient rituals:

> F. M. Cornford, in *The Origins of Attic Comedy*, suggested that invocation and abuse were the basic gestures of a nature worship behind Aristophanes' union of poetry and railing. The two gestures were still practiced in the 'folly' of Elizabethan Maygame, harvest home, or winter revel: invocation, for example, in the manifold spring garlanding customs, 'gathering for Robin Hood'; abuse, in the customary license to flout and fleer at what on other days commanded respect. The same double way of achieving release appears in Shakespeare's festive plays. There the poetry about the pleasures of nature and the naturalness of pleasure serves to evoke beneficent natural impulses; and much of the wit, mocking the good housewife Fortune from her wheel, acts to free the spirit as does the ritual abuse of hostile spirits.[8]

Insult is a source of mirth, entertainment; it is an integral part of the 'holiday humour' of which Orlando speaks in *As You Like It* (4.1.63). In his article devoted to erotic flyting, Warnke sees in this game of insult a celebration of the war of the sexes:

> But why should a man and woman who love each other express that feeling by engaging in games of combat? The answer is suggested by Huizinga when he proposes that, to the mind of 'the savage, the child and the poet,' reality presents itself as an 'agonistic structure,' and that processes in life and the cosmos are seen as the eternal conflict of opposites which is the root principle of existence. The amorous agon is an expression of the opposition of male and female, but it is a *celebration* of that opposition.[9]

Part of the festive mood of the play resides in Beatrice's wit that is so 'forcible' (5.3.53) that she 'turns [...] everyone the wrong side out' (3.1.68) or 'fright[s] the word out of his right sense' (5.2.52-3) and even turns compliments into insults. Seemingly sympathizing with Benedick, during the trap scene, Hero describes her destructive art of mocking:

> If I should speak,
> She would mock me into air. O, she would laugh me
> Out of myself, press me to death with wit!
> Therefore, let Benedick, like covered fire,
> Consume away in sighs, waste inwardly.
> It were a better death than die with mocks
> Which is as bad as die with tickling.
>
> (3.1.74–80)

Hero's recommendation is that being silent is better than exposing oneself to Beatrice's scorn by speaking. Verbal cannibalism is typical of men and women of wit who use the speech of the other as a support for their own insulting remarks. Insulters imitate and transform at leisure the words of the others. This idea finds its most conspicuous illustration in Don Pedro's narration of Beatrice's art of reversal:

> I'll tell thee how Beatrice praised thy wit the other day. I said thou hadst a fine wit. 'True,' said she, 'a fine little one.' 'No,' said I, 'a great wit.' 'Right,' says she, 'a great gross one.' 'Nay,' said I, 'a good wit.' 'Just,' said she, 'it hurts nobody.' 'Nay,' said I, 'the gentleman is wise.' 'Certain,' said she, 'a wise gentleman.' 'Nay,' said I, 'he hath the tongues.' 'That I believe,' said she, 'for he swore a thing to me on Monday night, which he forswore on Tuesday morning. There's a double tongue; there's two tongues.' Thus did she an hour together trans-shape thy particular virtues. Yet at last she concluded, with a sigh, thou wast the properest man in Italy.
>
> (5.1.157–68)

THE 'MERRY WAR': INSULT AS A LOVE GAME

Wit is both the means and the topic of this witty merry war. Beatrice uses Don Pedro's speech to formulate her sarcastic praises that become insults when they are repeated to Benedick by Don Pedro. The irony is all the greater as 'Lady Disdain' transforms laudatory words into insults, this trans-shaping process showing how close to one another insult and its opposite, compliment, can be. To insult is here to transfigure the words of the other. It is in this sense that one can describe the insulter as 'a corrupter of words', as Touchstone is called in *Twelfth Night* (3.1.30). Beatrice engages in this corrupting art of reversal from the very beginning of the play, for example, when she addresses the messenger who praises Benedick:

MESSENGER
    And a good soldier too, lady.
BEATRICE
    And a good soldier to a lady; but what is he to a lord?
MESSENGER
    A lord to a lord, a man to a man, stuffed with all honourable virtues.
BEATRICE
    It is so, indeed, he is no less than a stuffed man. But for the stuffing – well, we are all mortals.

(1.1.51–7)

If Beatrice turns compliment into insult, Benedick, once blinded by love, disfigures Beatrice's insults, or at least her sharp remarks, into compliments, once he has been gulled by his fellow men:

Ha! 'Against my will I am sent to bid you come in to dinner' – There's a double meaning in that. 'I took no more pains for those thanks than you took pains to thank me' – that's as much as to say, 'Any pains that I take for you is as easy as thanks.'

(2.3.248–52)

Once again, the borderline between words of hate and words of love seems very thin and the tongue again proves 'double'.[10] The meaning of the words is flexible and slippery, and all speeches are subject to interpretation.

The playful and erotic contract that Beatrice and Benedick seem to have concluded should turn their exchanges into a verbal ping-pong with no consequences, the insults being hurled for pleasure. In *Much Ado About Nothing*, Warnke notes:

> the match is perfect: no reader or viewer (of a proper production) could possibly feel that either Beatrice or Benedick is outmatched. It is part of the meaning of the play that they are perfect matches for each other (the pun is intentional – perfect partners in a couple, and perfect opponents).[11]

Yet this equality of forces is debatable. Isn't Benedick always the first who abandons the game? Isn't he the one who feels Beatrice's words are 'poniards'? Shakespeare indeed repeatedly stages the friction between playful and serious insults, suggesting the fragility of the verbal balance on which such erotic flyting is based. Insult is a love activity that requires complicity and harmony. It is tempting to see in this paradoxical verbal complicity an intimation of the wedding that will take place at the end of the play. Yet the ball episode stages the potential shift of the insult from the merry mode to the serious mode.

BEATRICE
  Will you not tell me who told you so?
BENEDICK
  No, you shall pardon me.
BEATRICE
  Nor will you not tell me who you are?
BENEDICK
  Not now.

BEATRICE
That I was disdainful, and that I had my good wit out of *The Hundred Merry Tales*! Well, this was Signior Benedick that said so.

BENEDICK
What's he?

BEATRICE
I am sure you know him well enough.

BENEDICK
Not I, believe me.

BEATRICE
Did he never make you laugh?

BENEDICK
I pray you, what is he?

BEATRICE
Why, he is the prince's jester, a very dull fool; only his gift is in devising impossible slanders. None but libertines delight in him, and the commendation is not in his wit, but in his villainy, for he both pleases men and angers them, and then they laugh at him and beat him. I am sure he is in the fleet: I would he had boarded me.

BENEDICK
When I know the gentleman, I'll tell him what you say.

BEATRICE
Do, do. He'll but break a comparison or two on me, which, peradventure not marked or not laughed at, strikes him into melancholy, and then there's a partridge wing saved, for the fool will eat no supper that night. We must follow the leaders.

BENEDICK
In every good thing.

BEATRICE
Nay, if they lead to any ill I will leave them at the next turning.

(2.1.113–40)

The scene begins *in media res* but we may reconstruct its beginning in Benedick's words as they are reported by Beatrice.

Benedick debunked her wit by associating it with a popular book of comic stories and jokes, insinuating that Beatrice is a poor plagiarist of unsophisticated jests. Beatrice in her turn debunks Benedick's art of insulting comparison in his very presence. In *The Politics of Courtly Dancing in Early Modern England*, Skiles Howard points out that Beatrice's lines, by their length and complex syntax, break the rhythm of the dance and transgress its regular pattern.[12] This transgression of the dancing codes goes together with a transgression of the playful pact of aggression that is supposed to govern the relationship between the two characters. The balance is broken because Beatrice then leads the dance. Benedick's reaction to Beatrice's assaults shows that we switch from insult without effect to the insulting effect. Integrated into a false misunderstanding allowed by the use of masks, the insult changes moods. The general pattern of contradiction on which the scene is based is somehow perverted by this true-false game of deception that prevents Benedick's immediate reply and implies frustration of the pleasure of the counter-attack. If Beatrice's insults leave a bitter taste in his mouth, it is because he cannot reply or contradict his opponent without transgressing the festive code of the masked ball. That is why he can only void his rheum a little later:

> O, she misused me past the endurance of a block. An oak but with one green leaf would have answered her; my very visor began to assume life and scold with her! She told me, not thinking I had been myself, that I was the Prince's jester, that I was duller than a great thaw, huddling jest upon jest with such impossible conveyance upon me that I stood like a man at a mark, with a whole army shooting at me. She speaks poniards, and every word stabs. If her breath were as terrible as her terminations there was no living near her, she would infect to the North Star.
>
> (2.1.219–29)

This speech takes an ironic twist if one notices that, like Dogberry later, Benedick emphasizes the insult and makes it prosper by repeating it, instead of neutralizing it. When Benedick asks Don Pedro to send him to the other end of the world in order to escape from this 'harpy' (2.1.248), the playful contract between the insulting and the insulted seems to be broken. Benedick leaves the game. It seems that Beatrice's attacks have had an insulting effect and that Benedick has become a victim while he should have remained a mere target. The complaint he pours into Don Pedro's ears transforms Benedick into a kind of plaintiff in a lawsuit, a defamation case. Beatrice's insult 'The Prince's fool' (2.1.187) turns into a slander, an attack on reputation for which Benedick wants to be revenged:

> I am not so reputed: it is the base, though bitter, disposition of Beatrice that puts the world into her person and so gives me out. Well, I'll be revenged as I may.
> (2.1.189–92)

Shakespeare here offers a euphemistic and comical version of the fate Hero suffers a little later, in public.

'I jest not'

In the scene of the aborted wedding, the playwright exploits the telescoping of the playful and serious modes:

FRIAR
   You come hither, my lord, to marry this lady?
CLAUDIO
   No.
LEONATO
   To be married to her, Friar; you come to marry her.
                                                (4.1.4–7)

This church scene is based on a major insult when Claudio answers the Friar's ritual question with a 'No' that probably constitutes the most spectacular moment in the play. During this scene, the playwright represents the passage from the word that is mere wind to the word that kills. The spectators on- and off-stage have become accustomed to the playful mode of the witty insult and to the amorous Agon. Leonato's reaction shows that one needs time to adapt to the change of register. Leonato contradicts the Friar by re-dressing Claudio's 'No' into a witty answer. We witness here the transition between two modes of insult. Leonato then appears as an absorber of shock that hides the insult behind a play on words, offering a verbal shield euphemizing the violence of the 'No'.[13] Then Benedick's reaction signals the change of mood: 'How now? Interjections? Why then, some be of laughing, as ha, ha, he' (4.1.19–20). Speaking of 'interjections' Benedick reveals the shift from a spiritual to an emotional mode of insult. Yet the parodic reference to William Lyly's *Short Introduction of Latin Grammar* (1538)[14] preserves the witty mode for a moment. Both Leonato and Benedick use verbal shields to maintain the ludic mode; but these shields will not last long. The sequence in which Benedick challenges Claudio is also based on the overlapping of the two moods of insult. While Claudio and Don Pedro both playfully practise insult, Benedick uses it as a prelude to the act. When he 'warns' Claudio that he is not joking ('You are a villain, I jest not', 5.1.143), Benedick underlines and counters the possible gap between the emission and the reception of the insult. In a world where words seemed to be nothing more than wind, the characters find it difficult to reinvest them with meaning. Insult is food for interpretation. From the outset Leonato presented it as such by saying to the messenger 'You must not, sir, mistake my niece' (1.1.57). However, the three episodes we have just mentioned show the ineffectiveness of this warning by revealing a series of misunderstandings committed by characters of which Dogberry will ultimately only be a magnified reflection.

The codes of courtesy that the merry war rests on in *Much Ado About Nothing* are challenged and put in danger in *A Midsummer Night's Dream*.

'Killing courtesy' in *A Midsummer Night's Dream*

> Pretty soul, she durst not lie
> Near this lack-love, this kill-courtesy:
> (2.2.80–1)

Here is how Puck misinterprets the tableau of Hermia and Lysander sleeping at a distance from one another on the wood's 'dank and dirty ground' (2.2.79), wrongly pitying Hermia, whom he takes for Helena, as the victim of a discourteous man. This scene is an illustration of the infernal comedy of errors dramatized in the play. Puck, a bad decipherer of signs, confuses the couples and takes for disdain what is in fact a sign of courtesy. He should indeed read the distance that separates the two sleeping lovers as a mark of respect, a gesture imported from the court and a testimony of courteous love. Puck's misunderstanding appears to the spectator all the more strikingly ironical since, a few lines before, Hermia had herself asked for this distance as a marker of courtly manners:

> But gentle friend, for love and courtesy,
> Lie further off, in human modesty:
> Such separation as may well be said
> Becomes a virtuous bachelor and a maid,
> So far be distant, and good night, sweet friend.
> (2.2.60–4)

If we consider the context in which Puck's mistake is set, it appears that Oberon's servant is not entirely wrong. The 'Athenian' in question has just transgressed good manners by making an indecent proposal to Hermia (2.2.45–6) and Puck's error is proleptic of the odious way in which Lysander will treat Hermia when he wakes up. Beyond an immediate ironic effect, this episode has other resonances. Indeed, it suggests that in the dark night of the wood, the codes of courtesy are put into question. They become blurred and unreadable, making the identity of the courtiers itself undecipherable. In the light of this misinterpretation, the nightmarish world of *A Midsummer Night's Dream* appears, in which Shakespeare constantly plays on the discrepancies between the emission and the reception of signs, and, more specifically, where the kind gesture becomes a mark of cruelty, and where words of love become insults.

This journey to the end of the night shakes and 'disfigures' courtesy, which ends up haunting the play with its absence-presence. One can indeed read the journey of the lovers as a return to the state of nature, which is measured by the transgression of the codes of courtesy and rules of civility, of the good manners learned at court, a transgression that goes hand in hand with a caricatured and parodic distortion of courteous love. But if courtesy is debunked in the noisy world of *A Midsummer Night's Dream*, it is to better resurface, in grotesque and incongruous forms, in the miniature world over which Titania reigns, but also in the play staged by the mechanicals. Bottom and his companions keep expressing their concern about possibly offending the nobility. They do their best so that their show is not discourteous. Being thus reconstructed, courtesy becomes a mirage, an illusion, a spirit that contradicts the letter: Quince's Prologue, this monstrous marriage of insult and compliment, appears then as the expression of the disturbance of courtesy in this play.

'If you were civil...'

'If you were civil and knew courtesy / You would not do me thus much injury' (3.2.147–8),[15] laments Helena, paradoxically when she hears Lysander declare how much he loves her. If we consider the etymological meaning of the word 'courtesy', it appears that by leaving the *court* of Theseus, by going from culture to nature, the lovers objectively abandon courtesy at the same time. From the beginning of the play, Lysander and Hermia oppose the court and its manners by refusing to 'choose love by another's eyes' (1.1.140). 'I know not by what power I am made bold' (1.1.59), Hermia wonders, assigning her revolt to some superior, irrational power. Hermia departs from the codes of courtesy as they are, for example, detailed in John Della Casa's treatise *Galateo*, subtitled *Or rather A treatise of the manners and behaviours, it behoveth a man to use and eschewe, in his familiar conversation*. Published in English in 1576, the book contains the following recommendation:

> I call them FROMWARD people, which will in all things be overtwhart to other men: as the very worde it selfe doth shewe. For, *Fromewarde*, signifieth asmuche, as *shorne against the wooll*. Now, how fit a thinge this frowardnes is, to wyn the good will of men, and cause men to wyshe well unto them: that you yourself may easily judge, in that it consisteth in overtwharting other mens desiers: which qualitie never maynteineth friendship, but maketh friends become foes. And therefor let them that desire to be well thought of and welcome amongst men, endevour themselves to shunne this fault: for it breedes no good lyking nor love, but hatred and hurt. I would councell you rather to measure your pleasures by other mens willes: where there shal come no hurt nor shame of it: and therein alwayse to doe & to saye, more to please other mens myndes and fansies, then your owne.[16]

Although this manual of good manners is addressed to men, it seems that Hermia's reaction to Theseus corresponds to this description of 'frowardenes'. Hermia, the 'froward' woman, challenges the rules of the court. She takes the risk of displeasing by refusing 'To fit [her] fancies to [her] father's will' (1.1.118).

LYSANDER
  Or else it stood upon the choice of friends–
HERMIA
  O hell, to choose love by another's eyes.
                            (1.1.139–40)

The stichomythic duet of thwarted lovers formulates this rejection of courtly manners that constitute a corset to which love refuses to submit. Their stay in the woods can be interpreted as a return to some 'rude' state (3.2.262), a nightmare where courtesy knows great disturbance, revealing the character's 'fierce' vein (3.2.82; 3.2.325; 4.1.68).

Behind the good manners implied by the word 'courtesy' there is also a whole philosophy of life, 'Courteous behaviour; courtly elegance and politeness of manners; graceful politeness or considerateness in intercourse with others' (*OED*).[17] This courtesy can be learned from books ('courtesy books') which, during the Renaissance, reflect a culture that allows the individual to sculpt an identity and a personality of his own. Taken in this humanistic sense, it seems that, in the noise and fury of that summer night, courtesy is doomed to 'dissolve' and 'melt' (1.1.245), taking with it the identity of lovers who become unrecognizable.

In *A Marxist Study of Shakespeare's Comedies*, Elliot Krieger defends the stimulating idea that, if the lovers flee from social conventions, it is to better reconstruct them outside Athens: 'While trying to get beyond one set of laws, the formal Athenian laws, the lovers – both couples – stay within the confines of social laws, the laws of decorum and propriety'.[18] It is true that courtesy is often mentioned in the play, by the fairies, the mechanicals, the lovers alike. But in the night of this *Dream*, courtesy becomes ghostly, turning lovers into ghosts of themselves.

If the wandering couples refer to good manners, it is above all to underline their fragility and absence. The image of courtesy is conjured up in a hypothetical mode that highlights its absence: 'I thought you lord of more true gentleness' (2.2.136), 'If you were civil and new courtesy' (3.2.147), 'If you were men, as men you are in show / You would not use a gentle lady so' (3.2.151–2), 'None of noble sort / Would so offend a virgin' (3.2.159–60), 'If you have any pity, grace or manners / You would not make me such an argument' (3.2.241–2), 'Have you no modesty, no maiden shame, / No touch of bashfulness?'

(3.2.285–6). If images of courtesy and gentleness crop up in the forest of *Dream*, it is to better be denied and challenged. As Barber notes about *Twelfth Night*, liberty is here 'testing courtesy'.[19]

The first words delivered by Demetrius when the lovers arrive in the forest seem to set the tone and reveal that love in this play will be discourteous: 'I love thee not, therefore pursue me not' (2.1.188). In this summer night, the varnish of courtesy can only peel off. It is neither a time nor a place to cultivate good manners and to 'speak fair' (2.1.199); it is time for 'passionate words' (3.2.220), and for a 'fierce vein' (3.2.82). Act 2 dramatizes a transitional stage in a journey that leads the quartet of lovers from courtesy to insult. The dialogue between Helena and Demetrius (2.1.188–244) brings out the threat and temptation of a journey back to the wild. 'Tempt not too much the hatred of my spirit / For I am sick when I do look on thee' (2.1.211–12): when Demetrius threatens Helena, she takes refuge behind the codes of courtesy ('Your virtue is my privilege', 2.1.220). But a few lines later, she points out that the codes have been transgressed, declaring: 'Your wrongs do set a scandal on my sex' (2.1.240) or 'We should be wooed, and were not made to woo' (2.1.242). In the next scene, the debate between Lysander and Hermia reproduces this tension between nature and culture. Confronted with Hermia's resistance ('Nay, good Lysander / [...] Do not lie so near', 2.2.47–8), Lysander uses the elegant verb and the witty word to dress up his misbehaviour and make it acceptable. Courtesy is revealed here as an artifice that fails to deceive the virtuous Hermia. The latter insists on the fact that she is a well-bred young girl: 'Now much beshrew my manners and my pride / If Hermia meant to say Lysander lied' (2.2.58–9). In both scenes, the women are the keepers of courtesy while the men threaten it. It is the women who seem to stand the test the longest. As soon as they arrive in the forest, Lysander and Demetrius forget their good manners, one by proposing to Hermia to make a common bed, the other by threatening Helena with rape (2.1.214–19). As for the women's journey, it goes from courteous restraint to verbal violence. Act 3, Scene 2 develops in gradation. Hermia dominates the various degrees of verbal violence. She controls herself for a moment ('Now I do but chide', 3.2.45) before letting herself go to insult ('curse', 3.2.46). The barrier of courtesy gives way when she exclaims: 'Out, dog, out, cur! Thou driv'st me past the bounds / Of maiden's patience' (3.2.65–6). Hermia here exceeds the bounds of courtesy just as Helena does a little later:

> What, will you tear
> Impatient answers from my gentle tongue?
> Fie, fie, you counterfeit, you puppet, you!
> (3.2.286–8)

As the term 'tear' suggests, the gentle courtesy is torn to pieces here and the tongue becomes unbridled. Insult is presented as a transgression of the rules of courtesy. In a section entitled 'Gentle wordes in communication', Della Casa makes the following recommendation to the reader: 'You must accustome your selfe, to use suche gentle and courtious speache to men, and so sweete, that it may have no maner of bitter taste'.[20] It is clear that the words exchanged during this night of folly have a bitter taste (3.2.44; 306). The insults that punctuate this whole scene sound the knell of courtesy.

'As this their jangling I esteem a sport'

In *Dream*, the discord of love makes a great noise. We can already hear this noise when Titania reproaches Oberon with his quarrelsome mood by using the term 'brawl': 'But with thy brawls thou hast disturbed our sport' (2.1.87). The sound of the quarrels between the lovers also appears when Oberon notes that 'The noise they make / Will cause Demetrius to awake' (3.2.116). The term 'noise', derived from the French word '*noise*', which originally referred to a noise, a tumult and then to a quarrel or an argument, in itself associates quarrel with noise.[21] Puck uses another term to evoke these nocturnal dissonances when he comments on the lovers' quarrels: 'As this their jangling I esteem a sport' (3.2.353). This sound impact is skilfully emphasized in the film by Dieterle and Reinhardt (1935) where the words of insult are multiplied, in echo, by Puck's voice, when Lysander abuses Hermia: 'Hang off, thou cat, thou burr, vile thing let loose, / Or I will shake thee from me like a serpent' (3.2.260–1); 'Out, tawny Tartar, out! / Out, loathed medicine; O hated potion, hence' (3.2.263–4), 'Get you gone, you dwarf, / You minimus, of hindering knot-grass made, / You bead, you acorn' (3.2.328–30). These generous strings of insults are magnified by this echo effect.[22] In her article on 'Flyting in Shakspere's [sic] Comedies', Margaret Galway points out that, in *The Dream*, the exchanges of insults depart from the rules governing the verbal confrontation between man and woman in other Shakespearean comedies: 'the one exception to Shakespeare's observation of social etiquette in the flytings between lords and ladies occurs in *A Midsummer Night's Dream*'.[23] In *Much Ado About Nothing* or *Love's Labour's Lost*, the war between the sexes is constructed in a paradoxically courteous manner, that is to say, through innuendoes, puns and witticisms. Verbal violence is polished by innuendo. That is not the case in *Dream*, where the insults are direct, thus provoking Hermia's incredulous reactions: 'Why are you grown so rude?' (3.2.262); 'Do you not jest?' (3.2.265). In *Dream*, insults are unvarnished. Hermia is 'disfigured' *via* insults to become a monster; she is 'translated'. The body is indeed at the heart of these invectives that translate how much, for Lysander, Hermia has become a source of disgust, an object that hurts his senses, sight ('tawny tartar', 'Ethiop', 3.2.257), touch ('thou cat', 'thou burr', 'serpent') and taste ('hated potion', 'loathed medicine').

The rules of flyting are transgressed in many other ways in this central scene. A form of ritualized verbal combat, flyting is normally played on a one-to-one basis. This pattern is disturbed since Hermia does not respond to Lysander's insults but takes Helena as a substitute target. If we analyze the mechanisms at work in this war of the sexes, it appears that the insult is rarely reciprocal: Demetrius attacks Lysander (3.2.259), Lysander attacks Hermia (3.2.260), Hermia attacks Helena (3.2.282) who ends up answering her directly ('You counterfeit, you puppet, you', 3.2.288). Helena prefers defamation to insult, since she attacks Hermia in the third person, taking the men as witnesses (3.2.299–305, 323–5). Through Hermia and Helena, Shakespeare depicts two types of evil tongues, the insulting one and the defamatory one, that are, of course, both banned from courtesy books. As the exchanges between the characters are thus blurred, the spectator gets lost and perceives nothing but nocturnal din that is at once entertaining and painful, cruel and infantile, violent and fairylike. Drawing his insults from the lexicon of nature, plants and animals, Lysander gives discord magical resonances. By becoming an 'acorn' or a 'burr', Hermia becomes part of the cohort of fairies surrounding Titania (Peaseblossom, Cobweb, Mustardseed). The recurrent evocation of her small size propels her into the miniature world of the fairies. The insult generates at the same time monstrosity and enchantment. The interpenetration of the worlds manifests itself here through insult.

In the wake of this verbal violence, we catch a glimpse of the spectacular figure of the shrew. 'O me, you juggler, you canker blossom, / You thief of love!' (3.2.282–3): Hermia who tried to claim her good manners in Act 2 becomes a fury whose nails could scratch Helena's face (3.2.298), as the latter notes:

> O, when she is angry she is keen and shrewd.
> She was a vixen when she went to school;
> And though she be but little, she is fierce.
>
> (3.2.323–5)

After having shown Hermia in an ideal light by recalling childhood memories (3.2.209–11), Helena transforms her into a virago.

In *Henry IV*, the exchanges of insults between Falstaff and Hal delineate a quarrel between the fat and the lean, between Carnival and Lent. In *Dream*, the exchanges between Hermia and Helena constitute a quarrel between the tall and the little. To the 'you puppet' (3.2.288) answers the 'thou painted maypole' (3.2.296), an expression that inscribes the insult in a carnivalesque logic. However, if for the 'auditor', this verbal confrontation is an entertainment ('sport'), it is a suffering for the 'actors'. It is by playing on this shift in perception that Shakespeare turns the scene into potentially 'very tragical mirth' (5.1.57) based on the superimposition of festive and serious moods. This blurring of playfulness and seriousness appears when Hermia wonders if all this is a joke: 'Do you not jest?' (3.2.265).

In traditional flyting, words are not supposed to hurt. But here the 'game' of insult proves ambivalent:

> Puppet? Why so? Aye, that way goes the game.
> Now I perceive that she hath made compare
> Between our statures: she hath urged her height,
> And with her personage, her tall personage,
> Her height, forsooth, she hath prevailed with him.
> And are you grown so high in his esteem
> Because I am so dwarfish and so low?
> How low am I, thou painted maypole? Speak,
> How low am I? I am not yet so low
> But that my nails can reach unto thine eyes.
> (3.2.289–98)

The insult is all the more harmful because it is 'specific', that is to say that it uses a physical feature of the insulted character and is not disconnected from reality. The central scene of the *Dream* leads from words to deeds. Hermia and Helena are about to resort to a physical confrontation, while Demetrius and Lysander challenge each other (3.2.255–6; 336–8). By resorting to duelling, the two men try to rewrite their brawl through codes, to polish it, to frame it. However, by insulting each other, the two adversaries transgress one of the essential rules of the duel which, instead of being a 'fair quarrel', becomes a 'brawl ridiculous'. At first defused by the intervention of Hermia, who clings desperately to Lysander's neck, the duel is then disturbed by Puck who, as a good ventriloquist, comes to spoil the communication between the two men by stealing their voices. Through Puck's intervention, the courteous violence that a duel is supposed to be dissolves into insults multiplied by echoes (3.2.404–30). The insults that Puck hurls on behalf of Demetrius and Lysander are the most blatant illustrations of the ghostly insults that inhabit the *Dream*.

The insults of the *Dream* are all the more spectacular since they are accompanied by and contrasted with vivid manifestations of courteous love. The woman is idealized: 'O Helen, goddess, nymph, perfect, divine' (3.2.137); men make her promises: 'and then end life, when I end loyalty' (2.2.67); men fight for her: 'And run through fire I will for thy sweet sake' (2.2.107). Insults are contrasted with the idealization of beauty which becomes monstrous, discordant, incongruous. By juxtaposing insult and the fiery declaration of love ('My love, my life, my soul, fair Helena', 3.2.246), two speech acts which share the same bombastic rhetoric, the *Dream* dramatizes the confusion of ugliness and beauty. In this play, even the word 'love' is received as an insult. Helena only manages to hear the two men's words of love as an insult to her sex and herself: 'Our sex, as well as I, may chide you for it, / Though I alone do feel the injury' (3.2.218–19). Outrageous, the Petrarchan style in which Demetrius celebrates the beauty of Helena when he wakes up (3.2.137–44), becomes insulting ('injury', 3.2.148). Oaths and compliments ('To vow and swear and superpraise my parts', 3.2.153), by their excess, tumble into the realm of insult. Courtesy has become illegible: even when it is present, it is not perceived as such. In the *Dream*, insult is also created out of thin air by the imagination of Helena, for whom praise becomes injury, scorn, disdain, mockery, derision. If insults fuel Helena's passion (2.1.202–10), compliments, on the other hand, have an insulting effect on her.

Thus, when Lysander calls for the 'gentle day' (3.2.418), he emphasizes that the night has not been 'gentle' but rather 'rude'. Some directors express this dismantling of courtesy by showing the gradual disintegration of the clothes ('apparel') worn by the young Athenians who end up in tatters. The mud that disfigures the lovers in the theatrical version by Robert Lepage (1992), as well as in the film versions by Peter Hall (1968) and Michael Hoffman (1998), is also a good illustration of this disfigurement of courtesy. But while the lovers 'kill courtesy', the mechanicals, especially Bottom, paradoxically cultivate it and manifest their constant desire *not to abuse*.

'If we offend ...'

The last instruction Bottom gives to his companions before the performance of *Pyramus and Thisbe* is 'And, most dear actors, eat no onions nor garlic, for we are to utter sweet breath, and I do not doubt but to hear them say it is a sweet comedy' (4.2.37–9). This recommendation, which refers to the realistic conditions of performance, can be heard metaphorically. The mechanicals want to deliver words that will be 'sweet breath' to the ears of the nobility. We are not far from the 'gentle communication' recommended by Della Casa.

The 'hard-handed men' (5.1.72) want to be as gentle as possible. During the casting sequence, Bottom proposes to roar 'gently' (1.2.77) so as not to frighten the ladies. To convince him to play the role of Pyramus, Peter Quince describes the character as follows: 'You can play no part but Pyramus; for Pyramus is a sweet-faced man; a proper man as one shall see in a summer's day; a most lovely, gentlemanlike man. Therefore you must needs play Pyramus' (1.2.79–82). By playing Pyramus, Bottom becomes a gentle-man. Those whom Puck calls the 'rude mechanicals' (3.2.9)[24] want to show courtesy by offering their play to Theseus and his court. To do this, they turn themselves from men of action to men of letter. When Quince proposes to 'do it in action' (3.1.4–5), Bottom interrupts the impulse: 'There are things in this comedy of Pyramus and Thisbe that will never please. First, Pyramus must draw a sword to kill himself, which the ladies cannot abide. How answer you that?' (3.1.8–11). Bottom practices self-censorship by transforming himself into a Master of the revels. When Starveling suggests that they should 'leave the killing out' (3.1.13), Bottom replies that, 'to make all well' (3.1.15), action must be polished by words:

> Write me a prologue, and let the Prologue seem to say we will do no harm with our swords, and that Pyramus is not killed indeed; and for the more better assurance, tell them that I, Pyramus, am not Pyramus, but Bottom the weaver. This will put them out of fear.
>
> (3.1.16–20)

Gentle words are used to defuse and cushion the violence of deeds. As many commentators have pointed out, it is the fear of being hanged ('and that were enough to hang us all', 1.2.72) that prompts the company to spare the audience. When the will to be courteous emanates from fear, the art of pleasing becomes an art of not displeasing. The content of the Prologue, however absurd as it may seem, perfectly sums up the nature of a theatre where only the name 'Pyramus' is killed. As Lysander suggests, in the theatre only the name goes through the sword: 'Where is Demetrius? O, how fit a word / Is that vile name to perish on my sword!' (2.2.110–11). To make violence courteous, one must dress it with words that function as 'shock absorbers'. The second objection raised by Snout, and then by Bottom, concerning the unbearable spectacle of a lion's appearance on stage calls for the same solution:

> SNOUT
> Therefore another prologue must tell he is not a lion.
> BOTTOM
> Nay, you must name his name, and half his face must be seen through the lion's neck, and he himself must speak through, saying thus, or to the same defect: 'Ladies', or 'Fair ladies, I would wish you', or 'I would request you', or 'I would entreat you, not to fear, not to tremble'.
>
> (3.1.31–8)

This second prologue that takes the form of a very courteous address to the ladies in the audience contrasts with the rudeness of the lovers' dialogues. It is through this coating that the mechanicals intend to purge their play of its 'mortal grossness' (3.1.151).

In Titania's hands and arms, Bottom becomes a 'gentle mortal' (3.1.130) who has all the attributes of grace: voice ('note', 3.1.131), body ('shape', 3.1.132), virtue ('fair virtue', 3.1.133). Titania enjoins her cohort of servants to be courteous towards her *protégé*:

> Be kind and courteous to this gentleman.
> Hop in his walks, and gamble in his eyes.
> [...]
> And pluck the wings from painted butterflies
> To fan the moonbeams from his sleeping eyes.
> Nod to him, elves, and do him courtesies.
> (3.1.158–68)

For the Fairy Queen, being kind and courteous means serving, feeding, watching Bottom's sleep and bowing to him. The scene that follows gives us a glimpse of Bottom in his art of courteous conversation. He proves to be a master of civility. His lines are punctuated with such expressions as 'your worships' (3.1.170), 'good Master Cobweb' (3.1.173–4), 'honest gentleman' (3.1.175), 'I pray you' (3.1.177), 'I beseech you' (3.1.180). These demonstrations of courtesy continue in Act 4, when Titania literally 'polishes' – a word that is etymologically related to politeness – Bottom with her caresses and sweet words:

> Come, sit thee down upon this flowery bed
>   While I thy amiable cheeks do coy,
> And stick musk-roses in thy sleek smooth head,
>   And kiss thy fair large ears, my gentle joy.
> (4.1.1–4)

'Amiable', 'sleek', 'smooth' and 'gentle' are all terms that suggest the process of polishing and embellishment that

Bottom undergoes. The mechanical shows his fine manners by multiplying polite addresses to 'Monsieur', 'good Monsieur', 'Signor' and other 'Cavalerie' (4.1.10–26), thus complying with some of the instructions dictated by Castiglione in *The Courtyer*. However, while cultivating the art of courtesy, Bottom also denounces its incongruity. 'Pray you, leave your courtesy, good Monsieur' (4.1.20): by asking Mustardseed not to bow and scrape, Bottom points out that the artifices of courtesy are out of place here. He emphasizes the discrepancy between the text and its context, between the words and the characters who utter them. Courtesy is marred at the very moment it is made, just like the 'courteous' (5.1.176) soon becomes the 'wicked' wall that separates Pyramus from Thisbe.

It is no more fitting for an ass to be a gentleman than it is for a wall to be 'courteous'. Yet, in *Dream*, walls, asses, lions and even the moon are courteous. They are and they are not. 'Here come two noble beasts in a man and a lion' (5.1.215–16), 'A very gentle beast' (5.1.225), 'Truly, the Moon shines with a good grace' (5.1.260–1): the ironic comments made by the members of the audience underline and erase in one breath the courtesy of the mechanicals. The life of the Wall in Pyramus and Thisbe is emblematic of the reversal patterns that inhabit the *Dream*:

> *And thou, O Wall, O sweet, O lovely Wall,*
> *That stand'st between her father's ground and mine,*
> *Thou Wall, O Wall, O sweet and lovely Wall,*
> *Show me thy chink, to blink through with mine eyne.*
> [Wall parts its fingers]
> *Thanks, courteous Wall. Jove shield thee well for this.*
> *But what see I? No Thisbe do I see.*
> *O wicked Wall, through whom I see no bliss,*
> *Cursed be thy stones for thus deceiving me.*
> (5.1.173–80)

In an instant, from 'lovely', the wall becomes 'wicked'. As is the case with the lovers' inconstant speeches, praise is turned into insult. This tirade offers a variation on the metamorphoses undergone by Hermia and Helena, subject to the changes in the men's perception. It also reflects the ambivalence on which Quince's prologue is built:

If we offend, it is with our good will.
  That you should think, we come not to offend,
But with good will. To show our simple skill,
  That is the true beginning of our end.
Consider then we come but in despite.
  We do not come, as minding to content you,
Our true intent is. All for your delight,
  We are not here. That you should here repent you,
The actors are at hand.

(5.1.108–16)

This speech raises the complex question of insult and intentionality. If we offend, please believe it was not our *intention* to do so. In a few lines, we can see all the dysfunctions, all the discrepancies between the emission and the reception of the signs that inhabit this play and especially the cruel games of the lovers. This speech that is 'not in government' (5.1.124) is a comment on the reversals, the distortions, the wanderings that we have just examined. It is also the embodiment of the 'musical discord' (4.1.102–26) mentioned by Theseus and Hippolyta. 'How shall we find the concord of this discord?' (5.1.60), one may ask about Quince's Prologue. These passages resonate as comments on the overall functioning of the *Dream*. This apparently absurd prologue contains what can be called the polite insults of the play. The journeys of the mechanicals and the lovers intersect in Act 5 during the performance of *Pyramus and Thisbe*. We have already shown how courtesy becomes an insult in the troubled world of the lovers. Quince's Prologue is a condensed version of this reversal.

This text shows the contradiction between the spirit and the letter. The errors of punctuation that correspond to a poor breath control on the part of the amateur actor jeopardize the courteous intention underlying this text. One can imagine that it is the fear of displeasing, the fear of being discourteous and risking one's head that explains these pronunciation defects. In this scene courtesy kills courtesy as well as 'truth kills truth' (3.2.129). It is then up to the audience to re-dress the monstrous body of this ambiguous text. Many commentators point out that the compliment here turns into an insult. But one should note that this text is not received as an insult; it does not have any insulting effect. It is received as a courteous homage to the court of Theseus. This text does have the courteous effect intended. Theseus receives this prologue as a courtesy, as a sign of welcome, 'nothing impaired but all disordered' (5.1.124–5). Here appears the magic of a text that is 'translated' by the ear that hears it. We are witnessing the metamorphosis of an insult into a compliment. It is the translator, not the author/enunciator, who constructs the meaning. Quince's text is rewritten by the one who hears it. The ear that receives the words recreates the courtesy that is here shattered. The most astonishing thing is that this ghostly text thus imagined by the listener erases the source text. However, some critics have noted that the correction ('amend', 5.1.211), the rectification of the text could be an error. In effect, the audience makes a text say what it does not say. The spirit reconstructs the letter. But if one sticks to the words, as pronounced by Quince, the courtesy shown by the company of actors is undermined and may become a *trompe-l'oeil*. What is taken for a tribute can resound like a provocation. It is possible to interpret punctuation errors as a series of revealing slips of the tongue. The text oscillates between compliment and insult. Shakespeare suggests this ambivalence by twice using the expression 'against your/our nuptial' (1.1.125, 5.1.75). The 'against' here means 'in preparation for', but if one decides to hear it with another ear, the nuptial homage may turn into a provocation. Thus, this prologue undergoes a double metamorphosis: first distorted by Quince, it is then reconstructed by the listener who may decide to hear the courteous homage or to stick to the abusive words. The life of words is in the ears that hear them.

In his book on good manners, Della Casa banned the practice of what he called 'scorne':

> Doe not allow, that a man should scorne or scoffe at any man, what so ever he be: no not his very enimy, what displeasure so ever he beare him: for, it is a greater sign of contempt and disdaine, to scorne a man, then to do him an open wrong. [...] And the Nature and effect of a scorne, is properly to take a contentation and pleasure to do another man shame and villany: thoughe it do our selves no good in the world.[25]

Then he tries to distinguish between what he calls 'a scorne' and 'a mock':

> There is no difference betweene a scorne and a mocke: but the purpose alone and intent a man hath, in the meaning the one the other. For a man mockes and laughes otherwile, in a sport and a pastime: but his scorn is ever in a rage and disdain.[26]

According to Della Casa, what differentiates mockery from scorn is the intention of the enunciator. While mockery can be pleasant and entertaining, scorn may cause harm. If mockery is essentially playful, scorn is serious. After drawing this distinction, Della Casa notes how difficult it is nevertheless to know the intention of the speaker:

> It many times chanceth, in boording and jesting, one tackes in sporte, the other strykes againe in earnest: and thus from playing, they come to fraying.[27]

When it comes to mocking, therefore, one should be careful, because a joke can easily turn into an insult. The confusion of joking mockery and insult is at the centre of the play within the play and explains the discomfort it can cause in the spectator.

The courtiers, by their mocking comments, produce a courtly noise that is as unpleasant as it is pleasant. This scene can be read as a scene of courteous insult. The courtiers' sharp remarks constitute insulting and disturbing subtitles. If, in the forest, the courtiers practised direct insult, in the court, the insult takes the form of mockery that is pregnant with irony: 'It is the wittiest partition that ever I heard discourse' (5.1.166–7); 'A very gentle beast, and of a good conscience' (5.1.225), 'Well roared, Lion' (5.1.258), 'Well run, Thisbe' (5.1.259), 'Well moused, Lion' (5.1.262). Behind each of these words of praise, the spectators and the actors may perceive an insult.

In the light of this performance sequence, one can better understand Helena's reaction when she can only hear scorn and derision in the praises delivered by Demetrius and Lysander: 'Wherefore was I to this keen mockery born? / When at your hands did I deserve this scorn?' (2.2.127–8), 'Good troth, you do me wrong; good sooth, you do, / In such disdainful manner me to woo' (2.2.133–4), 'O that a lady of one man refused / Should of another therefore be abused!' (2.2.137–8), 'Never did mockers waste more idle breath' (3.2.168). In *The Courtyer*, Castiglione teaches women how to distinguish false love from true love: 'It were first needfull to teach her to know them that make semblant to love, and them that love in deede'.[28] The true lovers can be recognized by the fact that they do not speak much: 'true lovers as they have a burning heart so have they a colde tongue, with broken tongue and sodain silence. Therefore (may hap) it were no false principle to say, He that loveth much, speaketh little.'[29] A lady of the court, Helena knows that courtesy may be nothing but 'mocking', a word that can also mean 'deceit'.

'Odious savours sweet'

Thus, the ear will give words their courteous or insulting value. The same words can be 'sweet breath' and 'bitter breath'. Before the performance, Bottom tells his companions 'I do not doubt but to hear them say, it is a sweet comedy' (4.2.41–2). This formulation is not insignificant because it preserves a possible discrepancy between what is said ('they are going to say') and what we perceive of what is said ('we are going to hear them say it'). In this gap, which separates what is said from what is heard, lies interpretation. The epilogue pronounced by Puck echoes Quince's Prologue ('if we offend') and the epilogue both written and erased by Theseus (5.1.346–52). At the heart of these three texts is the evocation of an offense that the listener should forgive:

> If we shadows have offended,
> Think but this and all is mended:
> That you have but slumbered here,
> While these visions did appear.
> And this weak and idle theme,
> No more yielding but a dream,
> Gentles, do not reprehend:
> if you pardon, we will mend.
> (5.1.413–20)

Robin leaves it up to the listener to amend his own perception of the work. It is the listener who amends the hypothetical harm done to him ('think but this'). It is up to the listener to erase the insult ('If you pardon, we will mend'). Puck's words also suggest that when one dreams, one has every right, even the right to be discourteous. The disregard for courtesy that we have just evoked is closely linked to the dreamlike dimension of the *Dream*. In dreams, asses can be gentlemen and courtiers can be fools. In the *Dream*, 'Courtesy itself [can] convert to disdain' and be a 'turncoat' (*MA*, 1.1.116–18). Coarseness turns into civility, just as the sea evoked by Oberon is soothed by hearing the siren's song ('That the rude sea grew civil at her song', 2.1.152). From these exchanges of courtesy is born the harmonious discord of a *Dream* whose 'sweet scents' are also odious: 'odious savours sweet' (3.1.77). The term 'brawl' is emblematic of this ambiguity, since it evokes disputes but also dances that are more refined and courteous than the rounds orchestrated by Titania. The word 'noise' is also pervaded by this ambivalence: in French, 'noise' certainly refers to the harshness of quarrels, but in English it can designate all kinds of noise, including the pleasant noise made by the violins at a wedding. The noise that precedes the Athenians' wedding is made of this mixture of courtesy and violence.

3

'Quarrelling by the book': Insult and duelling codes

At a time when trial by combat, of medieval origin, was 'still alive in the English collective consciousness',[1] Elizabethan society experienced the emergence and development of private duelling, a phenomenon that came from elsewhere, especially from Italy and France, and that spread sufficiently for James I to prohibit this deadly fashion in 1613.[2] For the Elizabethans, duelling was essentially an art that could not be practised by everyone. It was a science that one learned in books. In Ben Jonson's *The Alchemist* (performed in 1610 and published in 1612), Kastril asks Face and Subtle for the recipe of duelling that will enable him to fight a duel according to the rules. He is promised a precious 'instrument' for those who want to discover the secrets of the art of quarrelling: 'a table / With mathematical demonstrations / Touching the art of quarrels […] / An instrument to quarrel by'.[3] The Elizabethan period saw the publication and circulation of these 'instruments', theoretical works and instructions for duelling, whether they were English texts, such as those written by William Segar (1590)[4] and George Silver (1599),[5] or translated texts, such as the manuals by the Italian masters of arms Giacomo di Grassi (1594)[6] and Vincentio Saviolo (1595).[7] These works answered all the questions that any duellist could ask, not only about combat techniques, weapons, passes, but also about the rules governing the initiation of the duel. For there to be a duel, and not a brawl, a tournament, or a war, a certain number of rules had to be respected. Moreover, to use François Billacois' words, 'a duel is inseparable from the quarrel of which it is the logical outcome'.[8] Before being an act, the duel is an act of language that relies on a certain number of codes. How does one go from words to deeds? What insult justifies the challenging of a friend, of an enemy or even a stranger? What are the rules of language that every good duellist should respect? The answer to all these questions can be found in these works that propose to tame violence by codifying it. The purpose of this chapter is to suggest that *Romeo and Juliet*, *As You Like It* and *Twelfth Night*, among other plays, show that Shakespeare was informed by these non-literary texts, and to explore to what extent his work draws on the phenomenon, whose dramatic potential the plays largely exploit.

'Do you quarrel, sir?': *Romeo and Juliet* as a story of insult

'From ancient grudge break to new mutiny': the third line of the prologue to *Romeo and Juliet* presents the story in terms of a 'grudge', a word that evokes past insults and creates a grumbling murmur. This prologue suggests that insults leave indelible marks on the present of the play and that, far from being merely what Beatrice calls 'foul wind' in *Much Ado About Nothing*, some words lead to action and death. The Prince complains about 'Three civil brawls bred of an airy word' (1.1.87). Insults, no matter how airy they are, prove lethal indeed in *Romeo and Juliet*.

'Gregory, on my word, we'll not carry coals' (1.1.1): the very first words of the play confirm that what is usually seen as a love story is also a story of insult. René Weis glosses the line as 'we will not "allow ourselves to be insulted, literally, do dirty work" '.[9] The expression 'carry coals' underlines the stain that an insult may constitute, while the words 'I strike quickly, being moved' (1.1.5) suggest that words lead to action. The word 'move' accords with the term 'insult' that etymologically means to 'jump on' (*in-sulto*), to 'triumph' and is in itself a programme of action. The term 'invective', from *invehi, invectus*, which means 'to rush against' (from *vehere*, to carry, to bear), also evokes this physical dimension. Insulting means assaulting the other person: no wonder then that it should lead to blows. Shakespeare evokes this telescoping of doing and saying when Mercutio calls for the act to be joined with the word: 'make it a word and a blow' (3.1.39). Words and blows constitute the first episode of the play that features one of the 'new mutinies' mentioned in the Prologue. This first scene places insults at the heart of Shakespeare's dramatic design.

The famous thumb-biting episode is pregnant with ill-digested duelling codes:

SAMSON
  Let us take the law of our sides; let them begin.
GREGORY
  I will frown as I pass by and let them take it as they list.
SAMSON
  Nay, as they dare. I will bite my thumb at them, which is disgrace to them if they bear it.
ABRAHAM
  Do you bite your thumb at us, sir?
SAMSON
  I do bite my thumb, sir.
ABRAHAM
  Do you bite your thumb at us, sir?
SAMSON [*aside to Gregory*]
  Is the law of our side if I say 'Ay'?
GREGORY [*aside to Samson*]
  No.
SAMSON
  No, sir, I do not bite my thumb at you, sir, but I bite my thumb, sir.
GREGORY
  Do you quarrel, sir?

ABRAHAM
Quarrel, sir? No, sir.
Samson. But if you do, sir, I am for you. I serve as good a man as you.
ABRAHAM
No better.
SAMSON
Well, sir.
[*Enter* Benvolio.]
GREGORY [*aside to Samson*]
Say 'better', here comes one of my master's kinsmen.
SAMSON
Yes, better, sir.
ABRAHAM
You lie.
SAMSON
Draw if you be men. Gregory, remember thy washing blow. *They fight.*
BENVOLIO [*Draws.*]
Part, fools!
Put up your swords, you know not what you do.

(1.1.37–63)

This thumb-biting has recently been studied by Miranda Fay Thomas as a 'shaming gesture' that performs 'toxic masculinity' in *Romeo and Juliet*.[10] Jill L. Levenson has suggested that this moment is based on a parody of duelling codes.[11] In *Shakespeare's Insults: A Pragmatic Dictionary*, I have shown how this episode is also evocative of the crucial difference duelling codes established between injury by word and injury by deed, as well as of the centrality of the lie[12] in the way duels were designed. Yet what this episode first and foremost throws into relief is the abuse of quarrels that turns what could be a duel into a mere brawl.

Duelling manuals of the Elizabethan period warn readers against the excesses of quarrels. The most famous and detailed book on the duelling art, its codes and rules, is *Vincentio*

Saviolo, His Practise, in Two Bookes, published in 1595 in England. The contents of its two books is summarized as follows in the frontispiece: 'The first intreating of the use of the Rapier and Dagger. / The second, of Honor and honorable quarrels.' The second part allows the reader to frame a quarrel and to grasp what insulting words or acts were supposed to trigger off a duel. Before defining the 'honourable quarrel', Saviolo describes what should not be considered as such, by enumerating the various ways in which a man may avoid useless duels and futile quarrels. An honourable duellist should be able to watch his tongue and his behaviour. In his address to the reader, Saviolo stresses the pedagogical value of his book and warns his disciples against all abuses of the duelling art:

> Exhorting all men of good mindes and noble spirites to learne and purchase the same, not to the end to abuse it in insolencies and injuries, but to use it in cases of necessitie for the defence of just causes, and to the maintenance of the honour of themselves and others.[13]

Saviolo advises his contemporaries not to misuse the duelling art that he is going to teach them:

> For whosoever will followe this profession must flie from rashnes, pride, and injurie, and not fall into that foule falt and error which many men incurre, who feeling themselves to be strong of bodie and expert in this science, presuming thereupon, thinke that they may lawfully offer outrage and injury unto anie man, and with crosse and grosse tearmes and behaviour provoke everie man to fight, as though they were the onely heirs of Mars.[14]

The opening scene of *Romeo and Juliet* is a lively illustration of these excesses and of the misuse of the art of duelling that is denounced by Saviolo. The frowning is the first provocation: 'I will frown as I pass by, and let them take it as they list': these words show again that in matters of insult, the reception is as important as the emission. The insulting gesture that follows is called 'la nique' in French: it is the gesture that consists in biting one's thumb while producing a snapping sound. Randle Cotgrave in 1611 defined this gesture as follows:

> faire la nique. To mocke by nodding, or lifting up of the chinne; or more properly, to threaten or defie, by putting the thumbe naile into the mouth, and with a jerke (from th'upper teeth) make it to knacke. The ailments ending in ique make the doctor ill: Prov. Such be Hydropic, Hectic, Paralitic, Apoplectic, Lethargic, etc, because they are hardly, or never, cured.[15]

In his *Encyclopedia of Swearing*, Geoffrey Hughes talks about 'coded provocation'[16] between the Capulet and Montague servants. The gesture is often associated with an explicitly obscene gesture, the fig, which is to be found in other Shakespeare plays,[17] an obscene dimension that is confirmed by the sexual allusions that pervade this opening scene, where, in a few lines, the servants talk of 'maidenheads', of a 'pretty piece of flesh' and of a 'naked weapon [that] is out' (1.1.24–32). Body language often becomes bawdy language. The combination of mouth and finger is loaded with obvious sexual symbolism and, even if it does not rest on any etymological link, the French Renaissance term 'nique' may find an echo in the contemporary popular French insults *nique ta mère* or *va te faire niquer*, in which the word is short for *forniquer* ('fornicate', which derives from Latin *fornix*, meaning 'brothel').

The opening scene of *Romeo and Juliet* seems to correspond to what Saviolo describes as quarrels deriving from mere trifles:

> I have seene and noted in diverse partes of mine owne countrie and in other places of the world, great quarrels springing from small causes, and many men slayne uppon light occasions.[18]

The particular quarrel Saviolo narrates opposes two Italian captains 'of great familiarity and acquaintance', the crux of the matter being an imprudent gesture. One of the two men's servants had been so bold as to touch lightly the sword of the other captain, who, in his turn, 'lent the boy a little blow'. Here is what ensued from this:

> The other Captaine (the boies master) taking this reprehension of his boy in worse parte than there was cause, after some wordes multiplyed began to drawe his sword.[19]

Several conclusions may be drawn from this incident that eventually caused the master's death. First, the servant's gesture was received as an outrage. Moreover, the master's reaction to the 'little blow' that the captain gave to his servant reveals how an insult may be transferred from one person to another. By striking the servant, the offended captain hit the master. This example also reveals that interpretation is at the heart of insult. Saviolo's comment on the incident shows that the gesture was mis-taken or taken 'in worse parte than there was cause'. The 'multiplication' of words is presented as the mechanism that leads to a dishonourable quarrel. When an insult calls for another insult, verbal conflict leads to physical combat and one finally switches disorderly from words to blows while in an honourable quarrel, as Markku Peltonen notes, 'A challenge was a polite response to an impolite word or act'.[20]

Saviolo advises all men to learn how to avoid quarrels when it is possible, especially between friends:

> I would wish that everie one should beware to offend any man either in wordes or deedes, and if you have offered offence, seeke to make amends, as a civill and honest man should, and suffer not the matter to grow to such extremitie and inconvenience, as wee see examples everie daie, whereby God is highly displeased.[21]

In the second book, he notes that the duelling fashion is based on wrong prejudices:

> For if a man frame himselfe to leade a civill and temperate course of life, some will saie hee is a foole: if hee be not quarrel-some, hee is a cowarde: if no gamester, hee is of base education: if no blasphemer, an hipocrite.[22]

As in the address to the reader, he denounces 'unnecessarie strifes and fruitelesse contentions'[23] that rest on an erroneous conception of morality and virtue. Two of the terms that are used here ('foole' and 'cowarde') are among the most recurrent abusive words in Shakespeare's plays. To know what is abuse and what is 'no abuse', a man needs to take into consideration the quality of his opponent and the situation in which the abusive words or acts intervene. The insulter may have extenuating circumstances. When the insult is proffered by a man who is under the influence of anger or drunkenness, it does not have the same impact as when it is coldly or soberly uttered. The import of an abusive word is not frozen once and for all, but changes as the same words do not or should not produce the same insulting effect, depending on the pragmatic circumstances of their enunciation.

Saviolo keeps warning his readers against any disproportionate reaction. If one wants to go from words to blows, one must first make sure that the insult is worth it:

> and so by multiplying of speeche, they may fall from words to blowes, whereby some or other may be spoyled upon a matter not worthy the talking of.[24]

The same image of the multiplication of words leading to deeds crops up again when Saviolo depicts another particular quarrel:

> To bee short, in the end one word added on the other, and one speech following the other, the matter came from saying,

to doing: and what the tung had uttered the hand would maintaine.[25]

The origin of the quarrel that is mentioned here was nothing but a gaze:

> I sawe two brethren, one a most honorable Captaine, and the other a brave and worthie souldier, who walking together in the streetes, were verie stedfastly eied of certaine young Gentlemen of the Citie, who stared the Captaine and his brother in the face something unseemly, and (as they tooke it) discurteouslie: whereuppon they asked the Gentlemen in verie curteous manner, whether they had seene them in anie place before, or whether they knew them. They answered no. Then replied the Captaine and his brother, Why then doo you looke so much upon us? They aunswered, because they had eies. That (sayd the other) is the crowes fault, in that they have not picked them out.[26]

The expression 'as they tooke it' once again reveals that insults are nothing *per se* but become insults only in so far as they are taken as such. After having enumerated the tragic consequences of this incident (one man deceased, two men injured and many men exiled), Saviolo concludes by saying that if those men 'had more curteouslie and wiselye demeaned themselves',[27] nothing would have happened. Yet the author starts by blaming the men who took pleasure in 'eying' passers-by on the street:

> There be also certaine undiscreet men, whose grosse fault I cannot overslip without blaming: these men use as they either stand or go in streets, so to stare and looke men passing by them in the face, as if they woulde for some reason marke them: which breedeth such an offence unto some men so marked, that they cannot take it in good part, and therefore it is verie dangerous.[28]

This cannot but remind us of the opening scene of *Romeo and Juliet* and its offensive 'frowning'. According to Saviolo's criteria, this quarrel cannot be an honourable quarrel. The Capulets' servants illustrate the anarchic tendency to quarrel over the slightest peccadillo. In Act 3, Scene 1, Mercutio accuses Benvolio of being a quarreller:

> Thou – why, thou wilt quarrel with a man that hath a hair more or a hair less in his beard than thou hast. Thou wilt quarrel with a man for cracking nuts, having no other reason but because thou hast hazel eyes. What eye but such an eye would spy out such a quarrel? Thy head is as full of quarrels as an egg is full of meat, and yet thy head hath been beaten as addle as an egg for quarrelling. Thou hast quarrelled with a man for coughing in the street, because he hath wakened thy dog that hath lain asleep in the sun. Didst thou not fall out with a tailor for wearing his new doublet before Easter, with another for tying his new shoes with old riband, and yet thou wilt tutor me from quarrelling!
>
> (3.1.16–29)[29]

Shakespeare's text reflects the excesses that were denounced in treatises on duelling such as Saviolo's. If we look at his treatise, we also understand that if the Capulets use a gesture and not a word, it is because they want the Montagues to be the challengers while they themselves try to be in the position of the defendants, to remain on the 'right side of the law'. The term 'injury' takes on its full meaning in this play where the insult is approached in terms of law (*jus*) within a process of quarrelling. In Saviolo's treatise, the section entitled 'A Rule and order concerning the Challenger and Defender' explains how the parts are distributed and how things are different depending on whether you insult in words or deeds:

> All injuries are reduced to two kindes, and are either by wordes or deedes. In the first, he that offereth the injurie ought to bee the Challenger: in the later, hee that is injuried.[30]

Saviolo gives two examples:

> Example, Caius sayth to Seius that hee is a traitour: unto which Seius aunswereth by giving the lie: whereuppon ensueth, that the charge of the Combat falleth on Caius, because hee is to maintaine what hee sayd, and therefore to challenge Seius.[31]

It is the lie that leads to the challenge. Things are different when the insult is expressed in a gesture:

> Now when an injurie is offered by deede, then do they proceed in this manner. Caius striketh Seius, giveth him a boxe on the eare, or some other waie hurteth him by some violent meanes: Wherewith Seius offended, saith unto Caius, that hee hath used violence towardes him, or that hee hath dealt injuriouslie with him, or that hee hath abused him, or some such manner of saying. Whereunto Caius aunswereth, Thou lyest: whereby Seius is forced to challenge Caius, and to compell him to fight, to maintaine the injurie which hee had offered him. The summe of all therefore, is in these cases of honour, that hee unto whome the lie is wrongfullie given, ought to challenge him that offereth that dishonour, and by the swoorde to prove himself no lyer.[32]

The chronology of words and deeds is essential and therein lies the explanation of 'let them [the Montagues] begin': the idea is to make them bear what William Segar in 1590 calls the 'burden' of challenge in his *Booke of Honor and Armes*:

> we call an act done contrarie to reason, *injurie*, or (as some do terme it) *Offence* or *Wrong*: and the Burthen, is a certeine naturall obligation, whereby a man standeth bound to repulse or mainteine the matter in question.[33]

It is for this reason that Samson and Gregory choose insult by deed and not by word. In *The Duel in Early Modern England*.

Civility, Politeness and Honour, Markku Peltonen quotes Simon Robson's (R. S.) *The Courte of Civill Courtesie* (1577):

> It followed that he who received 'the first reprocheful words' had his honour insulted and thus became the challenger. It was however expedient 'for pollicie sake' [...] to try to make the other to challenge 'to save my selfe from the daunger of the lawe.'[34]

Ironically, the gesture, instead of leading to a duel, leads to a multiplication of words, or what Saviolo would call 'multiplying' of words and speeches, quite unsuited to the duelling procedure, the expression 'bite your thumb' / 'bite my thumb' being repeated six times in a few lines. This multiplying of words leads to a brawl rather than to a proper duel.

What the first episode also reveals is that the 'lie' is the element that triggers off the duel. It is when Abraham says 'You lie' that the characters switch from words to blows. Beyond the precise meaning of the thumb-biting gesture, the scene is enlightening as to the relative status of the insult and the subtleties of interpretation on which the parties involved can play. Samson and Abraham play on the ambiguity of the gesture as one plays on words until the decisive 'You lie' is uttered, which was considered as key in the duelling process.[35]

In the chapter entitled 'What the reason is, that the partie unto whom the lie is given ought to become Challenger: and of the nature of Lies', Saviolo explains why the lie is essential in the design of a duel:

> Some men marvell why that hee unto whome the lie is given, ought rather to challenge the Combat, than hee that is called a traitor or a villaine, or by some other injurious name, seeing that it woulde seeme more reasonable, that hee which is most injuried, ought to become Challenger, and not the other, and that this is a greater injurie to saie unto a man, Thou art a theefe, thou art a villaine, & a traitor, than this, thou lyest. But the lawes have no regarde of the

wordes, or of the force or efficacie of them, but provide
that the burthen of the challenge shall ever fall on him
that offereth the injurie: for it is thought that everie man is
honest, just, and honourable untill the contrarie bee proved.
And therefore as in common triall by civill judgement and
order of lawe, whosoever is accused of anie crime, is by
simple denying the same delivered from condemnation,
unlesse further proofe thereof be brought agaynst him:
even so in this case, whosoever speaketh of another man
contrarie unto that which is ordinarilie presumed of him,
it is great reason that the charge of proof should lie uppon
him, to make that manifest unto the worlde by force of
Armes, that such a man is guiltie of such and such thinges
as hee hath laide to his charge.[36]

Duelling rules do not consider the force or degree of abuse
but they imply that the accusation of lying (termed 'the lie')
is the worst possible insult.[37] The basic principle on which
duels rest ignores the nature of the insult but considers it as
an accusation whose relevance should be proved. From this
point of view, one should note that the word 'challenge' is
etymologically related to the Latin 'calumnia' (calumny). The
'challenger' is the 'calumniator'. In the duelling field, abuse is
taken seriously in so far as it implies an accusation that must
find its justification in combat. To sum up Saviolo's rule, it is
the one who calls the other 'traitor' who has to prove what
he is saying by taking the initiative of the duel in being the
challenger. On the other hand, in the case if an injury in deed,
the man who physically hurts the other does not have to prove
that he has done so, and thus the offended party is to be the
challenger.

[I]f I beate or strike anie man, thereof it proceedeth no cause
of proofe, it is manifest that I offend or hurt him, and I
know no cause why I shoulde prove that I doo so. But if the
other saie unto mee, that I did not as a Gentleman worthie
to beare Armes, or that I dealt not honourably, or any such

thing, I repell his sayings with the Lie, and force him to maintaine what hee hath spoken: whereof I am acquitted with sole denial, till hee make further proofe.[38]

All this shows that in the duelling process, insults amount to accusations which one has to prove the truth of. As the answer to this accusation, the lie may be delivered in a number of different ways:

> Wherefore although the names of deniall are diverse, as Thou lyest, Thou sayest untruly, Thou speakest falsely, Thou sparest the truth, Thou tellest tales, Thou regardest not how falsely thou reportest a matter, Thou art wide from truth, This is a lie, a tale, a falsehood, &c. Yet all these manners of speech import the Lie, whether hee unto whome they were spoken spake injuriously or no.[39]

The lie is the hinge that leads the servants from words to blows in the opening sequence, in a complete misapplication of all duelling rules. The triggering of the fight through the utterance of the lie is parodic, because it is based on a simplistic vision of the rules. As a matter of fact, Saviolo warns 'That straightwaies vpon the Lye, you must not take armes',[40] a guideline that the servants do not respect.

The treatment of the 'lie' is crucial in the subsequent conflict between Tybalt, Mercutio and Romeo. While the Capulet and the Montague servants engage in a mockery of procedure that triggers a fight, the confrontation between Tybalt and Romeo is recurrently postponed until Act 3. The intervention of Capulet at the beginning of the play first defuses the fight that Tybalt was planning to wage with Romeo. Then, during the ball scene, it is Capulet again who restrains Tybalt and prevents him from challenging Romeo because the latter has insulted him by attending the ball to which he was not invited. We then understand that Romeo, not having received Tybalt's cartel, or letter of challenge, was unable to respond. By playing on the problems of transmission, that are so essential in *Romeo and*

Juliet, Shakespeare articulates the codes of duelling with the codes of the tragic genre and defers the reaction to the insult. Finally, in Act 3, Romeo adopts precise duelling codes to avoid the duel, by firstly only responding to Tybalt's insult 'thou art a villain' with 'villain am I none':

TYBALT
    Romeo, the love I bear thee can afford
    No better term than this: thou art a villain.
ROMEO
    Tybalt, the reason that I have to love thee
    Doth much excuse the appertaining rage
    To such a greeting. Villain am I none,
    Therefore farewell; I see thou knowest me not.
                                   (3.1.59–64)

One may assume that when Tybalt says to Romeo 'thou art a villain', he is referring to the lack of response to the challenge that the passionate lover should have received from Tybalt. In this sequence, Romeo first carefully avoids giving 'the lie' by just uttering the precise words 'Villain am I none'. Thus, he does not respond to the insult because the codes of love here interfere with the codes of honour. By not uttering 'thou liest', which would be the trigger for action expected by Tybalt, Romeo avoids the act. In order not to fight, he follows the advice of the duelling manuals, carefully avoiding the formulation of a direct lie. The application of the codes is part of a strategy of avoidance. In the same scene, Romeo evades the challenge a second time:

TYBALT
    Boy, this shall not excuse the injuries
    That thou hast done me; therefore turn and draw.
ROMEO
    I do protest, I never injured thee,
    But love thee better than thou canst devise
    Till thou shalt know the reason of my love.

> And so, good Capulet, which name I tender
> As dearly as mine own, be satisfied.
>
> (3.1.65–71)

Romeo knows how to play with words and uses *double entendre* to avoid conflict. Yet, if Tybalt's verbal assault does not have the expected insulting effect on Romeo, it does on Mercutio, who takes Romeo's place for a moment, to fight Tybalt. The insult triggers the action but Shakespeare manages to displace it by a process of substitution. The transfer of the insult is at work in this scene. When Mercutio denounces Romeo's inertia with the exclamation 'O calm, dishonourable, vile submission' (3.1.72), he evokes in one sentence all the debates about the duel of honour. This reaction illustrates the idea that not responding to insult is a sign of cowardice. Mercutio embodies the social pressure that rests on any man who, to avoid being seen as a coward, is bound to react to an insult. If Mercutio intervenes in the quarrel by substituting himself for Romeo, it is because he wants to guarantee his honour. But the substitution here leads to tragedy. By interposing himself between Tybalt and Mercutio, Romeo transgresses one of the rules laid down by Saviolo. He who wishes to separate two men who are fighting must ensure that his intervention does not harm or benefit either of them.[41] Romeo's reaction is fatal to Mercutio. It is this transgression of codes that turns the play into a tragedy:

> Now, Tybalt, take the 'villain' back again
> That late thou gavest me.
>
> (3.1.127–8)

With this sentence, Romeo does not deliver a 'lie' but returns the initial insult to its sender, putting Mercutio's death in parentheses, as it were. However, it is this death that turns the possible duel into a mere vendetta. The fight between Tybalt and Romeo is not a duel, because according to Saviolo, the duel should not be revenge: 'Combat [is] not ordayned for revenge'.[42] Romeo accepts the fight without respecting the letter of the duel which should make him say 'thou liest'. The first part of *Romeo and Juliet* is therefore based on a suspension of the passage from insults to acts. Once the deed is done, once Mercutio and Tybalt are dead, things become blurred and it is no longer clear who is to blame, who is the 'villain'. That is what the oxymoron 'honorable villain' (3.2.79) or the question 'What villain, madam?' (3.5.79), both uttered by Juliet, convey. At the heart of the crisis, it is ironically on Juliet that a rain of insults will fall.

If in *Romeo and Juliet*, the duel dissolves into vendetta, in *As You Like It*, it is reduced to mere words that Touchstone comically summarizes as 'the degrees of the lie'.

'The degrees of the lie' in *As You Like It*

To prove that he 'He hath been a courtier' (5.4.41), Touchstone argues that he has 'had four quarrels and like to have fought one' (5.4.46–7). The quarrel was then 'upon the seventh cause'. At Jaques' request, Touchstone explains what he means by this:

> Upon a lie seven times removed [...] as thus, sir: I did dislike the cut of a certain courtier's beard. He sent me word if I said his beard was not cut well, he was in the mind it was. This is called the 'retort courteous'. If I sent him word again it was not well cut, he would send me word he cut it to please himself. This is called the 'quip modest'. If again it was not well cut, he disabled my judgement. This is called the 'reply churlish'. If again it was not well cut, he would answer I spake not true. This is called the 'reproof valiant'. If again it was not well cut, he would say I lie. This is called the 'counter check quarrelsome' – and so to the 'lie circumstancial' and the 'lie direct.'
> (5.4.68–81)

Touchstone concludes by saying that he did not dare to go beyond the 'lie circumstancial', and that his opponent did not dare to give him the 'lie direct'. So they simply 'measured swords and parted' (5.4.86). After this account, Jaques asks him: 'Can you nominate in order now the degrees of the lie?' (5.4.87–8). Touchstone, performing on request, delivers the following speech:

> O sir, we quarrel in print, by the book, as you have books for good manners. I will name you the degrees. The first, the retort courteous; the second, the quip modest; the third, the reply churlish; the fourth, the reproof valiant; the fifth, the counter-check quarrelsome; the sixth, the lie with circumstance; the seventh, the lie direct. All these you may avoid but the lie direct and you may avoid that, too, with an 'if'. I knew when seven justices could not take up a quarrel, but when the parties were met themselves, one of them thought but of an 'if': as 'if you said so, then I said so'; and they shook hands and swore brothers. Your 'if' is the only peacemaker; much virtue in 'if'.
>
> (5.4.89–101)

This second speech uttered by Touchstone is a rewriting of the first one. Indeed, the recitation of a particular quarrel is followed by the recitation of the general rules it illustrates. Each episode of the quarrel recounted by Touchstone corresponds to a degree of the lie. Who else but a character called 'Touchstone' could have enumerated these degrees? The two speeches have a repetitive effect that produces a certain weariness in the listener, and that reflects the extremely enumerative form of the theoretical manuals devoted to the duel. For if to an uninitiated contemporary reader or spectator these tirades may sound enigmatic, the Elizabethan spectator, on the other hand, could probably hear in them a parodic rewriting of the duelling codes that were so subtle at the time. Saviolo's manual was printed in in England in 1595 while *As You Like It* was performed in 1599. Juliet Dusinberre rightly notes that

'The lines suggest a specific reference to *Vincentio Saviolo His practice (1595)*'.[43] Through Touchstone, Shakespeare mocks the extreme complexity of the distinctions drawn by duelling theorists between the various kinds of lie. To appreciate Touchstone's tirade, it is necessary to know that the lie was considered in duelling literature as the worst kind of insult. The 'thou liest' or, even worse, the 'thou liest in thy throat' was the insult that a man of honour could never tolerate. These words triggered the challenge and thus the duelling process. However, a 'thou liest' or 'thou speakest falsely'[44] should not be confused with, for example, 'this is not so' or 'the truth heereof I take to be otherwise' which did not commit a person to any fight, as was noted by Saviolo:

> But if he chaunce to saie onely thus, or after this manner unto mee, This is not so, or the truth heereof I take to be otherwise, &c. I cannot take anie such speech injuriously, for it may be the thing whereof I spake is not true, and yet I doo not lie [...]. [...] for a worde commeth sometimes to bee injuryous, and sometimes not, onelye by beeing sometimes injuriously spoken and sometimes not.[45]

Touchstone enumerates here all the forms of the lie that avoid physical confrontation because they are not accepted by the duelling technicians. The enumerative aspect of his speech perfectly reflects the organization of the books on duelling, which were divided into numerous chapters. Moreover, when we know that Saviolo speaks 'Of the manner and diversitie of Lies', then 'Of Lies certaine', then 'Of conditionall Lyes', then 'Of the Lye in generall', then 'Of the Lie in particular' and finally 'Of foolish Lyes',[46] we can clearly see in Touchstone's categorizing discourse an imitation of the pedagogical and legalistic style of these duelling manuals. By turning these manuals into books on manners, turning the technical names into witticisms and renaming the various kinds of lies, Touchstone hardly exaggerates but disguises these instructions sufficiently to achieve parody.[47] Moreover, if one remembers that the duelling theoretical works were full of examples supposed to enlighten the reader on extremely subtle distinctions, one savours with all the more pleasure the 'as "if you said so, then I said so"' uttered by the parrot-theorist Touchstone whose speech then borders on pastiche. Saviolo's book is full of these 'as ifs':

> As for example: If one man doo saye unto another, Thou sayest not true, hee dooth thereby make him a Lyer, and so hee doth injurie him. But if hee doo replye and saie in this manner, That which thou sayest is not so, or it is not true, &c. No such manner of speech or saying can bee injurious, for that, as I haue aboue sayde, the thing may bee false, and yet hee no Lyer, by reason that hee eyther maye bee euyll infourmed, or else not understande the matter as it was, or some suche other thing might happen, whereby hee might bee mooued to reporte and speake that agayne which is not true: wherefore anie such aunswere whatsoeuer cannot in anie sort fall burdenous unto him.[48]

The examples given by Saviolo enlighten Romeo's reaction to Tybalt's provocation, and they are emblematic of the subtleties that are parodied in Touchstone's speech where one can hear the satire of an era in which courtiers quarrelled over such trivial matters as the cutting of a beard. Shakespeare's text mirrors the warnings of duelling theorists who denounced the abuse of duels. At the same time, Touchstone laughs at the subtle nuances presented by these theorists, who end up transforming the art of duelling into an art of avoiding duelling. Touchstone's speech, like the duelling manuals, constitutes a panorama of what is 'abuse' and what is 'no abuse' but also suggests that the subtleties of emission and reception might be so great that it becomes difficult to distinguish what is injurious from what is not. The codification of insulting words is a complex exercise.

The main idea conveyed by Touchstone's speech is simple: the art of quarrelling is the art of avoiding a duel. It is not surprising, therefore, that Shakespeare should embody the paradox of the aborted duel in the character of the coward. The idea that emerges is that only the cowardly ones can engage in this absurd application of codes, which is a means of avoiding the act. This idea appears in *Twelfth Night*, where the duellist is the anti-hero par excellence.

'Taunt him with the licence of ink': Writing insults in *Twelfth Night*

Cowardly duelling practices are an extremely effective comic, because paradoxical, device in Shakespeare's plays. In *Cymbeline*, the cowardly Cloten takes refuge behind a social code of duelling that forbids duelling with someone who is less noble than oneself: 'Would he had been one of my rank' (2.1.14–15), he says, which allows him to dodge a duel. Cloten's 'rank' allows him to be 'rank' to and insult everyone but also to carefully escape the consequences of his abuse, an idea summarized in his dialogue with the ironic Lord:

2 LORD
   It is not fit your lordship should undertake every companion that you give offence to.
CLOTEN
   No, I know that, but it is fit I should commit offence to my inferiors.

(2.1.26–9)

Cloten seems to be adopting social distinctions that are thrown into relief in Saviolo's *Practice*:

> Forasmuch as Duello is a proofe by armes, which appertaine to gentlemen, and that gentry is an honourable degree, it is not meet to admitte proofe by armes to any but to honorable persons, and therfore as before civile judges it is not permitted, that infamous persons can accuse anye

other, so in the judgement of gentrie, an honourable person cannot bee accused but by an honourable person: for how shal he be able to accuse another of any defect of honour, that in the like is faultye himselfe.[49]

One should oppose a person of an approximately equal rank, as is suggested in Saviolo's chapters that speak 'Of the inequalitie of noble men, and cheefely of commaunding Lords' and 'Of the inequalitie of private Noblemen' or that describe 'With what persons a Knight ought to enter Combate, and with what he ought not'.[50] In *King Lear*, Oswald takes refuge behind another rule according to which one should not fight against someone who is too old when he explains to Cornwall that he 'spared' Kent's life 'at suit of his grey beard' (2.2.60–1), thus avoiding to react to Kent's insults. In *All's Well That Ends Well*, it is Paroles who hides his cowardice behind the same rule when, responding to Lafeu's insults, he claims: 'Hadst thou not the privilege of antiquity upon thee –' (*AW*, 2.3.209–10). The rules of the duel are thus a means of avoiding physical combat, a safety valve that prevents one from going from words to deeds.

The most comical duel of cowards in Shakespeare's work is probably the duel that Andrew Aguecheek tries to trigger in *Twelfth Night*. The character, whose name specifically evokes cowardice ('ague' meaning fever, and evoking the pallor that accompanies it), is described at the beginning of the play as follows:

MARIA
[...] He's a very fool and a prodigal.
SIR TOBY
Fie that you'll say so! He plays o'th' viol-de-gamboys, and speaks three or four languages word for word and hath all the gifts of nature.
MARIA
He hath indeed, almost natural, for besides that he's a fool, he's a great quarreller, and, but he hath the gift of a coward to allay the gust he hath in quarrelling, 'tis

thought among the prudent he would quickly have the gift of a grave.

SIR TOBY

By this hand they are scoundrels and substractors that say so of him. Who are they?

MARIA

They that add, moreover, he's drunk nightly in your company.

SIR TOBY

With drinking health to me niece. I'll drink to her as long as there is a passage in my throat and drink in Illyria. He's a coward and a coistrel that will not drink to my niece till his brain turn o'th' toe, like a parish top.

(*TN*, 1.3.22–40)

This dialogue illustrates the inversion of values that was denounced by such authors as Thomas Northbrooke in his *Treatise* 'against dicing, dancing, plays and interludes with other idle pastimes':

It is a world to see and behold the wicked people, how they wrest and turne the names of good things, unto the names of vices. As if a gentleman have in him any humble behaviour, then the Roysters cal such a one, by the name of Loute, a Clinchpoup, or one that knoweth no fashions: if a man talke godly or wisely, the wordlings deride it, and say the yong Fox preacheth, beware youre Geese, and of a yong saint groweth an old devil: if a man will not dice, and play, then he is a nigard and a miser, and no good fellow: if he be no dauncer, he is a foole and blockhead, &c. If a man be a Royster, & knoweth how to fight his fight, then he is called by the name of honesty: if he can kil a man, & dare rob upon the highway, he is called a tall man, and a valiant man of his hands: if he can Dice, playe and daunce, hee is named a proper and a fyne nimble man: if he wil loyter and live idlely upon other mens labours & sit al day and night at Cards and Dice, he is named a good companion, and a shopfellow: if he can sweare and stare, they say he hath a stout cowrage. If he be a whoremaister, they say he is an amorous lover and *Venus* byrde, it is the course of youth, he will leave it when he is olde &c.[51]

In this carnivalesque context, the metamorphosis of words reveals a reversal of values, confusing words of praise and abuse. The duel in *Twelfth Night* must be assessed in this context. A drunkard is 'as tall a man as any's in Illyria' (1.3.18) and the man who does not drink is termed 'a coward and a coistrel' (1.3.38). To rewrite the duel, Shakespeare paradoxically stages the figure of the quarrelsome and cowardly drunkard that is so often mentioned in the texts of his time. For example, Joseph Swetnam, a few years later, will insist upon the link between drinking and quarrelling:

thy enemy if he be but a ranke coward, upon drink or fury, or upon hot blood, will be so desperate, that if you favor him he will endanger thee.

There is seldom or never any quarrell begun but in an afternoone, for then commonly the drinke is in and the wit is out, although thou knowest thy selfe in good case, and not to have received more drinke then to suffice thy want, yet dost thou not know how little drinke will overcome the wits of another man; and this I know, and by good experience I speake it, there is no ods during the time betwixt a madde man and a drunkard.[52]

Swetnam warns the reader against granting too much importance to a drunkard's words:

Goe not into the field with one that is knowne to be a common drunkard, no though thou take him never so sober, for if thou chance to hurt him, the vulgar sort will deeme that he was drunke, so thou dost hazard thy life, and get no credite, then take no exceptions at a drunkards words, for what he speaketh is not regarded amongst men of discretion, yet many times it so falleth out, that a drunken madde-braine meetes with a prodigall unwise fellow, and they do quickely upon a word, nay upon a looke, make a sodaine brawle, to the disturbance of the rest of the company.⁵³

According to Swetnam, a drunkard's words should not have any insulting effect.

In Andrew Aguecheek, cowardice, drinking and duelling go hand in hand. He prefers the art of writing a letter of defiance to the art of fighting. With the help of his companions, Fabian and Sir Toby Belch, he sets out to challenge his supposed rival, Viola-Cesario, with his pen, following Sir Toby's writing advice:

SIR ANDREW
   Will either of you bear me a challenge to him?
SIR TOBY
   Go, write it in a martial hand, be curst and brief. It is no matter how witty so it be eloquent and full of invention. Taunt him with the licence of ink. If thou thou'st him some thrice, it shall not be amiss; and as many lies as will lie in thy sheet of paper, although the sheet were big enough for the bed of Ware in England, set 'em down. Go, about it. Let there be gall enough in thy ink – though thou write with a goose-pen, no matter. About it.
   (3.2.38–48)

The term 'goose-pen' is, of course, ironic here in that it refers to a goose-feather-quill, while the goose, by its whiteness, is an emblem of cowardice. Andrew Aguecheek writes with a 'goose-pen', that is a coward's pen.

Sir Toby's advice contradicts most of the rules laid down by a theorist like Saviolo, who, in a chapter entitled 'Of the form of Cartels, or Letters of Defiance', gives recommendations on the writing of cartels:

When cartels are to be made, they must be written with the greatest brevity that may be possible, framing the quarrell with certaine, proper, and simple wordes. [...]

And in such manner of writing, the least eloquence and copie of woordes that maye be must be used, but with naked and cleere speeche must knit up the conclusion. [...][54]

And heere I will not stay to tell you, that it seemeth unto me a most gentleman-like thing, in all manner of writings to speake honourably of his enemie, for so a Gentleman or Cavalier doth honor to himselfe, shewing thereby to have quarrell with an honorable person: whereas otherwise, hee dishonoreth himselfe, and sheweth himselfe rather to have minde to fight with the pen then with the sworde.[55]

A proper challenge should be clear and brief. Sir Toby's opening advice 'be curst and brief' seems to abide by that rule but the image of a letter that is 'eloquent and full of invention' contradicts Saviolo's recommendation. The cartel should not be insulting, Saviolo prescribes. By dictating both insults, in the triple use of an offending 'thou',[56] and 'as many lies as will lie in thy sheet of paper', Sir Toby's advice goes against the distribution of roles in a duel and in a letter of challenge in which you either accuse or you deny, but you certainly cannot do both at the same time.

Sir Andrew Aguecheek's letter of challenge reflects the aberrations and contradictions formulated by his duelling professor, Sir Toby Belch, whose very name reveals that he cannot but be a bad teacher.

The wording of the letter is presented to the spectators a bit later:

SIR ANDREW

Here's the challenge, read it. I warrant there's vinegar and pepper in't.

FABIAN

Is't so saucy?

SIR ANDREW

Ay – is't? I warrant him. Do but read.

SIR TOBY

Give me. [*Reads.*] *Youth, whatsoever thou art, thou art but a scurvy fellow.*

FABIAN
Good, and valiant.
SIR TOBY [*Reads.*]
Wonder not nor admire not in thy mind why I do call thee so for I will show thee no reason for't.
FABIAN
A good note, that keeps you from the blow of the law.
SIR TOBY [*Reads.*]
Thou com'st to the Lady Olivia, and in my sight she uses thee kindly. But thou liest in thy throat; that is not the matter I challenge thee for.
FABIAN
Very brief, and to exceeding good sense [*aside*]-less.
SIR TOBY [*Reads.*]
I will waylay thee going home, where if it be thy chance to kill me –
FABIAN
Good.
SIR TOBY [*Reads.*]
Thou kill'st me like a rogue and a villain.
FABIAN
Still you keep o'th' windy side of the law – good.
SIR TOBY [*Reads.*]
Fare thee well, and God have mercy upon one of our souls. He may have mercy upon mine, but my hope is better, and so look to thyself. Thy friend, as thou usest him, and thy sworn enemy,
Andrew Aguecheek.
If this letter move him not, his legs cannot. I'll give't him.
(3.4.139–67)

This letter of defiance could be defined as monstrous in that it transgresses all the rules of challenges laid down by the duel theorists. They have obviously been ill-digested, whatever Fabian and Sir Toby may say in their ironic comments. Sir Andrew accuses Cesario of lying, which contradicts his very position as a challenger. The codes are not assimilated; the distribution of roles is not done correctly. Aguecheek illustrates

Saviolo's description of those who prefer to fight with their pen rather than with their sword and who do not respect the limits of language imposed by duelling codes. It is not appropriate to insult one's opponent, but one should rather respect him. It is dishonourable to indulge in a stream of insults. A good duellist must make a rigorous use of his tongue. He must reject all linguistic excesses, which is far from being the case in Sir Andrew's letter. The challenge is to define and frame the quarrel with appropriate terminology and precise language. This rigorous formulation is necessary for the duelling process to run smoothly. In short, instead of a letter of challenge, Sir Andrew writes an incomprehensible letter of abuse, while a letter of challenge should precisely not be a letter of insult.

But one of the most blatant transgressions is that the challenge is addressed to Viola, who may be in disguise but who is nonetheless a woman. The duel belonging to an exclusively male universe, the very choice of such an opponent invalidates the whole procedure. Finally, let us not forget that this cartel remains a pure comic writing exercise since it will never be sent, which constitutes the most obvious obstacle to the act. Produced but never sent or received, this letter of challenge remains a dead letter.

Thus, in *Twelfth Night*, the duel paradoxically becomes the preferred exercise of the coward, which translates a vision of the duel as a futile activity that in no way reveals a man's worth but, at most, his stupidity. Given this carnivalesque subversion, it is not surprising that in many of his plays Shakespeare should favour the duel as a mode of evasion. The recurrence of the aborted duel confirms the idea that the art of duelling is more about bluffing than bravery, more words than deeds. In *The Merry Wives of Windsor*, nothing comes of Pistol's raging, bombastic challenge to Slender:

> I combat challenge of this latten bilbo.
> Word of denial in thy *labras* here!
> Word of denial! Froth and scum, thou liest!
> (*MW*, 1.1.150–2)

The lie as the supreme insult seems to be the only memorable idea that comes out of all the very subtle duelling codes. In the same play, nothing will come of the challenge issued by the most enthusiastic of duellists, Doctor Caius, a character who seems to be cut out for duelling because he is French. He too sends a letter of challenge, to Sir Evans, for the same reason as Sir Andrew in *Twelfth Night*: a love rivalry that is certainly not one of the noblest causes of honour cited by duelling theorists. Here is how Caius expresses his warlike intentions:

> You, Jack'nape, give-a this letter to Sir Hugh. By gar, it is a shallenge: I will cut his troat in de park, and I will teach a scurvy jackanape priest to meddle or make. [...] By gar, I will cut all his two stones. By gar, he shall not have a stone to throw at his dog. [...] By gar, I vill kill de Jack-priest; and I have appointed mine host of de Jarteer to measure our weapon. By gar, I will myself have Anne Page.
> (*MW*, 1.4.100–5; 108–11)

Once again, the codes of duelling are exploited for comic and burlesque purposes by Shakespeare. The character's accent deflates the solemnity of his enterprise. The baseness of the threatening words he uses ('I will cut all his two stones') reinforces the burlesque discrepancy between the supposed nobility of the quarrel and its formulation. Once again, Shakespeare plays on this transgression of codes into mere insulting words that can only lead to an aborted duel. The duel does not take place indeed, as the Host of the Garter Inn plays with the two adversaries by giving them different meeting places. Thus, they will wait for each other without ever seeing the other coming. The show will not take place. The opponent chosen by Caius is the opposite of a duellist. There is little to expect in terms of honourable quarrels from a parson who declares several times: 'I will knog his urinals about his knave's costard' (3.1.13–14) or 'I will knog your urinal about your knave's cogscomb' (3.1.81). Everything thus leads the spectator to foresee the failure of this duel, the defusing of which relies on another element: the justice of the peace, Shallow, who also stands in their way. His role is to preserve order, and this type of public confrontation is a source of disorder. Shallow is a comical and mocking embodiment of the law that was trying to combat this duelling fashion.

Shakespeare dramatizes the thwarting of the duel on numerous occasions: in *A Midsummer Night's Dream*, in *Love's Labour's Lost*, *Much Ado About Nothing* or *Henry V*. While the tragic design of *Romeo and Juliet* stages the switch from words and blows, in the economy of comedies, words cannot slide into deeds. Yet, *Twelfth Night* may be seen as constituting an exception to this rule and an in-between case: blood is actually shed at the end of the play. There is a shift from words to deeds, from wordy quarrel to blows. The swords are truly drawn. Sir Andrew and Sir Toby arrive on stage wounded, with bloody heads, and they call for a surgeon. However, the laws of the genre dictate that this bloodshed is comic blood. The codes of comedy prevail over the codes of duelling. Indeed, it is by using one of the constitutive elements of comedy, the substitution of identity, that Shakespeare transforms the duelling codes and defuses their tragic potential. Through misunderstanding (made possible by the twin nature of Viola and Sebastian), Shakespeare transforms the planned duel into a completely irregular fight, since there will be a case of mistaken identity. Thus, it seems that when the playwright evokes the duel in all its rites and codes, it is to ridicule it, to deflate it, to exploit it for burlesque and parodic purposes. In order to integrate the duel into comedy, Shakespeare reduces it to quarrels and dissolves it into proceedings and insults.

4

Insults as actionable words

If reception and interpretation are central in the duelling rules we have just studied, they are also at the heart of the legal actions that involve insulting words.

In *Interpretation and Meaning in the Renaissance, The Case of Law*, Ian Maclean defines defamation as follows:

> Defamation is an injury to the person affected by words, writings, gestures, images or ritual acts, rather than physical force; but the degree of violence suffered is no less great for all that, for as St Gregory points out, words can inflict greater distress than physical assault ('aliquando plus turbant verba quam verbera').[1]

Although the two terms cannot be equated, defamation is closely related to insult (*convicium*) and the confusion between the two, as we shall see, is very frequent in the courts. Shifts from defamation to pure insult are very frequent, and the two categories overlap so much that it is sometimes very difficult to make a distinction. In fact, the main question is to know which insults can be considered as defamatory and therefore 'actionable'.

Insult and defamation

In an article entitled 'Language, power and the law: women's slander litigation in early modern London', Laura Gowing expresses the close link between insult and defamation:

> Slander in London was determined by urban circumstances, but it was expressed in a language of insult whose themes are recorded in defamation cases across the country.[2]

Defamation most often involves insult, but not every insult can be considered defamatory. That is the link between these two concepts. Defamation implies intention, and it can be considered a sin, a tort and a crime:

> The crime of defamation is intentional; one component of any successful prosecution must in theory be proof of malicious intent (*animus iniuriandi*). It can relate to all sections of society; its remedy may be sought in civil, criminal or ecclesiastical courts and involves the restitution of the good name of the injured party, as well as (in different contexts) monetary damages, and the punishment of the offender.[3]

W. S. Holdsworth explains the difference between defamation as a crime and defamation as a tort:

> The wrong of defamation is sometimes a crime pure and simple, sometimes a tort pure and simple and sometimes it can be treated either as a crime or as a tort at the option of the injured person. Defamation is a crime when it consists of the publication of seditious obscene or blasphemous speeches, or the publication of writings or the utterance of speeches which directly incite to a breach of the peace. Defamation is a tort when it consists of the publication of writings or the utterance of speeches which hold another person up to hatred contempt or ridicule, provided, in the case of speeches, special damage can be proved or is

presumed. Defamation can be treated either as a crime or tort at the option of the injured person, if it consists of the publication of writings which hold him up to hatred, contempt or ridicule.

There is nothing anomalous in the fact that defamation is thus treated sometimes as a crime, sometimes as a tort, and sometimes as either a crime or a tort; for it is obvious that defamatory writings or speeches may, according to their contents, either (i) affect the stability or the peace of the State, or the morals of its subjects; or (ii) cause loss of reputation or pecuniary loss to an individual; or (iii) be both dangerous to the peace of the State and harmful to an individual.[4]

Defamation can be a crime of *lèse-majesté*. That is why Elizabeth, in the first year of her reign, recalled a statute that was dear to her in 'An Act for the explanacion of the Statute of Seditious words and Rumors' (1 Eliz I. c. 7). Twenty-two years later, defamation was still on the agenda in the royal texts: 'An Act against seditious words and rumours uttered agaynst the Queenes most excellent Maiestie' (23 Eliz I. C. 2). During the reign of James I, the issue also seems to have been of concern, as evident from the publication of 'A Proclamation commaunding that no man abuse the Earl of Tyrone' (8 June 1603) and 'A Proclamation touching a seditious rumor suddenly raised' (22 March 1606).[5]

In the context of defamation, the question arises as to which words become 'actionable', that is to say lead to legal action. What words were considered by Elizabethan society as liable to legal action and in what precise circumstances? Shakespeare's plays dramatize the complex relationships between insult and slander or defamation, and stage a wide range of cases. Defamation can be a matter of state, as it is, for example, in *Measure for Measure* where Lucio defames the Duke, committing a crime of *lèse-majesté*, a felony. But it is also part of Elizabethan daily life in various forms. It can be committed orally, but it can also be conveyed through written documents, libels or 'ballads'. Frederick Emmison gives us an example of this by citing the Chelmsford Ballads, which circulated in

1600. These were libels[6] in verse, which questioned the morals and morality of an entire community.[7] Traces of this form of defamation can be found in Shakespeare's scripts, for example, when Falstaff brandishes 'ballads' as a threat:

> An I have not ballads made on you all and sung to filthy tunes, let a cup of sack be my poison.
>
> (*1H4*, 2.2.43–5)

In *All's Well That Ends Well*, Helen risks being exposed to this public insult if she fails to cure the king:

> Tax of impudence,
> A strumpet's boldness, a divulged shame;
> Traduced by odious ballads, my maiden's name
> Seared otherwise;
>
> (*AW*, 2.1.168–71)

In the same play, Paroles slanders Bertram through a written poem:

> *Dian, The Count's a fool, and full of gold*
> *[…]*
> *When he swears oaths, bid him drop gold, and take it.*
>   *After he scores, he never pays the score.*
> *Half-won is match well made; match, and well make it.*
>   *He ne'er pays after-debts; take it before.*
> *And say a soldier, Dian, told thee this:*
> *Men are to mell with, boys are not to kiss.*
> *For count of this, the count's a fool, I know it,*
> *Who pays before, but not when he does owe it.*
>   *Thine, as he vowed to thee in thine ear,*
>   *Paroles.*
>
> (*AW*, 4.3.207; 219–28)

Bertram reacts to this slanderous poem in an aside: 'He shall be whipped through the army with this rhyme in's forehead' (*AW*, 4.3.229–30).

Cleopatra is afraid she might be subjected to this kind of humiliation at the end of *Antony and Cleopatra:*

> Saucy lictors
> Will catch at us like strumpets, and scald rhymers
> Ballad us out o'tune. The quick comedians
> Extemporally will stage us and present
> Our Alexandrian revels; Antony
> Shall be brought drunken forth; and I shall see
> Some squeaking Cleopatra boy my greatness
> I'th' posture of a whore.
>
> (AC, 5.2.213–20)

Ballads and theatrical satire appear as conveying defamation that can also be expressed through gesture. Laura Gowing notes that breaking the windows of a house designated it as harbouring people of dubious morals: 'Broken windows were supposed to mark a bawdy house, and some women had their windows broken to show their whoredom'.[8] Some folk rituals also conveyed slander:

> Like the rituals of rough music recorded in other areas, the banging of basins and pans at women was used to accuse them of whoredom or scolding, and this too found its way into the vernacular of defamation.[9]

According to Emmison, the term 'libel' could refer to a wide variety of forms of insult:

> Dalton[10] reminds us that libel might be committed not only in writing, in 'book, ballad, epigram or rhyme, either in metre or prose', or in 'words, scoffs, jests, taunts or songs, maliciously repeated or sung in the presence of others', but also by 'pictures or signs of shame, as pictures of the gallows, pillory, cucking-stool, horns or such like'.[11]

Shakespeare mentions these 'pictures and signs of shame' in *Much Ado About Nothing* when Benedick swears he will never get married, to avoid having to face this kind of public humiliation:

DON PEDRO
I shall see thee, ere I die, look pale with love.
BENEDICK
With anger, with sickness, or with hunger, my lord, not with love. Prove that ever I lose more blood with love than I will get again with drinking, pick out mine eyes with a ballad-maker's pen and hang me up at the door of a brothel-house for the sign of blind Cupid.
DON PEDRO
Well, if ever thou dost fall from this faith, thou wilt prove a notable argument.
BENEDICK
If I do, hang me in a bottle like a cat and shoot at me, and he that hits me, let him be clapped on the shoulder and called Adam.
DON PEDRO
Well, as time shall try. 'In time the savage bull doth bear the yoke.'
BENEDICK
The savage bull may, but if ever the sensible Benedick bear it, pluck off the bull's horns and set them in my forehead; and let me be vilely painted, and in such great letters as they write 'Here is good horse to hire', let them signify under my sign, 'Here you may see Benedick, the married man.'

(*MA*, 1.1.231–49)

Benedick agrees to submit to the scorn of popular judgement if he breaks his word, which he does in the end, stating that, after all, he does not 'care for a satire or an epigram' (*MA*, 5.4.100–1). Thus, defamation is a protean phenomenon whose themes are obviously varied. However, one trend has been clearly identified and stands out very clearly. Women are almost always the victims of *sexual* defamation. It is this type of insult that leads them to seek redress in ecclesiastical courts, as J. A. Sharpe shows in his study entitled *Defamation and Sexual Slander in Early Modern England: The Church Courts at York*.[12] In *Othello*, *Much Ado About Nothing*, *Cymbeline* and *The Winter's Tale*, Shakespeare reflects a society where women are often stigmatized as whores, under names that constitute the worst of insults. In *Othello*, these words seem to kill Desdemona even before Othello strangles her; in *The Winter's Tale*, Leontes' accusations of adultery symbolically kill Hermione. In *Much Ado About Nothing*, Hero is symbolically killed by words even if, in this play, the playwright also questions the actionability of words in the comic mode.

The stale and the ass: Noting in *Much Ado About Nothing*

The 'noting' that we can hear in the 'nothing' of its title signals *Much Ado About Nothing* as a play that has much to do with accusation and slander. The verb 'note' means, among other things, 'To accuse *of* a fault, defect, or wrongdoing; to mark with the stigma *of* a fault' or 'To mark or brand *with* some disgrace, defect, or fault'.[13]

Falling 'into a pit of ink'

During the church scene, after being publicly called 'this rotten orange' (4.1.30), 'an approved wanton' (4.1.43), and after being said to be 'more intemperate [...] / Than Venus, or those pampered animals / That rage in savage sensuality', Hero is called a 'common stale' (4.1.64) by Don Pedro. He seems to have borrowed the insult from Borachio who had referred to Hero as 'a contaminated stale' (2.2.23) when planning her disgrace with the help of Don John. The word 'stale', which originally refers to a decoy-bird and then to a prostitute 'used by thieves to lure victims',[14] is particularly significant in a play in which *trompe-l'oeil* has a central role. The church sequence questions the limits of truth and illusion:

> DON PEDRO
> I stand dishonoured that I have gone about
> To link my dear friend to a common stale.
> LEONATO
> Are these things spoken, or do I but dream?
> DON JOHN
> Sir, they are spoken, and these things are true.
> BENEDICK
> This looks not like a nuptial.
> HERO
> True? O God!
> CLAUDIO
> Leonato, stand I here?
> Is this the prince? Is this the prince's brother?
> Is this face Hero's? Are our eyes our own?
> LEONATO
> All this is so, but what of this, my lord? (*MA*, 4.1.63–72)

Slander here is to be related to its French root *esclandre*, which Cotgrave (1611) defined as follows:

> A slaunder; a defamation, detractation, unjust imputation; also, a slaughter; also, a mishap, danger; tumult, uprore; mischiefe. *À grand pecheur esclandre*: Prov. Great sinners ever come to shame.

Claudio and Don Pedro's slanderous words trigger an uproar, a great tumult (*esclandre* in French). In a context of deception, it is not fortuitous that the word 'stale' should be used, which makes the dialogue above ironical. Indeed, the spectators know that Hero is not a 'stale', i.e. a prostitute, and at the same time they see that she is used as a 'stale', that is as a decoy to lure and trap the victims of Don John's plotting and blotting. That is why the things that are spoken are both true and untrue. The text insists on the insult constituting a 'blot' on Hero's name (4.1.80), an image that is enhanced by Leonato's speech:

> O, she is fallen
> Into a pit of ink that the wide sea
> Hath drops too few to wash her clean again,
> And salt too little which may season give
> To her foul-tainted flesh.
> (*MA*, 4.1.139–43)

Leonato attributes the blot to Hero's behaviour while the blot, the spectators know, is due to the slanderous words. Thus, ironically again, his words are both true and untrue. The slander has acted as a blot, and saying Hero is a 'common stale' amounts, in Leonato's words, to transforming her into that name and leaving her 'for dead' (4.1.201). The efficiency of the words of abuse is spectacularly dramatized when she falls down in a faint (4.1.109). The semblance of death that the Friar wants to use to restore Hero's honour suggests that only death can wash a blotted name. In this case, slander does not lead to a defamation case at court but to a mock duel that appears when Leonato comically defies Claudio (5.1) and then when Benedick challenges Claudio on Beatrice's behalf, who laments about Hero's fate: 'She is wronged, she is slandered, she is undone' (4.1.310–11). Here are Benedick's words of challenge, delivered as an aside to Claudio:

> You are a villain. I jest not. I will make it good how you dare, with what you dare and when you dare. Do me right, or I will protest your cowardice. You have killed a sweet lady, and her death shall fall heavy on you. Let me hear from you.
> (*MA*, 5.1.143–8)

Benedick resorts to a duel, although it is eventually cancelled, to respond to Hero's slander. Yet Shakespeare offers us another Elizabethan type of reaction to insult and/or slander especially in Dogberry's reaction, which constitutes a comical counterpart to Hero's defamation and reflects a judiciary trend in Shakespeare's days: the proliferation of defamation cases.

'Write me down an ass'

In *Much Ado*, it is ironically the 'ass' who unmasks the villains and it is ironically the ass who points to the impact of words and wants to find satisfaction in an intellectual way, rather than through physical confrontation, by calling for judiciary means.

Conrade abuses Dogberry in 4.2, during an examination scene that comes just after the church episode. This sequence of comedy constitutes an anticlimactic moment that contrasts with the tension we have just experienced, but at the same time can be seen as an interesting comment on it:

CONRADE
 Off, coxcomb!
DOGBERRY
 God's my life, where's the sexton? Let him write down the prince's officer coxcomb! Come, bind them. [*to Conrade, who resists*] Thou naughty varlet!
CONRADE
 Away! You are an ass, you are an ass!
DOGBERRY
 Dost thou not suspect my place? Dost thou not suspect my years? O, that he (i.e. the sexton) were here to write me down an ass! But masters, remember that I am an ass; though it be not written down, yet forget not that I am an ass. No, thou villain, thou art full of piety, as shall be proved upon thee by good witness. I am a wise fellow, and which is more, an officer, and which is more, a householder, and which is more, as pretty a piece of flesh as any is in Messina, and one that knows the law – go to! – and a rich fellow enough – go to! – and a fellow that hath had losses, and one that hath two gowns, and

everything handsome about him. – Bring him away. – O that I had been writ down an ass.

(*MA*, 4.2.71–88)

For Conrade, as for the audience, Dogberry is an 'ass', i.e. a fool. 'Ass' here is to be taken figuratively but Dogberry's reaction to this insult brings us closer to the literal meaning of the word. The confusion of 'suspect' with 'respect' and the pun on 'years' and 'ears'[15] confirm that Dogberry is an ass indeed who himself unwittingly extends the insult by attributing to himself one of the physical characteristics of the donkey: the long ears.[16] Dogberry can be reassured: nobody will now forget that he is an ass. What we retain from this self-portrait, logically intended to contradict Conrade and to 'disabuse' the audience, is precisely that Dogberry is an ass. Thus, an insult that might have gone unnoticed in this play is ironically highlighted and emphasized by the insulted character himself. 'You are an ass' is replaced by 'I am an ass', as if Dogberry did not know indirect speech. Act 5, Scene 1 will confirm that he has not digested the insult:

Come, bring away the plaintiffs. By this time our sexton hath reformed Signor Leonato of the matter. And masters, do not forget to specify, when time and place shall serve, that I am an ass.

(5.1.243–6)

Only in the end will he finally use indirect speech:

Moreover, sir, which indeed is not under white and black, this plaintiff here, the offender, did call me ass. I beseech you let it be remembered in his punishment.

(5.1.294–7)

The confusion of the roles of plaintiff and offender suggests that abuse goes together with self-abuse in Dogberry's words. Both the plaintiff (himself) and the offender (Conrade) called him an ass. Yet behind this comic repetition of insults, one can find a trace of the defamation cases that were so numerous in Shakespeare's days. Dogberry obviously wants to engage with a 'case for words'.

All legal scholars and historians observe a marked increase, and even a proliferation, of suits for defamation in the Elizabethan period. This is noted by J. A. Sharpe in his article '"Such Disagreement betwyx Neighbours": Litigation and Human Relations in Early Modern England':

> From the mid-sixteenth century onwards, the tribunals of both the common and ecclesiastical law experienced a rapid increase in the number of suits for defamation.[17]

It should be noted that until the early sixteenth century, defamation suits were reserved for the ecclesiastical courts. Until then, the Common Law did not provide any remedy for defamation. In the Middle Ages, defamation was considered a sin, not a crime or an offence. Therefore, it was part of the ecclesiastical legal domain. Helmholz notes that legislation on defamation dates back to the thirteenth century:

> It rests upon ecclesiastical legislation of the early thirteenth century, by which excommunication was ordained for those who maliciously impute crimes to persons who are of good fame, so that they have to clear themselves at least by compurgation or are otherwise harmed.[18]

The legislation that is referred to by Milsom dates back to 1222 and reads as follows:

> Excommunicamus omnes illos qui gratia odii, lucri, vel favoris, vel alia quacunque de causa malitiose crimen imponunt alicui, cum infamatus non sit apud bonos et graves, ut sic saltem ei purgatio indicatur vel alio modo gravetur.
>
> We excommunicate all those who, for the sake of hatred, profit, or favor, or for whatever cause, maliciously impute

a crime to any person who is not of ill name among good and serious men, by means of which at least purgation is awarded to him or he is harmed in some other manner.[19]

This 'constitution', which was enacted by the Council of Oxford, shows that defamation was originally a spiritual offence of imputing a crime to another. According to Helmholz, libel suits were a significant part of the litigation in the medieval courts: 'They were a regular and important part of canonical litigation throughout the later medieval period. The Oxford constitution was central to these proceedings.'[20] It determined which words were 'actionable' and which were not. The words that could trigger a trial were those that implied that a crime had been committed. Calling someone a 'thief' could lead to a trial if it implied that the other person had committed a crime:

> It was defamatory to call someone a thief, as in a London action where a man said, 'Thow art the woman that stolest the kyetyll from the Old Swan.' It was actionable to name another man as a 'public perjurer', as in a Canterbury case from 1373. Likewise, imputation of forgery, of heresy, of manufacturing false evidence, of adultery, of procuring the death of an innocent man were all actionable.[21]

On the other hand, calling a woman a 'scalde' could not trigger a trial because the word did not imply any crime and was merely an insult. However, Helmholz adds that words that were mere insults were often present in court reports because, technically, they implied a crime in their proper sense:

> Some of the phrases one finds in the court books were doubtless nothing but common insults. To shout that a woman was a 'strong harlot' was probably no more than a term of general abuse. But the words technically included a crime punishable in a public court. Therefore they were enough to give rise to a claim for defamation. Words which were merely abusive were not.[22]

This shows how thin the line was between defamation and insult. Insults, unlike defamation, were not actionable. However, the two categories could often overlap and intersect, and in such cases, suits were brought for words that might only be considered as insults. Crimes did not need to be specifically named for defamation to arise, in contrast with the subsequent position under the Common Law. The mere insinuation of a crime was sufficient to trigger a libel suit.

While in the Middle Ages ecclesiastical courts were supposed to deal only with allegations of spiritual crimes, leaving other crimes to the secular courts, this distinction was not respected in practice and religious courts had free rein in defamation cases.[23]

In 1285, the statute of 'Circumspecte Agatis' (13 Edw. 1)[24] stipulated that ecclesiastical courts could only impose spiritual penalties on defamers: 'No money damages were to be available'.[25] However, the person condemned always had the possibility of redeeming the corporal punishments inflicted on them with a sum of money. But they usually had to do penance in public and suffer other such 'spiritual' punishments, the worst of which was excommunication. Helmholz notes that these spiritual punishments were ultimately more likely to bring justice to the victims and cleanse them of slander than financial compensation would later be:

> But as a tool to restore a man's tarnished reputation, they [money damages] are a blunt instrument indeed.
>
> The ecclesiastical remedy in the Middle Ages, whatever its other limitations, fulfilled this function better than the later Common Law action. Sometimes, we find in the records, the complainant was content with a simple sentence of the court upholding his innocence. The judge 'restored him to good fame.'[26]

Helmholz quotes the following example:

> In a Hereford action,[27] the defendant had again to publicly ask pardon during divine service and to say 'that he had uttered the words out of evil will, not from zealousness, and

that he had been moved by anger'. It is no romanticism, I think, to suggest that penalties such as these more effectively restored an injured reputation than the award of money damages would have.[28]

He adds that 'the Church courts provided a useful remedy for men injured by harsh and insulting words'.[29]

Action on the case for words

In *Much Ado About Nothing*, the symbolic amends that Leonato imposes on Claudio and Don Pedro to restore Hero's name recall the public penances that ecclesiastical courts imposed on defamers, as appears once Leonato has accused Borachio and the two men of having killed his 'innocent child' with their 'breath' (5.1.253–4) in the following dialogue:

CLAUDIO
    I know not how to pray your patience;
    Yet I must speak. Choose your revenge yourself.
    Impose me to what penance your invention
    Can lay upon my sin. Yet sinned I not
    But in mistaking.
DON PEDRO
                        By my soul, nor I.
    And yet to satisfy this good old man
    I would bend under any heavy weight
    That he'll enjoin me to.
LEONATO
    I cannot bid you bid my daughter live –
    That were impossible. But, I pray you both,
    Possess the people in Messina here
    How innocent she died. [*to Claudio*] And if your love
    Can labour ought in sad invention,
    Hang her an epitaph upon her tomb
    And sing it to her bones. Sing it tonight.
                                              (5.1.261–75)

Slander is here characterized as 'sin' that leads to a symbolic and spiritual penance. The only satisfaction that Leonato can ask for is spiritual. Until the sixteenth century, it was the ecclesiastical courts that dealt with defamation. As Baker points out, the Common Law provided satisfaction for damage caused by actions rather than words:

> Words can be more harmful than deeds, and in some circumstances honour may be more tender than personal safety. Yet the common law has always been more reluctant to provide remedies for damage caused by words than for damage caused by deeds.[30]

However, it should be remembered that in the fifteenth century, when a man called another man 'villein', he was liable to prosecution under the Common Law, as this called into question his status as a free man. In addition, the defamation of 'the great', i.e. certain ecclesiastical dignitaries and judges, known as *Scandalum Magnatum*, could lead to legal action in the Common Law courts. Apart from these two types of action, defamation was a matter for the spiritual courts.

But from about 1500 onwards, the Common Law dealt with an area that had previously been almost exclusively reserved for the ecclesiastical courts. Certain words thus became 'actionable' in the secular courts. Insulting became a 'tort'. And the number of lawsuits increased so much that, as early as 1557, some people complained that libel suits were being brought 'for every trifling thing'.[31] The Elizabethan era was a transitional period for defamation, which depended on both the secular and the spiritual fields of justice. Sometimes too subtle distinctions were made between the two types of action at a time when defamation could be considered both a sin and an offence, even a crime when it threatened national peace and the security of the state.

Dogberry's reaction to the 'ass' insult is emblematic of a time that saw the increase in defamation cases and that questioned what words were 'actionable'. Dogberry insists that Conrade's insult is actionable. Yet the essence of the secular legal action lies not in the insult, but in the damaging effect that the words produce: 'in terms of recognisable temporal loss'.[32] Lawyers generally distinguish between three types of words liable to be sued, known as 'action on the case for words'.

First, there are words that endanger the life and liberty of others. Baker talks about 'Words alleging crime or endangering liberty'.[33] Accusing someone of stealing or killing or of being a 'villein' was one such case. Imputing professional incompetence on others was also grounds for prosecution, as it was tantamount to causing temporal damage by causing harm to the plaintiff in his profession:

> By Elizabethan times it was established that imputations might be actionable when it touched the plaintiff in his occupation, even if they would not otherwise have been actionable. Thus, it was not in itself actionable to call someone a bankrupt; but to call a merchant a bankrupt would obviously threaten his livelihood, and subject him to statutory penalties.[34]

In the same way, one has the right to call someone an ignorant, as long as he is not a lawyer, for example, because this insult could be prejudicial to his profession. So, it all depends on who is being addressed. The pragmatic status of insult is here confirmed again. Finally, during the sixteenth century, you could bring a civil suit against someone who called you syphilitic:

> A third special category of slander actions, which has enjoyed a separate existence in the textbooks down to the present day, was that associated with the 'French pox' (syphilis). It was not actionable to say that someone was ill, unless the illness affected his calling. But the imputation of French pox, which became epidemic in Tudor England, was regarded as peculiarly offensive and harmful. The only other disease said to have been included in the same category was leprosy, because lepers could be ostracised by process of law (the writ *de leproso amovendo* to put them in quarantine).[35]

From the sixteenth century onwards, the secular courts were therefore responsible for these temporal matters, while the ecclesiastical courts dealt with spiritual matters. However, there were many overlaps between the two areas, as Emmison points out:

> Defamation in the ecclesiastical courts was the counterpart of slander in the secular courts. The former term was used primarily by the Church lawyers, but the parties generally referred to slander. [...] Only if slanderous speech bore on the moral character of the plaintiff could the church courts prosecute; though it was asserted, but not always maintained, that they had cognizance in all causes where a minister was defamed. If the slander included 'spiritual mixed with temporal words', the action lay in the civil courts; but calling a man 'bastard' was a secular offence as it 'tended to a temporal disinheritance'. There were other curious distinctions. To designate a woman 'bawd' rendered the speaker liable to citation by the Church; to declare that a man or woman kept a bawdy house, however, was a lay offence. [...] Such, at any rate was the law as explained by Burn.[36]

There was a thin line between what was supposed to be the responsibility of the religious courts and what was the responsibility of the secular courts. Emmison notes that cases involving defamation and insult were much more common in the ecclesiastical courts than in the secular courts, which is hardly surprising when one considers the texts we have studied above. Apparently, therefore, insulting others was more often a sin than a crime. Emmison formulates the following paradox:

> In the age when Shakespeare has shown that rude attributes were bandied about almost indiscriminately, it is surprising that so many who thus voiced their feelings were presented for defamation: a term which in later times postulated graver denigration of character than some of the commonplace Elizabethan invective.[37]

According to Baker, this type of action proliferated in the Common Law courts:

> Within half a century of its first appearance, the action for words had become part of the everyday business of the common-law courts, in particular the King's Bench.[38]

When Dogberry asks for the Sexton to 'write [him] down an ass', the play reflects what had emerged as an Elizabethan fashion: legal action for words. His reaction to the insult contrasts with Hero's lack of words and vulnerability to slander. Whether being called an 'ass' could be a cause for action is questionable but Dogberry's insistence on the words being written in black and white provides a comic image of what a defamation case could be. It would be for a court to decide whether the words 'you are an ass' constituted defamation and whether the constable's obsession with these words was 'much ado about nothing' or not. Whether the insult 'ass' would have been considered as defamatory or not, Dogberry's reaction interrogates the spectators about the degree of insult and the impact of words, an aspect that is also dramatized in *Measure for Measure*.

'Scandalum Magnatum' in *Measure for Measure*

John C. Lassiter has devoted an article to what is called 'Scandalum Magnatum' and confirms the essentially pragmatic status of the insult, which is all the more serious since it is addressed to people of high rank. Lassiter reminds us that in the sixteenth and seventeenth centuries, the value of the insult depended upon the quality of the insulted:

> English jurists of the sixteenth and seventeenth centuries regularly maintained that legal relief for defamatory words depended not only on the nature of the words themselves,

but also on the 'quality of the person of whom the words (were) spoken.' In an age which understood society as a divinely ordained hierarchy ascending by degrees of 'quality', it could only follow that 'disgraceful words and speeches against eminent persons' constituted a far more serious offence than those directed against individuals of less quality.[39]

The degrees of insult

Lassiter quotes William Sheppard's 1662 *Action upon the Case for Slander. Or A Methodical Collection under certain heads, of Thousands of Cases Dispersed in the many Great Volumes of the Law, of what words are Actionable, and what not*. In its second chapter, entitled 'Some general things of Actions of the Case for words', the author emphasizes the different degrees of insult. The fifteenth of the general rules laid down in this chapter is the following:

> 15. That the Quality of the person of whom the words are spoken, doth much tend to the maintainance of the Action. And therefore some words that in themselves are not Actionable; relating to some persons, may bee Actionable. So that albeit it will not bear an Action to call an ordinary man **Papist**, yet it will bear an Action to call the Archbishop of Canterbury **Papist**. So albeit it will not bear an Action to say of an ordinary man, **Hee is no true Subject**; yet to say so of a Privy Counsellor, Justice of Peace, Sheriff of a County, Captain of a Troop of Horse, about the King, may be Actionable.[40]

The rule known as *Scandalum Magnatum* is a mere application of this principle:

> Words spoken in derogation of a peer [...], though they be such as would not be actionable in the case of a common

person, yet when spoken in disgrace of such high and respectable characters, they amount to an atrocious injury.[41]

The rule of *Scandalum Magnatum* was instituted in the thirteenth and fourteenth centuries to combat political disorder and to limit the circulation of rumours and slander about the country's leaders. Defaming a person of high rank was a political crime. But towards the end of the fifteenth century, the courts began to grant civil 'remedy' for the defamation of a person of high social status, which meant that any nobleman could claim compensation for the contempt he had suffered:

> Thus the peer who was victim of verbal abuse might bring against his abuser an action for *scandalum magnatum*, stating it to be on behalf of the king as well as himself (*tam pro domino rege quam pro se ipso*), and alleging damages in a sum sufficient to compensate for the harm done to his reputation as a noble peer of the realm and one of the king's 'hereditary councillors.'[42]

In the light of these descriptions, we can measure, for example, the seriousness of Hal's giving a 'box of the ear' (1.2.194–6) to the Lord Chief Justice in *2 Henry IV* but also the new King's cruel memory of having been 'committed' for that (5.2.67–100), as if it could be retrospectively considered as a form of *Scandalum Magnatum*.

Lassiter notes a rise in such trials for *Scandalum Magnatum* from the reigns of Henry VII and Henry VIII onwards and especially in the sixteenth and seventeenth centuries. The peers of the realm, it seems, turned to the law to redress an insult. To explain this phenomenon, Lassiter first mentions the reason that is most frequently cited in seventeenth-century law books, which saw this trend as a substitute for the physical violence that peers resorted to when they were verbally assaulted: 'law provided them with an acceptable alternative to violent revenge in cases of slander'.[43] These trials were thus a step away from the barbarity of the medieval period, characterized by physical violence, and a way to a more polished form of justice:

> 'In those days,' observed Sir Francis Pemberton before the Court of Common Pleas in 1677, 'when a man was injured by words, he carved out his own remedy by his sword.' This was especially the case with nobles and, given their capacity for violence, made the provision of a civil remedy for even the slightest verbal abuse the more essential for the sake of law and order.[44]

Lassiter cites one of the earliest such cases, brought by Buckingham in 1512 against one named Lucas who had dared to say to him: '(you have) no more conscience than a dog'. The court awarded the plaintiff £40 in damages.[45] The rise of these lawsuits apparently was in coherence with the royal desire to combat violence and, more particularly, duelling.

However, Lassiter also sees this as the mark of an aristocracy eager to reinforce an apparently contested or at least fragile social status. In this he adopts Lawrence Stone's view, who, in *The Crisis of the Aristocracy, 1558–1641*,[46] showed that the nobility was experiencing a crisis of confidence at the time and was trying to compensate for the loss of respect owed to them through legal action:

> Thus the action for scandalum magnatum, more than simply providing an alternative to aristocratic violence, became a way of reinforcing – albeit artificially – old and weakening social boundaries.[47]

To confirm this hypothesis, Lassiter notes that most of the words that triggered a trial involved the honour and dignity of these peers, i.e. their social status rather than their political or religious behaviour:

> After 1600, charges of baseness[48] far outnumbered charges of being a traitor, a papist, or a crook. Indeed, it was the

express purpose of the law to remedy such disparaging language, which if spoken of a commoner would not have been held actionable at all.[49]

Disputes between neighbours

Beyond the particular case of *Scandalum Magnatum*, some other aspects may explain the multiplication of defamation cases. This trend can be seen as the sign of a society where relations between neighbours were becoming increasingly strained. This confirms Stone's thesis that there was a 'lack of warmth and tolerance in interpersonal relations at the village level' and that:

> The Elizabethan village was a place filled with malice and hatred, its only unifying bond being the occasional episode of mass hysteria, which temporarily bound together the majority in order to harry and prosecute the local witch.[50]

In this, Stone corroborates the view of an author such as John March who, taking up the argument of a Justice of the time, described this development in 1647 as the mark of increasing human wickedness:

> Well therefore might Wray Chiefe Justice[51] say, that the malice of men doth most increase in these times, then in times past.[52]

J. A. Sharpe qualifies this interpretation by pointing out that litigation enabled Elizabethans to settle their disputes within the framework of the ecclesiastical courts, which tended to advocate reconciliation or an 'amicable' settlement of the matter:

> On the evidence of the York archives, we may safely conclude that the system of ecclesiastical justice in Tudor

and Stuart England allowed every chance for a more or less amicable settlement to be reached between litigants. Given this, the initiation of a suit for defamation might be interpreted as the first step towards bringing neighbourly tensions to a close, as well as a symptom of such tensions as already existed [sic].[53]

The increase in defamation actions in Common Law courts may be due to more material reasons. Whereas ecclesiastical courts did not award damages to the plaintiff, secular juries sometimes awarded exorbitant sums that were disproportionate to the damage caused by the insult. This pecuniary aspect may have played a role.

Helmholz also notes a major development in the ecclesiastical courts that may explain this proliferation:

Legally, the most noticeable sixteenth-century change was a continuation of a medieval development: the expansion of the ecclesiastical remedy to encompass abusive words not necessarily amounting to imputation of a crime. […] A new form of pleading, not based on the Constitution, was adopted alongside the older form. Under it any *convicium* (= abuse) tending to the diminution of the good fame or status of the plaintiff could be punished by ecclesiastical sanctions. The act books show the result: causes brought for calling someone 'a drunkard', or a 'crafty old knave', or 'a hypocrite', all appear.[54]

Thus, in the ecclesiastical courts, the concept of defamation was broadened to include any insult. If legal actions proliferated, it was because the mere insult became sufficient to bring one's neighbour before the courts. Finally, the legal principles applied to defamation were prone to many excesses, since the courts decided early on that the harm caused by defamation did not need to be proven:

One reason for the increase in slander litigation which Dyer and Staunford JJ lamented was that the courts had decided early on that the damage was not traversable which meant that it could be presumed or fictitious.⁵⁵

In any case, this rise in defamation cases in both the secular and spiritual courts seems to show that the Elizabethans attached great importance to their 'good name', as Sharpe notes: 'The contemporary Englishman was unusually willing to protect his reputation through waging law'.⁵⁶ This interest in 'good name' is notably mocked by Iago in *Othello* when he laughs at Cassio's nostalgia for his 'reputation' (2.3.258–67), but also by Falstaff on the battlefield when he debunks honour as being a mere word (*1H4*, 5.1.127–40).

It seems that Shakespeare prefers to settle disputes between his characters through violence rather than through justice. Nevertheless, the fashion for defamation cases can be felt on several occasions in his work, sometimes so comically that it is easy to assume that he is poking fun at the new fad of his contemporaries. We have already mentioned the case of Dogberry, who intends to sue Conrade for insulting an officer. *Measure for Measure* is another interesting case where one finds a hint of such an action in a quarrel between Pompey and Elbow, who brandishes the lawsuit as a threat:

ELBOW
O thou caitiff, O thou varlet, O thou wicked Hannibal! I respected with her before I was married to her? If ever I was respected with her, or she with me, let not your worship think me the poor Duke's officer – prove this, thou wicked Hannibal, or I'll have mine action of battery on thee.
ESCALUS
If he took you a box o'th' ear, you might have your action of slander too.

(2.1.167–73)

Elbow, as usual, confuses two terms, 'battery' and 'slander', which makes his threat more comical than impressive. On the other hand, the clown's malapropism, is, as is often the case, quite revealing, in so far as it displays the combination of words and deeds that characterizes the act of insulting and the violence that words constitute. One finds the same confusion as in Dogberry's words between 'respected' and 'suspected', which makes his words even more ironical.

Mitior sensus

Faced with the excesses of such procedural behaviour, courts and lawyers tried to find ways of controlling this new fashion, mainly by using what is commonly called the 'mitior sensus' rule. The opening pages of John March's treatise reflect the spirit of the jurists of the time, who saw evil in this proliferation of litigation. March defines the purpose of his treatise as follows:

> I do not undertake this work, with an intent to encourage men in giving ill and unworthy language, or to teach them a lawless dyalect, but (as my Lord *Cook* speaks) to direct and instruct them rightly to manage that, which [though but a little member] proves often the greatest good, or the greatest evil to most men. And withall to deterre men from words, which are but wind (as he further speakes) which subject men to actions, in which damages and costs are to bee recovered, which usually trench to the great hinderance and impoverishment of the speaker.[57]

March echoes religious texts that recommend people to rule their tongues:[58]

> It is the saying of the Prophet David; I will take heed to my ways, that I offend not with my tongue, I will keepe my mouth as it were with a bridle.[59] It were happy for all men if they could make the like resolution.[60]

March's treatise upon actions of slander is 'as a Bridle for all rash and inconsiderate tongues; that seeing the mischiefe they may the better know how to avoyd it'.[61]

To combat this multiplication of lawsuits, several principles were adopted by the secular courts. The plaintiff was required to be able to prove the damage he or she had suffered. Second, words uttered for fun or in anger were no longer liable to prosecution. It was then up to the plaintiff to prove malice. March expresses this principle in the following terms:

> that words only of brangle, heate and choler, might not be so much as mentioned in those high and honourable Courts of Justice. For I professe for my part, I judge of them as a great dishonour to the Law, and the professors thereof; especially when I consider that they are used only as instruments to pronounce the malice, and vent the spleene of private jarres and discontents amongst men.[62]

In the 1570s, another policy emerged that consisted in taking ambiguous words only in their milder sense (*in mitiori sensu*):

> The third and most effective attack was launched in the 1570s, when the courts began the policy of construing ambiguous and doubtful words in the milder sense (in mitiori sensu) so that they would not be actionable.[63]

While, in 1575, anyone who called someone a 'rogue' was liable to prosecution,[64] in 1580 this was no longer the case for the reasons expressed by Wray, chief justice:

> at this day these actions on the case are so increased and so common – for one cannot say any word which slightly discredits any other but he will bring an action on it – that it is good to restrict them as much as we can, and by that means to abridge the multitude of suits which there would otherwise be here. For this reason it has recently been held in this court that if a man calls another a 'rogue', 'cozener' or 'a false knave', or such like, the action on the case shall not be given for it [...] and he further said that these words 'knave', 'rogue', and so forth, are words more of anger and for the most part spoken hastily and without any advisement.[65]

Thus, the legal status of words changes over the years. The so-called *mitior sensus* rule undoubtedly leads to some aberrations. Baker mentions a few extreme examples such as the following:

> it was not even actionable to say that a physician had killed a patient with his pills; the patient might have choked or suffered an unusual reaction, and so there was not necessarily an allegation of medical incompetence, let alone murder.[66]

The word 'pox' was also subject to subtle manipulation and interpretations:[67]

> The 'pox' cases were similarly restricted, so that a mere imputation of 'pox' would be taken to mean small pox and therefore (for some reason now obscure) not actionable. A great deal of subtlety was expended on expressions such as 'pocky whore', which might be taken to carry an indication of the kind of pox intended.[68]

'Treasonable abuses'

In *Measure for Measure*, Lucio is comically seen slandering the disguised Duke, and in fact unwittingly insulting him to his face. The comic situation of double and mistaken identity transforms indirect words of slander into direct words of insult. Believing he is addressing Friar Lodowick, Lucio slanders Duke Vincentio, comparing him to the 'ungenitured agent' (3.1.432), Angelo:

> The Duke yet would have dark deeds darkly answered; he would never bring them to light. Would he were returned. [...] The Duke (I say to thee again) would eat mutton on Fridays. He's now past it, yet (and I say to thee) he would

mouth with a beggar, though she smelt brown bread and garlic. Say that I said so. Farewell.
(3.1.433–42)

Lucio, who can be seen as an embodiment of Rumour,[69] associates Vincentio, the 'duke of dark corners' (4.3.154), with lechery, while describing Angelo as one 'begot between two stockfishes' (3.1.372). Lucio's words are heard as calumnious by the Duke, who comments on them once the latter has left the stage:

No might nor greatness in mortality
Can censure scape; back-wounding calumny
The whitest virtue strikes. What king so strong
Can tie the gall up in the slanderous tongue?
(3.1.443–6)

The irony of the sequence is striking when one considers that Lucio is in fact completely wrong in his apprehension of the two characters, which is not surprising in a play that, like Elbow, confuses 'benefactors' and 'malefactors' (2.1.49–51) as well as 'varlets' and 'honourable' men (2.1.82–83). Escalus, whose name evokes a scale of values, could say the same about Lucio as about Elbow: 'Do you hear how he misplaces?' (2.1.84). Ironically too, the Duke does not consider that, in Lucio's scale of values, lechery is higher than 'stricture and firm abstinence' (1.3.12), which explains the slanderer's wishes that the old Duke were back and transforms what is potential abuse into potential compliment. This is confirmed when in a later scene Lucio again tells 'pretty tales of the Duke' (4.3.161) to the Duke himself, still thinking he addresses a friar:

Friar, thou knowest not the Duke so well as I do; he's a better woodman[70] than thou tak'st him for.
(4.3.157–8)

The adjective 'better' shows that Lucio's speech wavers between abuse and compliment. Yet his confidences to the Friar not only question Vincentio's virtuous behaviour but also his intelligence and braveness, when he declares, as secret revelations, that 'he's a very superficial, ignorant, unweighing fellow' (3.1.400) or that he was 'a shy fellow' (3.1.393). Lucio ironically later attributes these words to the Friar, that is, to the Duke himself, denouncing them as being calumnious and deserving punishment:

LUCIO
[...] Come hither, goodman Baldpate. Do you know me?
DUKE
I remember you, sir, by the sound of your voice. I met you at the prison, in the absence of the duke.
LUCIO
O, did you so? And do you remember what you said of the Duke?
DUKE
Most notedly, sir.
LUCIO
Do you so, sir? And was the Duke a fleshmonger, a fool, and a coward, as you then reported him to be?
DUKE
You must, sir, change persons with me ere you make that my report. You indeed spoke so of him, and much more, much worse.
LUCIO
O, thou damnable fellow! Did not I pluck thee by the nose for thy speeches?
DUKE
I protest, I love the Duke as I love myself.
ANGELO
Hark how the villain would close now after his treasonable abuses.

(*MM*, 5.1.325–41)

Lucio's words are identified as 'treasonable abuses', which associates them with *Scandalum Magnatum* that David Cressy describes as 'An especially transgressive form of abusive speech'.[71] Lucio speaks 'scandalously about his social superiors'[72] and will soon have to face a political punishment for having committed a political crime of *lèse-majesté*. At the end of the play the Duke appears as a judge who treats all the parties according to their deserts, in a sequence in which Lucio's case is settled:

DUKE
> [*To Lucio*] You, sirrah, that knew me for a fool, a coward,
> One all of luxury, an ass, a madman:
> Wherein have I so deserved of you,
> That you extol me thus?

LUCIO
> 'Faith, my lord. I spoke it but according to the trick. If you will hang me for it you may, but I had rather it would please you I might be whipped.

DUKE
> Whipped first, sir, and hanged after.
> Proclaim it, Provost, round about the city.
> If any woman wronged by this lewd fellow –
> As I have heard him swear himself there's one
> Whom he begot with child – let her appear,
> And he shall marry her. The nuptial finished,
> Let him be whipped and hanged.

LUCIO
> I beseech your highness do not marry me to a whore. Your highness said even now I made you a duke; good my lord, do not recompense me in making me a cuckold.

DUKE
> Upon mine honour, thou shalt marry her.
> Thy slanders I forgive and therewithal
> Remit thy other forfeits. Take him to prison;
> And see our pleasure herein executed.

LUCIO

Marrying a punk, my lord, is pressing to death, whipping, and hanging.

DUKE

Slandering a prince deserves it.

(*MM*, 5.1.500–24)

The offender is here a felon and must suffer a penalty because 'slandering a prince deserves it'. The codes of comedy dictate that this punishment is more moral than physical. However, this punishment is probably a resurgence of what jurists call the *Scandalum Magnatum*, which stipulated that insults to princes should be severely punished. It appears that the punishment gives the insult a political dimension that brings it closer to felony or treason. Only a prince could inflict this type of punishment, which reveals, as Lindsay Kaplan has shown,[73] the power of the clown's words when they compete with the slanders devised by the prince himself.

5

Insult and the taming of the tongue

Shakespeare's society attempted to regulate and control use of the tongue and fight against all sorts of sins of the tongue. Sermons and homilies such as 'The Taming of the Tongue'[1] or 'An Homelie Agaynst Contention and Braulynge'[2] forbid insult in all its forms, be it insults to God (swearing, blasphemy), to man (railing, scoffing, back-biting, slandering) or both (cursing, banning). This politics of the tongue is illustrated in titles of publications as evocative as *The Co[n]vercyon of Swerers*,[3] *An Invectyve agenst the moost wicked & detestable vyce of swearing*,[4] *A Swoord agaynst Swearyng*,[5] *A Treatise of the Good and Evil Tongue*,[6] *A Direction for the Government of the Tongue according to God's Worde*[7] and *The Araignement of an Unruly Tongue*.[8] The multiplication of handbooks or political texts on duelling and the proliferation of defamation cases[9] confirm this impression. The evil tongue is the tongue that lies, flatters, forswears but also rails, insults, blasphemes, slanders or curses. The key message of such texts is that the tongue must be tamed, in contradiction to James' Epistle 3, according to which 'the tongue can no man tame' because '*it is an unruly evil, full of deadly poison*' (James 3: 7–8). The aim of this chapter is to explore how Shakespeare inscribes insults within the context of the politics of the tongue, and to study the taming of the tongue in his plays, especially in *Richard III* and *The Taming of the Shrew*, which dramatize but also question the very efficiency of such bridling enterprises.

Richard III or the lessons in cursing

'Why should she live to fill the world with words?' asks Richard when Edward prevents him from killing Margaret at the end of *3 Henry VI* (5.5.44). With this question-answer Richard presents the *raison d'être* of a character who seems to have been introduced and recycled by Shakespeare only to shower words of abuse on the world of *Richard III*. Both conveying the vanity of words and the restlessness engendered by these words, this question already reveals, in all its ambivalence, Richard's relation to the power of words.[10] Here words are signs of powerlessness; they are the only means Margaret still has when she can no longer act, and at the same time the question is pregnant with their destructive potential. Moreover, with this question, Richard reduces Margaret to being an organ: from then on, she will be a mere tongue, an evil tongue, whose curses will resound throughout *Richard III*. As early as Act I, Scene 2, Anne summarizes the situation as follows:

> For thou hast made the happy earth thy hell,
> Filled it with cursing cries and deep exclaims.
> (*R3*, 1.2.51–2)

I aim to explore those 'cursing cries and deep exclaims' with which Richard's world is filled, by analyzing the use of insult and malediction in a play where verbal violence not only plays a dramatic part but is also the object of complex and ambivalent theoretical considerations. I will also show how Richard, the evil tongue *par excellence* in the play, ironically becomes the censor or controller of tongues by delivering most of the commandments dictated by theologians.

'Teach me how to curse'

If one considers the entire Shakespearean corpus, it appears that it is *Richard III* that contains the most numerous occurrences of the term 'curse' in all its forms ('curs'd', 'curse', 'cursed', 'curses', 'cursing'). In this play, insults are often integrated into cursing speeches. This eminently spectacular speech act plays an essential dramatic role. From the very beginning of the play, maledictions, whether they are voiced by Lady Anne (1.2) or Margaret (1.3), are at the heart of the tragic project, even if they sometimes sound so excessive that they verge on comedy. In contrast with Marlowe's *Tamburlaine*, where curses are, according to Wolfgang Clemen, 'fundamentally vague and unrealizable',[11] maledictions make up the dramatic fabric of *Richard III* where Margaret's curses are 'exactly fulfilled and remembered by the victim' and 'occupy an important place in the general design of the play and of the scene in which they occur'.[12] Many other commentators, such as A. P. Rossiter[13] and Alice Lotvin Birney[14] consider that malediction is at the heart of the play's structure and gives it its unity. *Richard III* may be read as a journey from the enunciation to the fulfilment of the curses, execration thus merging with prophecy. The characters who are cursed end up being punished throughout a play that seems to represent the work of an unrelenting Nemesis, as is suggested when Grey exclaims: 'Now Margaret's curse is fall'n upon our heads' (*R3*, 3.3.14).

In the light of such a reading, it is tempting to interpret the play as the representation of the active and destructive, even magical potency of words. However, one may consider that the maledictions are not 'exactly fulfilled', as is stated by Clemen, Elizabeth being the most obvious exception to this rule. At the end of the play, she becomes a woman of action again, giving the lie – at least provisionally – to the prophetic curse. Shirley Carr Mason has shown how the play rests on an ambivalent conception of language, more precisely on what she synthetically calls 'an interplay of superstition and scepticism'.[15] If part of the dramatic action seems to illustrate a belief in the magical power of words, the metalinguistic discourses that pervade the play reflect a more ambiguous conception. Imprecation is inscribed in a dialectic of acting and suffering, of vanity and efficiency that reveals the complex articulation of saying and doing.

Characters curse *because they cannot* act; characters curse *in order to* act: here are the two logical links that the speech act can imply. In *Richard III*, malediction is the prerogative of female characters, who thus seem to reveal their powerlessness but also their belief in the power of words. *Richard III* seems to contain a perfect illustration of the sexist opinion conveyed by Thomas Adams in his sermon 'The Taming of the Tongue':

> 'She is loud,' saith Solomon, Prov vii. 11; 'a foolish woman is ever clamorous,' ix. 13. She calls her tongue her defensive weapon; she means offensive: a firebrand in a frantic hand doth less mischief. The proverb came not from nothing, when we say of a brawling man, he hath a woman's tongue in his head.[16]

In *Richard III*, it is first women who are 'clamorous' and who are presented as evil tongues. Both Lady Anne and Margaret evoke the figure of the shrew whose 'exclaims' are both a sign of power and powerlessness. It is not fortuitous that we find the figure of Margaret next to that of Joan of Arc in Thomas Heywood's *Gynaikeion* (1624), within a chapter that is entitled 'Of English Virago's, & of Joan the Pucil'.[17] Several times described as a witch,[18] Margaret embodies the faith in the magic power of words:

> Can curses pierce the clouds and enter heaven?
> Why then give way, dull clouds, to my quick curses.
> (1.3.194–5)

First expressed in the interrogative form, this faith is confirmed throughout the play and notably appears in the following exchange:

QUEEN ELIZABETH
  My words are dull. O, quicken them with thine.
QUEEN MARGARET
  Thy woes will make them sharp and pierce like mine.
                                                     (4.4.124–5)

Margaret mimics Archilochus, a figure that was well known in Elizabethan times, whose maledictions were supposed to cause the death of his victims.[19] To be efficient, malediction must be poetic and only Margaret seems to be endowed with that artistic 'know-how', as is suggested by Elizabeth when she implores:

O thou, well skilled in curses, stay awhile
And teach me how to curse mine enemies. (4.4.116–17)

The evil tongue is a poetic tongue. The Duchess of York also underlines the power of words when she sets to cursing her son:

If so, then be not tongue-tied. Go with me,
And in the breath of bitter words let's smother
My damned son, that thy two sweet sons smothered.
                                                     (4.4.132–4)

When they do not consider the play's female characters as a chorus of mourners, commentators place the ghostly figure of Margaret at the heart of *Richard III*, because her imprecations overwhelm each stage of the dramatic action. By using asides and echoes, Shakespeare creates an absent-present character. The repetition of her initial curse enlarges the presence of the character and allows an essentially absent Margaret to have a pervasive presence on stage. This *trompe-l'œil* or rather *trompe-l'oreille* technique that lets us hear Margaret's voice even when and perhaps *especially* when she is absent should not make us forget the climax that is reached when the Duchess curses Richard:

> Therefore take with thee my most grievous curse,
> Which in the day of battle tire thee more
> Than all the complete armour that thou wear'st.
> My prayers on the adverse party fight,
> And there the little souls of Edward's children
> Whisper the spirits of thine enemies
> And promise them success and victory.
> Bloody thou art; bloody will be thy end.
> Shame serves thy life and doth thy death attend. *Exit*
> (4.4.188–96)

In this play, imprecation follows a *crescendo* pattern. Numerous Elizabethan texts reveal that of all verbal forms of violence, none is worse than the malediction a parent delivers to his child. In one of his pamphlets, Samuel Rowlands evokes the 'unkind parents' who, in the grip of anger, curse their children:

> You that in rage and fury, most unkinde,
> Will utter Curses where you ought to blesse:
> For which God often yeeldeth to your minde,
> And sayes Amen, to wished ill successe.
> You that from all humanitie have ceast,
> Man-like in shape, in manners but a beast.
>   Ile Stabbe yee.[20]

This pamphlet recycles many edifying stories told by theologians to deter parents from cursing their offspring. Religious texts present as the supreme transgression that which consists in cursing one's own flesh and blood.[21] According to Plato, parental maledictions were the most efficient,[22] and there are numerous traces of this belief in the examples chosen by sixteenth-century theologians. Thus, for an Elizabethan spectator, the final curse delivered by Richard's mother must have been a dramatic climax.

In *Richard III*, malediction means endless recurrence, as Shakespeare cultivates the memory of words. Curses make Buckingham's hair 'stand on end' (1.3.303) and everyone remembers them when their time has come. Most of the characters see in their death or misfortune the result of the curse, the evidence that curses can kill, that one can do things with words. Anne curses Richard at the beginning of the play (1.2.14–28), and she recalls her hateful words in Act 4 (1.70–76), reporting them to Elizabeth and the Duchess. Remembering this original curse, she becomes aware of all the irony it was pregnant with. As for Richard, he lets us hear the voice of his father (1.3.173–81) cursing Margaret in *3 Henry VI* (1.4.164–6), which is only one example among many of the words that circulate within the tetralogy. In Act 4, Margaret too remembers the invectives she hurled at Elizabeth in Act 1:

> I called thee then vain flourish of my fortune;
> I called thee then, poor shadow, painted queen,
> The presentation of but what I was,
> The flattering index of a direful pageant,
> One heaved a-high, to be hurled down below,
> A mother only mocked with two fair babes,
> A dream of what thou wast, a garish flag
> To be the aim of every dangerous shot,
> A sign of dignity, a breath, a bubble,
> A queen in jest, only to fill the scene.
> (*R3*, 4.4.82–91)

These words show how curses rest on a web of insults and they are a rewriting of Margaret's words to Elizabeth in Act 1:

> Poor painted queen, vain flourish of my fortune,
> Why strew'st thou sugar on that bottled spider,
> Whose deadly web ensnareth thee about?
> Fool, fool, thou whet'st a knife to kill thyself.
> The time will come when thou shalt wish for me
> To help thee curse this poisonous bunch-backed toad.
> (*R3*, 1.3.240–45)

Insults are constitutive of the rhetoric of cursing that pervades the play. Grey and Rivers (3.3.14–22), Hastings (3.4.91–2) and Buckingham (5.1.25–7) all remember Margaret's curses before they die, thus showing the impact of such words. In *Richard III*, to deliver maledictions means to imagine the magic power of words that become weapons and prolong the body.[23] When Lady Anne spits at Richard's face (1.2.147), this deed, in which Miranda Fay Thomas sees a means to 'tame the beast',[24] is the physical version of malediction. At this moment, words dissolve into deeds. But the words that leave a trace in memories are at the same time expressions of powerlessness. ''Tis bootless to exclaim' (3.4.101): leading Hastings to death, Lovell underlines the vanity of words.

To know how to curse, one has to suffer. This idea is at the heart of Margaret's cursing lesson:

> Forbear to sleep the nights, and fast the day;
> Compare dead happiness with living woe;
> Think that thy babes were sweeter than they were,
> And he that slew them fouler than he is.
> Bettering thy loss makes the bad causer worse.
> Revolving this will teach thee how to curse.
>
> (4.4.118–23)

Misfortune is the source of malediction. This link is thrown into relief by the Duchess of York, when she asks: 'Why should calamity be full of words?' (4.4.126). For Elizabeth, the only virtue one can attribute to invective is that it relieves the heart of the weak:

> Windy attorneys to their clients' woes,
> Airy succeeders of intestate joys,
> Poor breathing orators of miseries,
> Let them have scope, though what they will impart
> Help nothing else, yet do they ease the heart.
>
> (4.4.127–31)

Even if they are 'windy' and 'airy', even if they are a mere breath, curses and insults are worth being delivered because they 'ease the heart'. To curse means to try to do things with words, but it also means that you belong to a world that suffers. That is why in this play imprecation merges with lament, a ritual that Puttenham describes as follows:

> Lamenting is altogether contrary to rejoising, euery man saith so, and yet it is a peece of joy to be able to lament with ease, and freely to poure forth a mans inward sorrowes and greefs wherewith his minde is surcharged.[25]

When the reader discovers a little later Puttenham's description of imprecation, one cannot but associate the two modes of expression:

> but either in deede or by word, he [man] will seeke revenge against them that malice him, or practise his harmes, ... This made the auncient Poetes to invent a meane to rid the gall of all such Vindicative men: so as they might be a wrecked of their wrong, & never bely their enemie with slaunderous untruthes. And this was done by a maner of imprecation, or as we call it by cursing and banning of the parties, and wishing all evill to a light upon them, and though it never the sooner happened, yet was it great easment to the boiling stomacke: They were called *Dirae*, such as *Virgill* made aginst *Battarus*, and *Ovide* against *Ibis*: we Christians are forbidden to use such uncharitable fashions, and willed to referre all our revenges to God alone.[26]

Two expressions of suffering, lamenting and cursing are the ways men and women have found to 'ease their boiling stomacke[s]'. The tirade Anne utters in front of the corpse of Henry VI reflects how discourse slides from lament ('To hear the lamentations of poor Anne', 1.2.9) to malediction ('O, cursed be the hand that made these holes', 1.2.14). Those two modes of speech are characterized by a catalogue rhetoric, based on accumulation and often anaphoric enumeration, which gives the speech its ritual incantatory dimension. As far as lament and malediction are concerned, it never rains but it pours. Curses never come alone in this play, like the four hundred lines of exempla one can read in Ovid's *De Ibis*.[27] This rhetorical feature tends to show that words do not do things, that they are and will remain ever insufficient, ever inadequate. Ever unsatisfied, and *though* or *so* ever at work, the evil tongue never *stops* cursing. That is why Margaret needs Richard to interrupt the torrent of words she showers on him:

QUEEN MARGARET
[…]
Thou elvish-marked, abortive, rooting hog,
Thou that was sealed in thy nativity
The slave of nature and the son of hell;
Thou slander of thy heavy mother's womb,
Thou loathed issue of thy father's loins,
Thou rag of honour, thou detested –
RICHARD
Margaret!

(1.3.227–34)

As Margaret cannot 'make the period' (1.3.237) to her curse, Richard does so in a sequence that is pregnant with a comic potential as it rests on a boomerang principle. Richard's reaction underlines the almost comic excess that emerges from curses. One of the main features of malediction is that it is *endless*. This passage is also emblematic of the shift that occurs from cursing to insulting. When Margaret beseeches Richard to let her 'make the period' to her curse, the spectator has just heard in fact a stream of *abuse* rather than a *curse*. Insult, as the fruit of anger, merges with malediction. Of course, the two speech acts differ from one another as insult rests on a binary relationship between the enunciator and the co-enunciator, whereas malediction is based on a triangular relationship since the enunciator invokes a higher authority. Insult is very often devoid of a verbal nucleus while malediction is built round a verb. Moreover, those two speech acts do not have the same relation to time, as insult strikes in the instant while the curse postpones the damage and relegates it to the future. Different as they are, those two speech acts have something in common: they are based on what Jean Laplanche calls 'mots projectiles';[28] that is why one often finds one in the wake of the other. The evil tongue curses and insults in the same breath. Insults constitute a 'web'[29] of 'bitter names' (1.3.235), at the centre of which one finds Richard, who is the other characters' favourite target.

If, in *Henry VI*, insults are part of martial speeches that are scattered throughout the plays, and are distributed between numerous characters, in *Richard III*, on the other hand, the treatment of abuse isolates Richard. The play literally dramatizes what Richard says of his existence when he declares 'That dogs bark at [him], as [he] halt[s] by them' (1.1.23). Richard's portrait is almost exclusively drawn by means of insults and curses. They contain the 'repetition', that is, the endless narration of what he has 'marred' (1.3.164). Insults have a descriptive value and recycle the self-portrait drawn by Richard. It is not surprising that a character who describes himself as 'the devil' (1.3.337) and as 'the formal Vice, Iniquity' (3.1.82) should recurrently be called 'devil'.[30] '[R]udely stamped', 'curtailed of this fair proportion', 'cheated of feature', 'deformed', 'unfinished', 'sent before my time', 'lamely', 'unfashionable': here are the terms Richard uses to draw his self-portrait at the beginning of the play (1.1.14–22). 'Thou lump of foul deformity' (1.2.57), 'thou elvish-marked, abortive, rooting hog' (1.3.227), 'this poisonous bunch-backed toad' (1.3.245), 'that bottled spider, that foul bunch-backed toad' (4.4.81): these are some of the abusive words that Anne, Margaret and Elizabeth hurl at him, words that prolong Richard's self-portrait. In this play abuse merges with description. Sometimes called 'dog',[31] sometimes 'spider',[32] sometimes 'cockatrice',[33] 'boar',[34] 'hog'[35] or 'hedgehog',[36] Richard undergoes, through insults, a series of distortions that are the verbal expression of his natural physical monstrosity.

The same words return again and again and they are so often used that they almost lose their insulting content and sound descriptive and objective. This is all the more striking since the circulation of those words involves not only *Richard III* but the whole tetralogy. In the whole Shakespearean corpus, the word 'toad' is almost exclusively reserved for Richard.[37] This image, as well as the images of the spider or the serpent, conjures up a physically 'abject' creature that inspires disgust but above all a poisonous figure.[38] It is not the least irony that a character who is considered as 'venomed'[39] should present himself as the controller of tongues. 'O do not swear, my Lord of Buckingham' (3.7.219), Richard piously orders, when his adviser lets out a sacrilegious 'Zounds' ('God's wounds'). Richard is probably the character who swears the most often in the play.[40] But with this injunction, he appears in the guise of the controller of tongues who cannot suffer anyone swearing in front of him. The sermons, homilies and religious texts of all sorts condemn the practice that consists in insulting God by taking his name in vain and dismembering, rending Christ's body.[41] To tame the tongue, you have to prevent it from swearing. Throughout the play Richard, the embodiment of the evil tongue, ironically makes it his duty to tame the evil tongues that assail and assault him. To do so, he displays most of the commandments that are dictated by theologians.

'Blessings for curses'

With Lady Anne, Richard first puts into practice one of the key-precepts concerning the good use of the tongue: 'bless them that curse you'. Replying to Anne's curses by praise, Richard becomes the mouthpiece of a rule that is expounded, for example, in 'An Homelie Agaynst Contention and Braulynge': 'saye well by them that saye evill by you.... Blesse them that curse you, blesse, I saye, and curse not.'[42] Richard not only applies this rule when he gives praise for abuse, words of love for words of hate, but he also explicitly reminds Anne of it, teaching her good verbal manners:

> Lady, you know no rules of charity,
> Which renders good for bad, blessings for curses.
> (1.2.68–9)

The marriage of contrarieties finds its dramatic expression in this scene that is both a wooing scene and a scene of insult. Shakespeare cultivates the union of extremes by utilizing all the resources of stichomythia, the rhetorical emblem of verbal union and divorce. In this scene, extremes meet; abuse answers praise and curses answer blessings in a series of rhetorical reversals. 'Angel' answers 'devil' (1.2.73–4), 'Sweet Saint' (1.2.49) answers 'Thou dreadful minister of hell' (1.2.46). Each party uses the other's words to better reverse them. What should be a verbal fight turns into a verbal form of union that ironically foreshadows the marriage of the two characters whose words intertwine at the same time as they intersect. Anne and Richard become verbally inseparable. It is in this scene that they are joined together in a verbal 'match'. Needless for Shakespeare then to stage a union that he has just represented through rhetoric.

The spectator feels, behind this scene, the presence of the comic shrew-taming tradition that Richard uses to empty Anne's invectives of their tragic content:

> But, gentle Lady Anne,
> To leave this keen encounter of our wits,
> And fall something into a slower method:
> (1.2.118–20)

With these words, Richard denies the tragic dimension of the scene and reduces it to the kind of 'amorous Agon' that one finds in a play like *Much Ado About Nothing*. Moreover, the expression 'fall into a slower method' conveys the image of a tongue that should be bridled and tamed. The injunction 'be not so curst' (1.2.49) plunges the spectator into the world of shrew-taming.

'Bless them that curse you': when Margaret leaves the stage after having showered strings of prophetic curses on the other characters, Richard hypocritically displays the same precept by declaring 'I cannot blame her' (1.3.305). Rivers makes Richard's reaction explicit when he comments:

> A virtuous and a Christian-like conclusion,
> To pray for them that have done scathe to us.
> (1.3.315–16)

In the following monologue, Richard ironically theorizes about his method:

> But then I sigh, and, with a piece of scripture,
> Tell them that God bids us do good for evil;
> And thus I clothe my naked villainy
> With odd old ends stol'n forth of Holy Writ,
> And seem a saint when most I play the devil.
> (1.3.333–7)

Most of the 'odd ends' that he draws from Scripture concern the use of the tongue.

'Curse not thyself'

'Do not curse, because, when you curse, you curse yourself': here is the second commandment that underlies Richard's words and deeds. The boomerang effect of malediction appears in numerous religious works. In the *Anathomy of Sinne*, for example, one can read that 'curses rebound upon the head of him that curseth'.[43] Shakespeare makes the most of this idea to produce irony. Richard first delivers this motto in the following exchange:

ANNE
> Black night o'ershade thy day, and death thy life.

RICHARD
> Curse not thyself, fair creature; thou art both.
> (1.2.134–5)

Then Buckingham, as is so often the case, echoes Richard when he declares:

> for curses never pass
> The lips of those that breathe them in the air.
> (1.3.284–5)

Curses always rebound on the person who utters them. After having theorized on that boomerang effect, Shakespeare immediately dramatizes it by having Anne voice imprecations that will turn against her. By cursing Richard's future wife, Anne curses herself 'And prove[s] the subject of [her] own soul's curse' (4.1.80). A little later, Richard puts that principle into action, by turning Margaret's curse against her. Richard needs only one word ('Margaret', 1.3.232) to interrupt and deflate the old Queen's endless string of curses and abuse. The restricted verbal means Richard uses contrasts with Margaret's logorrhoea. 'Thus have you breathed your curse against yourself' (1.3.239): here is Elizabeth's conclusion with which she ironically becomes Richard's ally in this verbal ambush. By staging this boomerang effect, the playwright puts into dramatic action a verbal principle that belonged to the Elizabethan world. Richard is both the theorist and the actor of this principle.

'That was in thy rage'

Richard plays with another rule of the tongue, in the following exchange:

> ANNE
> Arise, dissembler; though I wish thy death,
> I will not be thy executioner.

RICHARD
> Then bid me kill myself, and I will do it.

ANNE
> I have already.

RICHARD
> That was in thy rage:
> Speak it again and, even with the word,
> This hand, which for thy love did kill thy love,
> Shall for thy love kill a far truer love;
> To both their deaths shalt thou be accessary.
>   (1.2.187–94)

Evil words that are uttered in the grip of anger should not be taken seriously. This idea is recurrently developed in tongue-taming books, notably in books on duelling that are meant to placate the touchiness that seemed to characterize Shakespeare's contemporaries. This scene reveals Richard's legalism that he displays in his own interest. In Shakespeare's days, evil words that were uttered playfully or by someone who was in the grip of anger were not 'actionable'. Richard takes Anne's words *in mitiori sensu*[44] and dismisses them, like a court of justice, as not being actionable. He substitutes himself for a kind of court of justice, as will so often be the case in the play. Moreover, while letting Anne believe that she has the power to kill him with one word ('even with the word...'), he proposes to be the superior authority that can fulfil a curse. Richard becomes a mixture of judge and God who has a right to decide which words count and which words don't.

Drowning the exclamations

If Richard manipulates religious and judicial laws to tame the evil tongues that surround him, he uses other weapons at the end of the play when he silences his mother with drums and trumpets. Richard, who 'cannot brook the accent of reproof'

(4.4.159), reduces to mere noise the curses that his mother hurls at him by ordering martial instruments to sound:

> A flourish, trumpets! Strike alarum, drums!
> Let not the heavens hear these tell-tale women
> Rail on the Lord's anointed. Strike, I say! *Flourish. Alarums.*
> Either be patient and entreat me fair,
> Or with the clamorous report of war
> Thus will I drown your exclamations.
>
> (4.4.149–54)

Richard silences evil tongues with mottoes and trumpets, this taming thus appearing as a tyrannical act and strategy. Once he has achieved his end, the mask of the pious man falls down, revealing the image of a tyrant who controls everyone's words. The sound of war competes with the sound of the tongue, in a form of battle of noises that is evocative of what Petruccio, another tyrannical figure, describes in a more domestic play, *The Taming of the Shrew*, when he reduces the shrew to a mere noisy nuisance that is nothing compared to other sounds he has been confronted with, especially the sound of war:

> Think you a little din can daunt mine ears?
> [...]
> Have I not heard great ordnance in the field,
> And heaven's artillery thunder in the skies?
> Have I not in a pitched battle heard
> Loud 'larums, neighing steeds, and trumpets' clang?
> And do you tell me of a woman's tongue,
> That gives not half so great a blow to hear
> As will a chestnut in a farmer's fire?
> Tush, tush, fear boys with bugs.
>
> (*TS*, 1.2.198–209)

Like Petruccio, Richard is unimpressed by the women's tongues and his reaction aims specifically at reducing women to the status of what he calls 'tell-tale women' (4.4.150) or chattering tongues.

Charming the 'chattering tongue' in *The Taming of the Shrew*

TRANIO
   Faith, he is gone unto the taming school.
BIANCA
   The taming-school? What, is there such a place?
TRANIO
   Ay, mistress, and Petruccio is the master
   That teacheth tricks eleven-and-twenty long
   To tame a shrew and charm her chattering tongue.
                                     (*TS*, 4.2.55–9)

The word 'charm' means 'control' and is also used in *Othello* when Iago strives to control his wife's tongue: 'Go to, charm your tongue' (*Oth*, 5.2.179). Emilia refuses to be shut up: 'I will not charm my tongue. I am bound to speak' (*Oth*, 5.2.180) and exclaims a little later ''Twill out, 'twill out' (*Oth*, 5.2.217). A few scenes earlier, Iago had already tried to control her tongue by ordering her to 'speak within doors' (*Oth*, 4.2.146), that is, to 'keep [herself] within [herself]' (*AC*, 2.5.75) and hold her tongue within the double barriers of her lips and teeth.[45] In dictionaries of the period, the word 'chatter' is associated with such terms as 'brawler', 'contender' or 'scolder'.[46]

Hortensio gives the spectator an idea of the part insult plays in the picture of the shrew when he narrates how Kate 'broke the lute' to him:

I did but tell her she mistook her frets
And bowed her hand to teach her fingering
When, with a most impatient devilish spirit,
'Frets call you these?' quoth she, 'I'll fume with them,'
And with that word she struck me on the head,
And through the instrument my pate made way,
And there I stood amazed for a while,
As on a pillory, looking through the lute,
While she did call me 'rascal', 'fiddler',

And 'twangling Jack', with twenty such vile terms,
As had she studied to misuse me so.
(*TS*, 2.1.148–58)

It seems that Petruccio is going to be the one who 'studies to misuse' the Shrew. *The Taming of the Shrew* can be read as a do-it-yourself guide to taming an unruly tongue and yet the play questions who is eventually tamed and who the unruly and evil tongue is.

'Of all titles the worst'

When Grumio declares '"Katherine the Curst" – / A title for a maid of all titles the worst' (*TS*, 1.2.127–8), his words imply that the surname that is given to Kate is the most insulting name one can imagine and that Kate is cursed in being labelled as 'curst'.

In the sixteenth century, the words 'shrew' and 'scold' evoke a social reality, an ideological conception as well as a folkloric and literary type, three essential aspects that Shakespeare integrates into his dramatic work.[47] In Elizabethan times, the shrew is first and foremost a tongue that needs to be controlled. Numerous writings, whether religious texts, sermons, pamphlets, political treatises or legal reports, suggest that the tongue is too often used in the service of sin, vice or even crime and that it is an instrument of rough music, noise, slander, insults and blasphemy. The shrew seems to be the character that best epitomizes all these excesses of language. In *The Taming of the Shrew*, Shakespeare reflects his society's attempts and failure to control the excesses of this tongue.

The sociologist Martin Ingram defines the term 'scold' by first pointing out that it was not originally linked to the female gender:

> the verb to scold had a much stronger meaning than it does today: it meant to chide and to brawl and had undertones of violence and uncontrolled rage. A scold was a turbulent,

chiding, brawling person. The term could apply to either sex, but from the fourteenth century it was characteristically used of women and by about 1700 had become virtually exclusive to them.[48]

Shakespeare's time was a transitional period for a term that was not yet exclusively reserved for women, but was not far from being so, a period in which the term was increasingly used in the feminine. As David Cressy reminds us, 'Most foul speakers described as scolds were women but men could be guilty of the like offence'.[49] This transitional dimension is expressed in Shakespeare's play itself when Curtis notes that Petruccio 'is more shrew than she' (4.1.76).

Ingram also emphasizes the legal value of the term:

> It should be noted also that, while the words *scold* and *to scold* could be used in a variety of social contexts – for example to refer to a nagging wife – they did have strong *legal* connotations. This was especially true of the noun: the phrase *common scold* was a technical term in common law, and meant an individual liable to prosecution and punishment as a nuisance for continually disturbing the neighbours by contentious behaviour.[50]

The shrew is above all a figure of discord, of which there are many traces in Elizabethan court reports.[51] According to some historians and sociologists, such as D. E. Underdown, between 1560 and 1640 there was a proliferation of cases against this type of abuser. Underdown speaks of an epidemic which, in his opinion, reflects a strengthening of patriarchal authority in the Elizabethan period.[52] According to Ingram, on the other hand, prosecutions for this type of behaviour had existed since the fourteenth century. In any case, it should be noted that given the various jurisdictions in which this behaviour could be tried, it is very difficult to have a precise idea of the number of cases brought for 'scolding'. It is all the more difficult to establish statistics since many other terms, such as 'railing', 'cursing', 'brawling', or in Latin 'rixatrix', 'garrulatrix', 'objurgatrix', 'calomniatrix', 'litigatrix', 'perturbatrix pacis',[53] could be evocative of the behaviour of the shrew. Finally, the cluster of accusations against women also makes the statistics uncertain. In the imagination of the Renaissance, the shrew is not far from the witch. Reginald Scot, in *The Discovery of Witchcraft* (1584), defines witches as 'doting, scolds, mad, divelish'.[54] The witch is known for cursing her neighbours, and it is thus natural that the two figures should be associated. In the Renaissance imagination, the shrew is also a 'whore', her language being as unrestrained as her sexuality. Thus, a sort of blurring between the shrew, the witch and the harlot, is often found in court reports that contain the conjunction of these accusations.

Beyond this typological blurring that Shakespeare partly reflects in *Richard III* and *The Taming of the Shrew*, it seems that the Elizabethan period is characterized by a greater severity towards these troublemakers. Ingram, however, qualifies this assertion and the feminist interpretations that may ensue, pointing out that corporal punishment was not unknown before this period and that the severity of the punishments that were inflicted was not restricted to these women but was a general trend of the time.[55] However, if the shrew is still remembered, it is probably due to the symbolic physical punishment she had to undergo when she was condemned. It was in fact from the second half of the sixteenth century onwards that instruments such as 'the branks' or 'the bridle' appeared in certain regions of England to tame the shrew. The symbolic dimension of this instrument, which transforms the woman into a horse and turns punishment into taming, is striking enough to make us forget that it was only rarely used, according to Ingram:

> In any event it is plain that the scold's bridle had a very brief history and was never used at all in most parts of England. Robert Plot, describing a specimen from Newcastle-under-Lyne (Staffordshire) in 1686 referred to it as 'an instrument scarce heard of, much less seen'.[56]

This statement again qualifies the interpretations that tend to make women in general the victims of an increasingly patriarchal society but the existence of an object as symbolic as a bridle shows how important it was to tame the tongue by means of humiliation.

Other types of punishment were inflicted on shrews:

> Scolds were sometimes punished in the stocks, by being incarcerated in the town 'cage' or, occasionally, by being carted or paraded round the town with basins ringing before them.[57]

Cleopatra's expressing her fear of becoming the object of public mockery (AC, 5.2.208–12) evokes the spectacular punishments described here. In the sixteenth and seventeenth centuries, the characteristic instrument used to tame discordant shrews, which was apparently reserved for them, was the cucking stool, also known by the more evocative name of 'ducking stool', referring to a chair (sometimes with a hole in it)[58] in which they were placed before being repeatedly dunked in water, obviously in public. In 1675, the jurist William Sheppard described the course of events in the following terms:

> A scold is a troublesome and angry Woman, who by her brauling and wrangling amongst her Neighbors, doth break the Publick Peace, and beget, cherish and increase publick Discord.
>
> She is to be presented for it by and punished in the Leet, by being put in the Cucking stool, Ducking-stool, or Tumbrel, an Engine appointed for that purpose, which is in the fashion of a Chair: And herein she is to sit, and to be let down in the water, over head and ears, three or four times, so that no part of her shall be above water, diving or ducking down, though against their wills, as Ducks use to do under the water.[59]

Boose, writing about these practices, describes the cucking-stool as follows:

> a chair-like apparatus into which the offender was ordered strapped and then, to the jeers of the crowd, was dunked

several times in water over her head – water that might be a local river but was equally likely to have been a horsewash pond.[60]

This 'public shaming ritual'[61] was recommended in 'A Homilie Agaynst Contention and Brawlynge':

> And because this vice (contention) is so muche hurtefull to the societie of a common wealth, in all well ordred cities these common braulers and skolders bee punished with a notable kynde of pain: as to be sette on the cokyngstole, pillery, or suche like. And thei be unworthy to live in a common wealthe the whiche do asmuche as lieth in theim, with braulyng and skoldyng, to disturbe the quietnes and peace of thesame.[62]

Ingram tries to identify the criteria that led someone to the cucking-stool. He argues that the practice was not as common as is often believed, but was specific to certain regions and to a combination of charges, which he describes as follows:

> But charges of being a 'common scold' that were likely to bring women to the cucking-stool usually involved not merely brawling and abuse but also such offences as indiscriminate slander, tale-bearing, the stirring up of strife, the deliberate sowing of discord between neighbours, and sometimes also the pursuit of quarrels through needless lawsuits and legal chicanery.[63]

The shrew is a cluster of evil usages of the tongue. Whatever the quantitative importance is granted to these practices (the bridle, the ducking-stool or the cart), one cannot fail to see symbolic implications and to find traces of this phenomenon in Shakespeare's *The Taming of the Shrew*. The shrew is punished by public humiliation and the shame that ensues. Underdown associates this public justice with 'rough music',[64] which could also be called the 'skimmington ride':

Processional rituals of the charivari type were often an officially sanctioned component in punishments ordered by the magistrates for violations of sexual or gender norms. A procession making 'rough music' – to quote Cotgrave's dictionary, 'the harmony of tinging kettles and frying-pan music' – was a routine accompaniment to the 'carting' or 'riding' of a whore, the placarding or ducking of a scold.[65]

Popular justice thus meets the application of legal punishment and extends it. Shame is at the centre of these ritual punishments, whose spectacular and festive dimension was pointed out by Lynda E. Boose:

> The cucking of scolds was turned into a carnival experience, one that literally placed the woman's body at the center of a mocking parade. Whenever local practicalities made it possible, her experience seems to have involved being ridden or carted through town, often to the accompaniment of musical instruments of the distinctly 'Dionysian' variety, making sounds such as those that imitated flatulence or made some degrading association with her body.[66]

This enthronement of women can be seen as a carnivalesque reversal:

> Because scolds were seen as threats to male authority, their carnivalesque punishments of mocking enthronement partake of the inverted structure of 'world-upside-down' rites.[67]

In the light of this context, we can better understand what Gremio is doing in this brief exchange with the father of the shrew, Baptista:

BAPTISTA
   […]
   Leave shall you have to court her at your pleasure.

GREMIO
> To cart her, rather. She's too rough for me.
> (*TS*, 1.1.54–5)

Beyond the paronomasia that rewrites 'court' into 'cart', Shakespeare brings out in a single word the fate that Elizabethan society reserved for shrews and harlots. The full significance of Grumio's description of the newlyweds' journey on horseback is made clear:

> But hadst thou not crossed me, thou shouldst have heard how her horse fell, and she under her horse; thou shouldst have heard in how miry a place, how she was bemoiled, how he left her with the horse upon her, how he beat me because her horse stumbled, how she waded through the dirt to pluck him off me, how he swore, how she prayed, that never prayed before, how I cried, how the horses ran away, how her bridle was burst,
> (*TS*, 4.1.64–72)

The image of the bridle brings to mind the instrument of taming mentioned before. The woman, who is sometimes portrayed as frantically riding an abused husband, is forcibly loaded onto a horse before being subjected to a humiliating mud bath that is highly evocative of the ducking-stool being plunged into a dirty pond. Petruccio tames her with shame. The bride's reaction to the late arrival of her future husband shows how shame and humiliation are central to Petruccio's strategy. 'No shame but mine' (*TS*, 3.2. 8), she says, before continuing:

> Now must the world point at poor Katherine
> And say, 'Lo, there is mad Petruccio's wife,
> If it would please him come and marry her.'
> (*TS*, 3.2.18–20)

The whole 'charming' process implemented by Petruccio is based on noise, the shrew being punished and 'redressed' by the rough music that Petruccio imposes on her throughout the play. The *Taming of the Shrew* as a whole can be seen as a rough festive outburst. A carnival figure, a source of 'rough music' in the first part of the play, where François Laroque recognizes 'The Women's Day',[68] the shrew then becomes a victim of the 'rough music' that Petruccio orchestrates, notably by using insults and by becoming another shrewish figure in the play.

'More shrew than she'

Described as 'Katherine the curst' (1.2.127), 'rough' (1.1.55), 'fiend of hell' (1.1.88), 'hell' (1.1.124), 'curst and shrewd' (1.1.179), 'a shrewd, ill-favoured wife' (1.2.59), 'intolerable curst, / And shrewd, and froward' (1.2.88–9), 'an irksome brawling scold' (1.2.186), 'wildcat' (1.2.195), 'thou hilding of a devilish spirit' (2.1.26) or 'this proud disdainful haggard' (4.2.39), associated with the image of Socrates' Xanthippe (1.2.70), Kate (whose surname can be related to 'cat' or 'kite') becomes an imaginary presence. Characters talk about her more than she talks herself and she is recurrently transformed into a tale. Petruccio, on the other hand, proves very noisy and he paradoxically uses insults to tame Kate's unruly tongue.

If Kate's insults have no effect on Petruccio, his words of abuse are efficient on her. That is what Grumio's comment signifies:

> O'my word, an she knew him as well as I do, she would think scolding would do little good upon him. She may perhaps call him half a score knaves or so – why, that's nothing; an he begin once, he'll rail in his rope-tricks. I'll tell you what, sir, an she stand him but a little, he will throw a figure in her face, and disfigure her with it that she shall have no more eyes to see withal than a cat. (*TS*, 1.2.107–14)

According to Grumio, Kate's insults are 'nothing' while Petruccio's words will 'disfigure her'. Once again one perceives the idea that insults are not efficient or inefficient *per se* but that their effect depends on the ear that hears them. Petruccio's ear is proof against Kate's 'loud alarums' (1.1.126) and verbal assaults:

BAPTISTA
  Well mayst thou woo, and happy be thy speed.
  But be thou armed for some unhappy words.
PETRUCCIO
  Ay, to the proof, as mountains are for winds,
  That shakes not though they blow perpetually.
                                        (*TS*, 2.1.137–40)

Kate's foul words are considered as 'wind' and Petruccio's ears have no problem to 'endure the din' (1.1.172). To tame a tongue, having a deaf ear is useful.

Whatever the meaning one chooses to give to the complex 'rope-tricks',[69] Grumio's words make of insult (to 'rail' means 'to utter abusive language') one of the artificial 'tricks' that Petruccio has to tame the shrew. Read in the light of Grumio's commentary, the comic subterfuge, the masquerade that constitutes the scene of insult to the little tailor, presents us with a 'disfigured' Kate, a puppet that is now only animated by the ventriloquist Petruccio. The scene plays on the relationship between clothing and linguistic artifice, suggesting that behind the 'rope-tricks' one may well hear 'robe-tricks'.[70] Like many Shakespearean insult scenes, the sequence is a spectacle within a spectacle, of which Kate must be the privileged spectator. Franco Zeffirelli's film version, starring Richard Burton and Elizabeth Taylor (1966), translates this by accumulating shots of Kate. It is on Kate that this scene of insult is meant to have an impact. The episode has been carefully 'studied', as the monologue in which Petruccio outlines his tactics tells us: 'And if she chance to nod I'll rail and brawl / And with the clamour keep her still awake'

(4.1.195–6). Theatrical insult is used for educational purposes on a Kate who becomes an infant again ('*infans*', who does not speak), a baby who is shown what is not done. In order to teach Kate good manners, Petruccio shows her bad ones.

The scene with the little tailor is also part of what could be called Petruccio's 'mirage technique', which he uses three times in the play. He goes to Venice to find the finest attire for a husband, but returns in a ridiculous outfit, giving new meaning to his line: 'I will unto Venice / To buy apparel 'gainst the wedding-day' (2.1.318–19). It is not fortuitous that the playwright should choose the word 'against' to mean 'in preparation for'. Indeed, the 'unreverent robes' (3.2.111) worn by Petruccio constitute an insult to Kate. He creates a sartorial illusion by promising Kate a 'ruffling treasure' (4.3.62) before cutting to pieces the cap and gown presented to her.

The string of abuse that Petruccio hurls at the tailor is designed to have an effect on the shrew:

> O monstrous arrogance. Thou liest, thou thread, thou thimble,
> Thou yard, three-quarters, half-yard, quarter, nail,
> Thou flea, thou nit, thou winter-cricket, thou!
> Braved in mine own house with a skein of thread?
> Away, thou rag, thou quantity, thou remnant,
> Or I shall so bemete thee with thy yard
> As thou shalt think on prating whilst thou liv'st,
> I tell thee, I, that thou hast marred her gown.
>
> (4.3.109–16)

The tailor and his gown are 'disfigured' through Petruccio's robe/rope-tricks. Before assaulting the tailor, Petruccio assaults the objects, in a play that is full of objects:[71]

> Why, this was moulded on a porringer –
> A velvet dish. Fie, fie, 'tis lewd and filthy.
> Why, 'tis a cockle or a walnut-shell,
> A knack, a toy, a trick, a baby's cap.
>
> (4.3.66–9)

The same cap is described as 'a paltry cap, / A custard-coffin, a bauble, a silken pie' (4.3.83–4) when Petruccio subverts Kate's words of praise into words of dispraise. Kate is targeted through the attack on the gown:

> O mercy, God, what masquing stuff is here?
> What's this? A sleeve? 'Tis like a demi-cannon.
> What, up and down carved like an apple tart?
> Here's snip, and nip, and cut, and slish and slash,
> Like to a cithern in a barber's shop.
> Why, what i'devil's name, tailor, call'st thou this?
> (4.3.89–94)

Petruccio abuses his wife by assaulting the objects and the tailor, who become substitutes for the violence that is carried out against her. By insulting Kate's taste, Petruccio insults her, in a mechanism of substitution that is also at work when he uses the same 'mirage' technique by having some tempting food prepared for his wife before spoiling it. Controlling Kate's food and clothing amounts to controlling her tongue. In her article 'The Raw and the Cooked in *The Taming of the Shrew*', Camille Wells Slights notes that the play is about 'the cultivated and the brutish'[72] rather than about men and women. It is true that Petruccio's enterprise is reminiscent of the manuals on manners that were in vogue at the time. By controlling Kate's food, he is trying to control her language. By controlling the eating, he intends to tame the speaking. The scene with the little tailor is full of food references, which show that it is Kate who is being targeted and that food and clothing go hand in hand. At the heart of this burlesque scene, which seems to ignore Kate, it is the body of the shrew that is abused. The constant references to food within the sartorial discourse ('velvet dish', 'porringer', 'an apple tart', 'a custard coffin', 'a silken pie') constitute a veritable Tantalus torture. By mobilizing the food metaphor, creating a mirage of food, when Kate has not been able to eat for hours, Petruccio gives his words a truly physical impact. The many sexual allusions in this scene also reveal that Kate is the sole target of Petruccio's insults. About the cap, Petruccio says ''tis lewd and filthy' (4.3.67), thus questioning the morals of the woman who would wear it. The 'note of the fashion' (4.3.130) refers to a 'loose-bodied gown' (4.3.133), a formulation that relates the woman who would wear it to the figure of a prostitute. Finally, when Grumio pretends to misunderstand Petruccio's words and takes offence that he can put his wife's 'gown' into the hands of another ('Take up thy mistress' gown for thy master's use', 4.3.154–8), Kate symbolically becomes an object that men can shamelessly play with.

'No abuse?': here is a question one may ask again about the taming process in the play. Whether the tongue-taming enterprise is successful or not, whether Petruccio's insults are triumphant or not, depends on the ear with which one hears Kate's final speech. We are left with Lucentio's final sceptical line: ''Tis a wonder, by your leave, she will be tamed so.' (5.2.195).

6

The trauma of insult

It may seem anachronistic to speak of the trauma of insult in Shakespeare's plays, as the word 'trauma' was, of course, not present in the dictionaries of the period and the psychoanalytic concept did not exist. Yet the object of this chapter is to show that Shakespeare's plays dramatize what could be regarded as traumatic effects caused by the violence of language. The insulting effect studied by Larguèche can be considered as a traumatic effect[1] that reveals complex relationships between verbal abuse and memory. What traces or scars do words leave in the characters' minds and how does Shakespeare represent the emotional shock that words may cause? What happens on stage when words are indeed 'abuse'? How does Shakespeare stage the after-effects of insults? These are the questions that will be tackled in this chapter together with some of the concepts that are central to trauma studies.

Trauma studies have been a growing field since the 1990s, and yet relatively little has been written on Shakespeare and trauma, and even less on Shakespeare and *linguistic* trauma. In 2002, Deborah Willis wrote an article on 'Revenge, Trauma Theory and *Titus Andronicus*', where she explored the articulation of trauma and revenge in the play. Her work focuses on the impact of physical trauma, showing that revenge constitutes 'a perverse therapy for traumatic experience', in a play where characters are confronted with 'traumas of the most extreme kind'.[2] In *Performing Early Modern Trauma*,

Thomas P. Anderson shows that 'a sense of loss persists within poetic forms that commemorate the past and more important, that the early modern period uses a specific vocabulary with which to talk about the relationship of history, memory, progress and loss'.[3] Patricia A. Cahill's 2008 *Unto the Breach: Martial Formations, Historical Trauma, and the Early Modern Stage* also contends that 'traumatic representation deals with the profound impact of historical events'.[4] In *Shakespeare, Trauma and Contemporary Performance*, Catherine Silverstone explores how performances of Shakespeare's plays are conditioned by traumatic events.[5] She studies 'relationships between Shakespeare's texts in contemporary performance on stage and screen and violent events and histories through an engagement with critical work on trauma as it has emerged in a range of humanities disciplines'[6] but she does not seek to 'identify Shakespeare as an early trauma theorist'.[7] While I agree with this stance, the aim of this chapter is to show that, in some of Shakespeare's plays, verbal injury may be productively read through a trauma theory lens. After studying the articulation between words and blows, language and body, we will focus more specifically on the shattering effect of words as represented in *Othello*, *The Merchant of Venice*, and, in a more comic mode, *Cymbeline*. We will see how Shakespeare illustrates what Denise Riley formulates in *Impersonal Passion. Language as Affect*:

> The reach of a malevolent word's reverberation is incalculable; it may buzz in the head of its hearer in a way that far exceeds any impact that its utterer had in mind.[8]

Words that wound

In a chapter entitled 'Ophelia and Trauma Theory in Shakespeare's *Hamlet*',[9] Robert C. Evans shows that Ophelia displays signs of trauma. He notably analyzes Ophelia's two 'mad scenes' 'in light of recent writings about trauma by psychologists and others',[10] especially using the work by Ronnie Janoff-Bulman in a book entitled *Shattered Assumptions: Towards a New Psychology of Trauma*.[11] Evans relates the hypnotic state and the dissociation phenomenon that are identified as symptoms of trauma to Ophelia's behaviour in her 'mad scenes'. He summarizes the signs of trauma that are displayed by Ophelia as follows:

(1) general amnesia; (2) existence in a kind of hypnotic state; (3) dissociation; (4) lack of responsiveness; (5) troubling traumatic memories; (6) a sense of facing unsolvable problems; (7) a feeling that one's psychological resources are overtaxed; and an inability to (8) self-regulate; (9) self-organize; and/or (10) draw on relationships with others to regain self-control. In all of these ways, then, Ophelia seems traumatized in ways that seem literally clinical rather than merely metaphorical.[12]

Evans does not really focus on the causes of these symptoms, but Ophelia's behaviour in Act 4 seems to display first and foremost the impact her father's death has on her. Trauma studies do not take insults into account. The second edition of *Trauma. Contemporary Directions in Trauma Theory, Research, and Practice*, published in 2020, does not index the word 'insult'.[13] Neither is insult indexed in *The Future of Trauma Theory. Contemporary Literary Cultural Criticism* published in 2014.[14]

Yet, the word 'trauma', deriving from Greek τραῦμα, meaning 'wound', seems relevant to tackle the field of verbal abuse. In *Excitable Speech*, Judith Butler raises the question of linguistic injury and vulnerability: 'What if language has within it its own possibilities for violence and for world shattering?',[15] she asks. The traumatic potential of words lies in the fact that language acts, albeit in often invisible ways. Butler explores the relationships between language and the body by noting that '*speaking is itself a bodily act*'.[16] She refers to Shoshana Felman's book *The Literary Speech Act* to suggest that 'the relation between speech and the body is a scandalous one' because the speech act is 'always unknowing about what it performs'.[17] She notes that 'the idea of a fully intentional speech act is perpetually subverted by that in speech which subverts intentionality'.[18] This brings us back to the idea expressed in Claude Paradin's emblem 'Lingua, quo tendis?'[19] and to the essential unpredictability of the effects words may have. This brings us back to the close relation between speech and the body.

The materialization of insults is omnipresent in Shakespeare's scripts, especially when the characters suggest that what they say is like a punch in the teeth. In *The Comedy of Errors*, Antipholus of Syracuse exclaims against Dromio of Syracuse: 'dost thou jeer and flout me in the teeth?' (*CE*, 2.2.22). In *1 Henry IV*, Douglas boasts that he has 'thrown / A brave defiance in King Henry's teeth' (*1H4*, 5.2.41–2), while in *2 Henry IV*, Pistol addresses Silence with a 'Puff i'thy teeth' (*2H4*, 5.3.92). In *Julius Caesar*, Octavius provokes Brutus and Cassius with 'Defiance, traitors, hurl we in your teeth' (*JC*, 5.1.63). Insults have to do with blows that result in the addressee 'losing face'. Shakespeare's text also often conjures up images of words that are hard to swallow. In *Richard II*, when Bolingbroke hurls at Mowbray 'With a foul traitor's name stuff I thy throat' (1.1.44), the latter fights back by using the same physical image and referring to 'These terms of treason doubled down his throat' (1.1.57). Insult goes from to heart to the throat; it hinders the throat and hits the heart and the lungs, as is shown by Mowbray's words when he tells Bolingbroke 'as low as to thy heart / Through the false passage of thy throat, thou liest' (*R2*, 1.1.124–5) or by Hamlet's imagining someone giving him 'the lie i' th' throat / As deep as to the lungs' (*Ham*, 2.2.509–10).

The merging of verbal and physical assaults is found in *The Courtiers Academie* (1598), where Gualinguo explains that words can be more dangerous and wounding than deeds:

> one may bee more diffamed by burdensome and opprobrious wordes, than by the injury of deedes. As for example: he shal

remaine more dishonoured that swalloweth up the terme of
Traitour, murderer, or any such like brutish speach, without
making revenge, then shall another that takes the Bastanado,
a box on the eare, a blow, or any such like injurie of deede:
for not to attempt revenge of a blowe or bastanado, notes
small valour, and impotencie, but yet is without vice: but
closely to digest the name of traitor or murderer, carrieth
with it, not onely note of vility, but supposeth the vice in him
injuried, objected unto him by the injurier, and therefore
such a one shalbe much more infamous. It may be prooved
also by this other reason, that contumelious wordes are
apter to impeach an other mans honor then deedes. For they
affirme, who entreate of combate, there is not so grievous an
injurie indeed, which with words may not be lenified: which
could not be if wordes were not much more effectuall, as
wel in ablation, as restitution of honor.[20]

Words are described as being more efficient ('effectual') than
deeds. The man of honour should not 'swallow up' or 'digest'
'contumelious words'. The physical aspect conveyed by these
words is found in Shakespeare's plays where the materialization
of insults is often expressed in variations on the proverbial
formula: 'you lie in your throat'. In *1 Henry VI*, Suffolk uses
the same image: 'I'll turn my part thereof (i.e. of scorn) into
thy throat' (*1H6*, 2.4.79). In *Titus Andronicus*, Demetrius tells
Aaron that his rage will not abate until he has had his own
brother Chiron swallow the abuse he has just hurled at him:

>   till I have sheathed
> My rapier in his bosom, and withal
> Thrust those reproachful speeches down his throat,
> That he hath breathed in my dishonour here.
> (*Tit*, 2.1.53–6)

In *Henry V*, Pistol, in a more comic mode, deals 'soluses' as if
he were dealing blows:

NYM [*to Pistol*]
 Will you shog off? I would have you *solus*.

PISTOL
> *Solus*, egregious dog? O viper vile!
> The *solus* in thy most marvailous face,
> The *solus* in thy teeth, and in thy throat,
> And in thy hateful lungs, yea, in thy maw, perdy,
> And, which is worse, within thy nasty mouth!
> I do retort the *solus* in thy bowels.
>
> (*H5*, 2.1.45–52)

The word 'solus', that is comically mistaken for an insult, is used as a projectile that is hurled back to its supposed sender and is designed to penetrate, to lodge in the various parts of Nym's body, through a gradation, from the most superficial to the most profound ingestion, down to the bowels. The deeper the insult is stuck, the worse it is. The 'lie in the throat' is 'the most serious kind of lie, one uttered deliberately and inexcusably'.[21] It differs from the 'lie in the teeth', which Hunter describes as 'one for which some excuse was allowed on the ground of its having proceeded from haste or some palliating cause'.[22]

The overlapping of the verbal and the physical that is recurrently thrown into relief by Shakespeare is theorized by such scholars as Denise Riley who, in *Impersonal Passion. Language as Affect*, specifically explores the effect of reverberation that 'bad words' have:

> The tendency of malignant speech is to ingrow like a toenail, embedding itself in its hearer until it's no longer felt to come 'from the outside'. The significance of its original emanation from another's hostility becomes lost to the recipient as a tinnitus of remembered attack buzzes in her inner ear. The hard word reverberates – so much so that it holds the appeal of false etymology (it's easy to assume that *to reverberate* derives from characteristically self-repeating verbal actions, whereas it meant striking or beating back). That it reverberates, rather than echoes, places it well beyond the possibilities of ironic recuperation that Echo

offers; reverberation will only resound, to its own limit. And rancorous phrases, matted in a wordy undergrowth, appear to be 'on the inside' as one fights them down while they perpetually spring up again. This is where it's crucial to recall that the accusations originally came from the outside, and the rage they echo was another's rage.[23]

The effect of reverberation can be found in *Othello* where Othello's insults have Desdemona doubt that these abusive words come 'from the outside' and where the shattering effect of words is conspicuous.

'Half asleep' in *Othello*

In *Othello*, Shakespeare dramatizes the change from love speech to hate speech. The slippery limit between the two appears when Othello exclaims, once Desdemona has left the stage:

> Excellent wretch! perdition catch my soul
> But I do love thee! and when I love thee not
> Chaos is come again. (*Oth*, 3.3.90–2)

'Excellent wretch' can be both a phrase of endearment and an expression of abuse and the word 'perdition' is proleptic. Ironically chaos is and has already been on stage for a while at that moment in the person of Iago who immediately addresses Othello and proceeds to reverse the values of honesty and dishonesty, thus completely distorting language, bringing disorder and shaking 'degree', as Ulysses defines it in *Troilus and Cressida* (*TC*, 1.3.101). The spectacular emergence of hate speech in *Othello* is both the cause and effect of chaos in the play, creating an abyss of incomprehension and conveying an image of what could now be identified as a post-traumatic stress disorder.

While much has been written on slander in *Othello*,[24] less has been said about the emotional shock that Desdemona suffers as victim when Othello violently insults her in a scene that leaves her stunned. The shock is all the more striking, for the character and the audience, since the playwright presents Desdemona as 'a child to chiding' (4.2.116). After publicly striking and insulting her in 4.1, Othello goes on abusing her in private, symbolically writing 'whore' upon her (4.2.73),[25] calling her 'thou public commoner' (4.2.74), 'Impudent strumpet' (4.2.82), before ironically questioning these labels: 'Are not you a strumpet?'; 'What, not a whore?' before scathingly concluding:

> I cry you mercy then,
> I took you for that cunning whore of Venice
> That married with Othello.
> (*Oth*, 4.2.90–2)

The formulation of the accusation constitutes a verbal trap as the answer to it can only be wrong: Desdemona can neither confirm it nor deny it. She can neither answer 'yes, I am', nor 'no, I'm not' and so cannot but remain speechless. Expressed in this manner, the accusation cuts both ways. Shakespeare signals Desdemona's state of shock when Emilia comes back on stage and asks her: 'How do you, madam? How do you, my good lady?' and Desdemona answers: 'Faith, half asleep' (4.2.98–9). Othello's abuse has left her 'stunned, numb', as is glossed by Honigmann.[26] She is in a hypnotic state that signals a traumatic effect. Othello's words have left her half-dead and have disconnected her from herself and from reality, shattering her self-image, her world and her 'assumptions', that we can describe as, in Ronnie Janoff-Bulman's words, a belief in the 'benevolence of the world', in the 'meaningfulness of the world' and in 'self-worth'.[27] Emilia's question equates a stage direction that would indicate that Desdemona no longer looks like herself, that she is disfigured by way of insults and that her world has fallen apart. Shakespeare's script seems to evoke what could be identified as a form of traumatic dissociation that projects the victim into a parallel world:

EMILIA
   Good madam, what's the matter with my lord?
DESDEMONA
   With whom?
EMILIA
   Why, with my lord, madam.
DESDEMONA
   Who is thy lord?
EMILIA
                     He that is yours, sweet lady.
DESDEMONA
   I have none. Do not talk to me, Emilia;
   I cannot weep, nor answer have I none
   But what should go by water. Prithee, tonight
   Lay on my bed my wedding sheets; remember,
   And call thy husband hither.
EMILIA
                     Here's a change indeed!
                                (*Oth*, 4.2.100–8)

The change that Emilia sees in Desdemona echoes the change that Iago had ironically identified in Othello in the previous scene, saying 'He is much changed' (4.1.268). 'Chaos is come again' (3.3.92) for the two characters whose assumptions are 'shattered'. In Desdemona, the apparent indifference to suffering, which is one of the signs of trauma, is displayed by an initial absence of tears, as well as by the lack of words. The confusion between Othello and Iago in the reference to 'my lord' is revealing as it suggests that the whole matter originates in Emilia's lord, Iago, the source of this 'chaos'. Desdemona wept in the previous scene when Othello struck her. The violence of words seems to create more damage, as Iago had ironically indicated in the previous scene when he cryptically declared: 'yet would I knew / That stroke would prove the worst' (4.1.273–4). The violence of words seems worse at this stage, and it is not fortuitous that Desdemona should be attracted to her bed, which is going to be her death bed. One of the symptoms of the traumatic effect is the fact that the abuse one has suffered is unspeakable. That is what appears when Iago enquires about Desdemona, asking her 'How is't with you?' and she answers 'I cannot tell' (4.2.112–13). She literally *cannot tell* what has just happened to her, which leaves some space for Emilia to tell it herself. Desdemona's initial inability to repeat the word 'whore' that has shaken her is emblematic of this traumatic unspeakability:

DESDEMONA
  Am I that name, Iago?
IAGO
                                    What name, fair lady?
DESDEMONA
  Such as she said my lord did say I was.
EMILIA
  He called her whore. A beggar in his drink
  Could not have laid such terms upon his callat.
IAGO
  Why did he so?
DESDEMONA
  I do not know; I am sure I am none such.
                                    (*Oth*, 4.2.120–5)

The initial question, 'Am I that name, Iago?', reveals that Othello's insults have shattered Desdemona's image of herself and suggests that she would tend to forget that, as Denise Riley formulates it, the 'accusations originally came from the outside, and the rage they echo was another's rage'.[28] Desdemona's words are strangely echoed in Riley's description of the impact of interpellation:

> There is an anxiety of interpellation, in which its subject ponders incessantly to herself 'Am I that name; am I really one of those?'[29]

Othello's rage has Desdemona doubt about who she is, even if she concludes that she is 'none such'. She puts herself into question rather than putting Othello into question, as appears when she declares:

> 'Tis meet I should be used so, very meet.
> How have I been behaved that he might stick
> The small'st opinion on my great misuse?
> (4.2.109–11)

The complex formulation is ambivalent enough to imply that she considers herself as worthy of blame, and at the same time it reveals that the insulter is the agent who sticks 'the small'st opinion' on her. Desdemona's words blur the limit between 'meet' use and misuse, between the accuser and the victim, or the abuser and the abused. The lethal impact of words is then emphasized:

> Unkindness may do much,
> And his unkindness may defeat my life
> But never taint my love.
> (*Oth*, 4.2.161–3)

Verbal abuse, here called 'unkindness', may kill but Desdemona's attachment to her persecutor sounds like a sort of Stockholm syndrome that will be confirmed up to the moment of her death, her last words being: 'Commend me to my kind lord – O, farewell' (5.2.123).

The traumatic effect is ambivalent as it oscillates between obsession and avoidance or denial. Desdemona's question 'Am I that name?' shows that she cannot forget the name she has been called. But the circumlocution 'Such as she said my lord did say I was', used to avoid to say 'whore', shows escapism and leaves a blank in the story that Emilia is going to fill in. The mixture of unspeakableness and repetition appears when Desdemona ironically says what she claims she cannot say:

> I cannot say whore:
> It does abhor me now I speak the word;
> To do the act that might the addition earn
> Not the world's mass of vanity could make me.
> (*Oth*, 4.2.163–6)

The unspeakable word is obsessively repeated in the scene, in a process of 'addition', first by Emilia who keeps rubbing the wound, be it in the interrogative mode: 'To be called whore? would it not make one weep?' (4.2.129); 'Why should he call her whore?' (4.2.139); and then by Desdemona herself who paradoxically speaks the unspeakable 'whore' that reverberates in the word 'abhor'. The impact of the insult on the victim is best formulated by Emilia's summary to her husband:

> my lord hath so bewhored her,
> Thrown such despite and heavy terms upon her
> That true hearts cannot bear it.
> (4.2.117–19)

The merging of verbal and physical forms of abuse is expressed by the word 'bewhored', a coinage meaning that, by calling Desdemona a whore, Othello has transformed her into a whore. It is also conveyed by the use of the words 'thrown' and 'heavy' that express the materiality of words. The Willow Song that Desdemona sings in 4.3 may be considered as a sign of her disconnection or dissociation from herself and reality, and at the same time it translates the pain she feels. 'Let nobody blame him, his scorn I approve' (4.3.51): one of the lines of the song suggests that Desdemona integrates the abuse by not blaming the one whom Brabantio called 'an abuser of the world' (1.2.78). While Brabantio meant that Othello was a deceiver, at the end of the play one may hear another meaning in the word 'abuser'. *Othello* is one of the plays in which the word 'abuse' is the most recurrent and Shakespeare blurs the boundaries between the two main meanings of the word (deception and insult), insult being the fruit of deception. 'Dost thou in conscience think, [...] / That there be women do abuse their husbands / In such gross kind?' (*Oth*, 4.3.60–2), asks Desdemona: the two meanings of 'abuse' seem to overlap as adultery can be seen as an insult in deed that may be a source of trauma for the man. When Othello is abused and/or deceived by Iago in the dumb show scene, his trauma is expressed by the state of trance he falls in and by the dislocation of his speech (4.1.35–43). In this chaotic speech, the playwright includes an ambivalent phrase on the power of words: 'It is not words that shakes me thus' (4.1.41–2). Othello denies the power of words at the very moment Iago's abusive words shake him, completely dismembering his own speech. Words 'shake' or shatter – to use Janoff-Bulman's terminology – Desdemona. Behind the abuse addressed to Desdemona, one may hear the abuse that such characters as Othello, or Leontes in *The Winter's Tale*, hear when they think they are deceived by their wives: the word 'cuckold' may be uttered or unspeakable, as when Leontes replaces it with a 'so-forth' (*WT*, 1.2.216).[30] Bewhoring is the answer or counterpoint to imaginary cuckolding. Othello, like Leontes, abuses because he feels abused, in the two senses of the word. Trauma engenders trauma, in a logic of punishment or retaliation. Denise Riley, considering the 'largely uninvestigated forensics of spoken injury',[31] studies what she called 'the words' remorseless afterlife'.[32] Desdemona's reaction to the word 'whore' may illustrate what Riley formulates:

> Persecutory interpellation's shadow falls well beyond the instant of its articulation. There are ghosts of the word which always haunt any present moment of enunciation, rendering that present already murmurous and thickly populated.[33]

The whole play buzzes with the word 'whore' before and after Othello's violent accusation, the three women in the play being in their turn called 'whore'. It is in *Othello* that we find the most numerous occurrences of the word. According to Riley, while 'accusation often lodges in the accused', 'accusers themselves are forcibly spoken',[34] an idea that finds a spectacular illustration in *Othello* if we consider that Othello is 'spoken by' Iago. Riley expresses what could be read as a description of what happens to Othello:

> he is dispossessed of his own words in advance. The rhetoric of rage speaks him mechanically and remorselessly. However much the accuser feels himself to triumph in the moment of his pronouncement, he is prey to echo.[35]

Othello is 'prey to echo' and to 'impersonal passion' indeed, because he uses a word of abuse that is systematically hurled at women in Shakespeare's days as in ours.[36] 'Impersonal passion' is what Riley calls 'an automated verbiage, [...] an "it is speaking in me"'.[37] She notes that 'the orator of violence is merely an instrument of dictation by tics and reflexes' and that 'rage speaks monotonously'.[38] Othello is also 'prey to echo' because Iago has instilled in him the figure of the whore that he throws at Desdemona. Even if Othello is the first to utter the word, when he menacingly exclaims to Iago 'Villain, be sure thou prove my love a whore' (3.3.362), the image has been suggested to him by Iago, so much so that the spectator has the impression that it is Iago who associates the word with Desdemona, although he only uses it twice, once about Bianca (4.1.174) and once about his own wife Emilia, whom he calls 'Villainous whore!' (5.2.227) at the end of the play. As Riley formulates it, the insulter is 'poised somewhere halfway between "language speaks me" and "I speak language"'.[39] Iago speaks Othello and Othello speaks Iago. This makes Desdemona's question 'Am I that name, *Iago*?' all the more ironical as she addresses the one who has specifically planted the seed of abuse in Othello's mind.

The buzzing effect of abuse and the trauma of verbal violence are also at the heart of *The Merchant of Venice* but this time, it does not lead to any hypnotic state or to any Stockholm syndrome but to a logic of revenge.

The 'ancient grudge' in *The Merchant of Venice*

The *Merchant of Venice* is the story of an 'ancient grudge' (1.3.43) that derives from insults that Shylock cannot forget or that have lodged in his throat and in his mind. The 'ancient grudge' that Shylock refers to at the beginning of the play draws a link between insult and memory. Shylock is the main and almost only target of insults in the play and he, from the start, complains about being ill-treated, even before we hear the other characters abuse him:

> [*aside*] [...]
> If I can catch him [Antonio] once upon the hip,
> I will feed fat the ancient grudge I bear him.
> He hates our sacred nation, and he rails,
> Even there where merchants most do congregate,
> On me, my bargains and my well-won thrift,
> Which he calls 'interest'. Cursed be my tribe
> If I forgive him.
>
> (1.3.42–8)

The *OED* relates the word 'grudge' to the Old French 'groucier, groucher, grocier, grocher, grucer, grouchier', which means 'to murmur', 'to grumble'. The word 'grudge' means 'To murmur; to utter complaints murmuringly; to grumble, complain; to be discontented or dissatisfied'. This murmuring, buzzing aspect of insults is expressed in the form of Shylock's speech that is delivered in an aside giving us access to his inner speech: 'He hates our sacred nation', he tells us. Here is the first expression of a specific kind of insult that could be termed 'racist insult'. Beyond Shylock, or through Shylock, it is a whole nation that is insulted, as 'Cursed be my tribe if I forgive him' draws the link between the I and the tribe.

According to Larguèche, all insults are racist because they create kinds, sorts, species.[40] Calling someone names means that you put him or her into a category. In French, when you want to insult someone, you often use the expression '*espèce de...*' (sort of...).[41] Yet the specificity of the abuse that is at stake here is that it is not personal but collective and negates individuality. 'He hates our sacred nation': the specificity of racist abuse is that it both hurts the personal and the collective, the I and the tribe. By hurting the collective, it attains the personal and vice versa. It is both personal and 'impersonal'.[42] The abuse is all the more hurtful since it is proffered in public, 'even there where merchants most do congregate'. The phrase 'my well-won thrift which he calls "interest"' reveals that Antonio and Shylock do not speak the same language, do not have the same usage of words. This discrepancy in the use of words is the sign of an essential breach. Replacing 'well-won thrift' by the word 'interest' has an insulting effect.

Shylock again describes this 'ancient grudge' a few lines later, showing that there are words and deeds that cannot be forgotten:

> Signior Antonio, many a time and oft
> In the Rialto you have rated me
> About my moneys and my usances.
> Still have I borne it with a patient shrug,
> For sufferance is the badge of all our tribe.
> You call me misbeliever, cut-throat dog,
> And spit upon my Jewish gaberdine,
> And all for use of that which is mine own.
> Well, then, it now appears you need my help.
> Go to, then, you come to me, and you say,
> 'Shylock, we would have moneys.' You say so.
> You, that did void your rheum upon my beard
> And foot me as you spurn a stranger cur
> Over your threshold, moneys is your suit.
> What should I say to you? Should I not say,
> 'Hath a dog money? Is it possible
> A cur can lend three thousand ducats?' Or
> Shall I bend low and in a bondman's key,

With bated breath and whispering humbleness,
Say this: 'Fair sir, you spat on me on Wednesday last,
You spurned me such a day; another time,
You called me dog: and, for these courtesies,
I'll lend you thus much moneys.'
(1.3.102–24)

Contrary to the Fool, Shylock has 'planted in his memory an army' not of 'good' but of '*bad* words' (3.5.59–60) that seem to drive us into an endless circle, words ever reproducing, repeating one another in a spiral of exclusion that puts Shylock on the 'threshold' of the Venetian Society. To this tirade, Antonio answers: 'I am as like to call thee so again, / To spit on thee again, to spurn thee too' (1.3.125–6). The automatic, mechanical repetition of the same words gives them an obsessive dimension and shows that they are not connected to a reality but rather become a hateful reflex. A few lines later, Shylock declares that he is ready to 'forget the shames' he has been 'stained' with (1.3.135). Yet everything suggests that the abuse he suffers cannot be forgotten. In 3.1, he remembers that Antonio was 'wont to call [him] usurer' (3.1.42–3). 'He hath disgraced me, and hindered me half a million, laughed at my losses, mocked at my gains, scorned my nation, thwarted my bargains, cooled my friends, heated my enemies' (3.1.49–52): Antonio seems to have committed all the sins of the tongue at once by disgracing, laughing, mocking, scorning. This text provides a catalogue of all possible insulting effects, both on the addressee and on the witnesses.

In *Impersonal Passion*, Riley opens her chapter on 'Malediction' as follows:

The worst words revivify themselves within us, vampirically. Injurious speech echoes relentlessly, years after the occasion of its utterance, in the mind of the one at whom it was aimed: the bad word, splinterlike, pierces to lodge. In its violently emotional materiality, the word is indeed made flesh and dwells amongst us – often long outstaying its welcome. Old word-scars embody a 'knowing it by heart,' as if phrases had been hurled like darts into that thickly pulsating organ. But their resonances are not amorous. Where amnesia would help us, we cannot forget.[43]

What is striking in Shylock's memory of words is the physicality and materiality of the insults that he is referring to: spitting,[44] voiding one's rheum, spurning, footing. If insults are unforgettable, it is because they are 'made flesh', because they 'dwell among us', they are like 'darts', they are 'splinterlike', and no longer felt to come 'from the outside'.[45] With Shylock repeating the words he hears, we no longer know whether these words come from within or from without. Denise Riley goes on describing the effect of malicious words as follows:

> There is in effect a verbal form of post-traumatic stress disorder, marked by unstoppable aural flashbacks. Here anamnesia, unforgetting, is a linguistic curse of a disability. We hear much about the therapeutics of retrieved memory. The inability to forget, too, has been classified as a neurological illness.[46]

What Shylock gives us to hear, by reporting the insults he daily suffers, are the ghosts of the words which keep 'haunting' him and which keep 'buzzing' in his head and ears.[47] One can find in Shylock what Riley has identified as a phenomenon of 'audiation' and 'inner speech', in a chapter entitled 'A Voice without a Mouth'.[48] The aside that Shylock delivers constitutes his 'inner speech' in which he replays the words that have been hurting him from the outside. In the *Merchant of Venice*, these words do not come from one character but form a buzz of collective pre-judices. The word 'pre-judice' etymologically refers to ideas that precede the trial, the assessment, the judgement. The structure of *The Merchant of Venice* seems to follow this logic of prejudice, as it shows 'preceding judgement or decision, precedent, opinion formed in advance, preconception' (*OED*) and then only the judgement in the trial scene.

Shakespeare creates this buzz of insulting words by having the same derogatory terms come from all corners of the Venetian society. The play shows how the words of abuse that Shylock remembers circulate and are kept alive at all levels of the world of Venice. Whether or not Shylock hears his words – the text does not tell us –, Antonio compares him to 'the devil', to 'a villain with a smiling cheek', 'a goodly apple, rotten at the heart' (1.3.94–7). Lancelet, the Clown, also utters the same words when he tells the audience that 'the Jew my master [...] is a kind of devil', 'the very devil incarnation' (2.2.21–4), in a sort of comic reproduction process. 'I am a Jew if I serve the Jew any longer' (2.2.105), he says, expressing thus a fear of some kind of contamination, as if he could be converted into a Jew. But the two uses of the word show us that the word 'Jew' is and is not an insult and putting the two uses together amounts to blurring the limit between denotation and connotation. Salanio later says that the devil 'comes in the likeness of a Jew' (3.1.20; 3.1.70–1) as if he were saying 'Talk of the devil and he will appear'. Incidentally, it is interesting to note that in French the expression is *'quand on parle du loup...'* (talk of the wolf...). Salanio again, a little later, declares that 'It is the most impenetrable cur / That ever kept with men' (3.3.18–19). In 2.4, it is Lorenzo who refers to a 'faithless Jew' (2.4.38). Insult is here not the expression of a personal view but both the source and result of public opinion. By showing us the circulation of the word 'Jew' in the play from one mouth to another, associated with negative words, the play reveals what Judith Butler calls the 'historicity of the name':

Clearly, injurious names have a history, one that is invoked and reconsolidated at the moment of utterance, but not explicitly told. [...] The name has, thus, a *historicity*, what might be understood as the history which has become internal to a name, has come to constitute the contemporary meaning of a name: the sedimentation of its usages as they have become part of the very name, a sedimentation, a repetition that congeals, that gives the name its force.

> [...] The force of the name depends not only on its iterability, but on a form of repetition that is linked to trauma, on what is, strictly speaking, not remembered but relived and relived in and through the linguistic substitution for the traumatic event.[49]

The Merchant of Venice shows the historicity of names at work and presents how injurious names are lived and relived in an endless cycle. The performative power of what Judith Butler calls 'excitable speech' appears when Shylock says: 'Thou call'dst me dog before thou hadst a cause, / But, since I am a dog, beware my fangs' (3.3.6-7). You call me dog; therefore I am a dog, I become a dog: the play reveals the magic, performative power of words that are literally here turned into flesh, a pound of flesh. In *The Merchant of Venice*, one *does* things with *words*. The play tells the story of a metaphor that becomes literalized.

The word 'prejudice' is also related to the French word *préjudice* which means 'damage'. The play dramatizes three basic types of defence, or shields against the damage caused by insults or prejudices. The first defence against slander and insult consists in shutting one's ears.[50] Shylock is shown shutting the doors of his house: 'Lock up my doors' (2.5.28), 'But stop my house's ears – I mean the casement – / Let not the sound of shallow foppery enter / My sober house' (2.5.33–5). Shutting one's doors amounts to shutting one's ears. Shylock refuses to hear and 'gaze on the Christian fools with varnished faces' (2.5.32). Doing so, he excludes himself from a society that excludes him anyway. Closing one's ears to insults is one way of surviving, one way of bearing them.

Then with the famous speech 'Hath not a Jew eyes?' Shakespeare dramatizes another reaction to abuse: rhetorical contradiction.

> and what's his reason [for insulting me]? I am a Jew. Hath not a Jew eyes? Hath not a Jew hands, organs, dimensions, senses, affections, passions? Fed with the same food, hurt

with the same weapons, subject to the same diseases, healed by the same means, warmed and cooled by the same winter and summer as a Christian is? If you prick us do we not bleed? If you tickle us do we not laugh? If you poison us do we not die? And if you wrong us shall we not revenge? If we are like you in the rest, we will resemble you in that.

(*MV*, 3.1.52–61)

This speech is a judicial plea that tries to fight words with words and tries to avoid being categorized and considered as a special kind, not through insult but through logic, through reasoning. Then the play dramatizes another form of reaction to insult: revenge through legal action. With legal action we switch from insult to injury (*in-juria*) in the two meanings of the word (abuse and wound). What Shylock does in Act 4 is claim for compensation for racist prejudice, for the verbal damage that he has suffered. He wants reparation for what Butler calls 'linguistic injury'.[51] What he wants against this abuse is a *pound* of flesh.

Insults are a matter of exchange in life and in many of Shakespeare's plays. You often exchange a word for a word. In the world of *The Merchant of Venice*, the word 'Christian' is used negatively by Shylock in what seems to be a battle, an exchange between the Christian and the Jew. Yet, the play dramatizes an exchange that is not fair, that is not balanced. And the whole discomfort of the play comes from this imbalance of exchange. Shylock refers to the 'Christian fools' (2.5.32) but the potential insulting effect of his offensive words is not dramatized in the play. It is as if Shylock's insults remained what Riley calls, after Samuel Beckett,[52] 'a voice without a mouth', 'inner words', that is, 'solitude's talk'.[53]

His way of reacting to insults is verbal, financial, but, above all, physical. The man who is called old 'carrion' (3.1.32), a word that refers to the fleshy part of a body, becomes a carrion eater, sending the insult back to the insulter and at the same time ironically confirming it, through words but also deeds, symbolically becoming the werewolf he is accused of being: 'If I can catch him [Antonio] once upon the hip, / I will *feed fat* the ancient grudge I bear him' (1.3.42–3). 'Your worship was the last man *in our mouths*' (1.3.56), says Shylock to Antonio: although he means 'we were just speaking of you', the formulation is proleptic of Shylock's asking for Antonio's 'pound of flesh', an expression in which two sorts of measure overlap: mass and money (pound). In the commercial world of the play in which insults are embedded, it is not fortuitous that the word 'rate' should be related to insult. You have 'rated' me, says Shylock to Antonio. What does the word 'rate' mean here? In *An Alveary or Triple Dictionary, in English, Latin and French* (London, 1574), John Baret gives the following definition for 'to rate bitterly': 'To be caried in, to invade some bodie, to go furiously against some bodie, to rate one with wordes in anger. Invehor, veheris, vectus sum, invehi. Cicer. Estre porté dedens. Envahir aucun, aller contre aucun en fureur. Oultrager aucun de parolles par cholere. To rate: to defame with sharpe woordes.'[54] The word 'rate' also refers to an assessment, evaluation and to a portion. In John Florio's *A World of Words* (London, 1598), 'Portionare' is defined as: 'to portion, to share, to part, to rate, to measure'. The word means a lot in the context of a play in which Shylock asks for a portion of Antonio, a form of 'tax' in nature, a word (to tax) which is not present in *The Merchant of Venice* but which also means 'to insult'. This link between the economic language and the language of insult also appears when you read in Cotgrave's *Dictionary* that the French word 'Despriser' means 'To disesteeme, vilipend, neglect, make light of, set naught by, prize at a low rate; to despise, contemne, disdaine; also, to blame, condemne, dispraise, discommend'. It also appears if you read in the *OED* the definition of the word 'contempt': 'The action of contemning or despising; the holding or treating as of little *account*, or as vile and *worthless*'. To insult means to 'rate', that is to assess, to measure, to categorize, to detract a value, a worth. 'Rating' is also what Portia does when she 'rates' her potential husbands and establishes a form of catalogue, assessment form for each of them.

The Merchant of Venice reveals the economy of insults that can be found, for example in another word: 'detraction' (calumny), which comes from *de-trahere*, what you take. The play is the story of a stealth: the stealth or loss of one's flesh (Jessica). Larguèche notes that the word 'nation' is etymologically related to nature and birth.[55] By detracting Jessica, the Christians de-tract Shylock's whole nation. The play also dramatizes the detraction of one's name, that is to say of one's reputation but also literally of one's name, the name 'Shylock' being erased and replaced by the name 'Jew', which negates any kind of individuality. After the trauma of the Shoah, the insults of *The Merchant of Venice* are hard for an audience to hear. In *The Merchant of Venice*, abuse has no imagination. In this play, insults do not constitute a world of linguistic invention and innovation but rather of repetition. As Riley notes, 'Rage speaks monotonously'.[56] The text seems to be endlessly recycling the same words – 'dog' (with its variant, 'cur'), 'devil' and 'Jew' – that seem to be hollow words but are full of sound and fury; far from signifying nothing, their insulting impact and content are inescapable. If the insults in *The Merchant of Venice* are not funny, it is because they are a source of unrest, as the play dramatizes the traumatic effect they have and their impact on memory. Discomfort and trauma come from the fact that the play contains anti-Semitic abuse and that, notably after the Shoah, one cannot hear the word 'Jew', which is at the heart of this play and of the abuse of the play, with the same ear as Shakespeare's contemporaries.

'Whore' in *Othello*, 'Jew' in *The Merchant of Venice*: in the two cases that we have explored, the trauma of insults is embedded in issues of gender and race. In *Cymbeline*, where abuse is also related to gender through the slander of Innogen, the trauma is linked to social status, in a more comic way but in a way that suggests that insults can remain alive even posthumously.

Cymbeline and the memory of abuse

There are words that stick in your throat, words that you cannot digest, words that remain forever engraved in your memory: against all odds, Innogen's three words, 'his meanest garment' (2.3.133), are, for Cloten, among these indelible, murderous, indigestible words. At first sight these words seem quite harmless. They are certainly not among the 'forbidden words' studied by linguists Allan and Burridge in *Forbidden words. Taboo and the Censuring of Language*. And yet Shakespeare throws these words into relief by having them haunt Cloten's memory and feed his rancour until death.

> His meanest garment
> That ever hath but clipped his body is dearer
> In my respect than all the hairs above thee,
> Were they all made such men.
> (2.3.133–6)

Here is how Innogen, addressing Cloten, describes both her love for Posthumus Leonatus and her disgust for Cloten. The praise of the one and the insult to the other overlap and are uttered in the same breath. Praising one amounts to dispraising the other. The noble ('dear') and the ignoble ('mean') are reversed.[57] The 'meanest garment of Posthumus is dearer to me', says Innogen, 'than anything you, the son of a queen, could ever be or offer'. There is more nobility in the vilest garment of Posthumus than there could ever be in a thousand Clotens. This is, in essence, the meaning of Innogen's insult to Cloten at the heart of the play, in 2.3.[58] By evoking Posthumus' garment, Innogen responds in sartorial terms to Cloten's attack against Posthumus, who has been chosen by Innogen[59] and whom he has just called

> a base slave,
> A hilding for a livery, a squire's cloth,
> A pantler – not so eminent.
> (*Cym*, 2.3.122–4)

In other words, you have no right, Cloten says to Innogen, as the daughter of a king, to marry a 'base wretch', 'one bred of alms and fostered with cold dishes, / With scraps o'th'court' (2.3.113–15). Misalliances are acceptable among the lower classes ('though it be allowed in meaner parties', 2.3.116) but are inconceivable among the high-born. By consorting with such a 'slave', Cloten suggests, Innogen jeopardizes the image of the crown, dishonours her rank, and taints the reputation, renown and memory of the royal family: '[you] must not *foil the precious note* [emphasis added] of it [the crown] with a base slave' (2.3.121–2). Martin Butler points out that the word 'foil', which he translates as 'dishonour', has sometimes been emended to 'soil' or 'file',[60] terms that then refer to the defilement that Innogen's conduct brings to the world from which she springs. But the stain with which Innogen sullies the memory of her people is present in the word 'foil' itself, which means 'to trample' and which the *OED* tells us is related to 'foul'. The term evokes defilement, as the verb can mean 'to foul, defile, pollute' (sense III.6 in *OED*) and 'to cause filth, to drop excrement' (sense III.8 in *OED*). For Cloten, Posthumus, the 'base slave' (2.3.122), is a stain; he is a taint that tarnishes the crown and the royal lineage. At the heart of this insulting tirade, which precedes Innogen's reply, Cloten asks the rhetorical question: 'Yet who than he more mean?' (2.3.117): on the social scale, can one imagine anyone lower than Posthumus? Is there anyone below him? To signify his rival's social baseness, Cloten then describes Posthumus as 'a hilding for a livery'[61] and 'a squire's cloth' (2.3.123). Thus, when we hear Innogen draw her comparison between the two men, we cannot fail to appreciate the echo and boomerang effect of Cloten's words, which ironically come back to strike him and shatter his 'assumptions' and his vision of the social ladder. As a good rhetorician, Innogen turns Cloten's verbal weapons, and the sartorial metaphor he used, against him. She answers abuse with abuse and places Cloten, who is supposed to be a prince, at the bottom of the scale of society by comparing him to Posthumus' 'meanest garment'.

In Cymbeline. *Constructions of Britain*, Ros King questions the meaning of the insult:

> The euphemism is here meant to puzzle, – which garment does she mean? And how mean can a garment get? The Elizabethans did not wear underpants. But the meaning of the sound of the phrase is clear: it almost necessitates curling the lip and spitting out the consonants.[62]

In their book on clothing and memory, Ann Rosalind Jones and Peter Stallybrass note how, in *Cymbeline* in particular, clothing is pregnant with memory. They point out that, in the Renaissance imagination, clothes hold the memory of those who wear them, and that in the context of *Cymbeline*, where Posthumus is the absent lover, every bit of his clothing is cherished by Innogen. 'In the Renaissance', they write, 'clothes could be imagined as retaining the identity and the form of the wearer'.[63] They add that 'The garment bears quite literally the trace and the memory of the owner'.[64] Jones and Stallybrass analyze how the whole play retains this image and how the pattern of the garment circulates through the scenes and takes on a highly symbolic meaning. They show how, in the portraits of the period, it is the clothes that convey expressions and personalities: 'The clothes provide a specificity that the faces do not',[65] a remark that sheds light on the scene of false recognition in which Innogen discovers the headless body of Cloten/Posthumus (4.2.290–331), the clothes remaining the only signs to be deciphered. By using the sartorial image, Innogen de-faces Cloten, which has a traumatic effect on him. The trauma appears when he gets stuck in Innogen's words and proves unable to forget them:

CLOTEN
               You have abused me.
  His mean'st garment?
INNOGEN
               Ay, I said so, sir.
  If you will make't an action, call witness to't.

CLOTEN
 I will inform your father.
INNOGEN
 Your mother, too.
 She's my good lady and will conceive, I hope,
 But the worst of me. So I leave you, sir,
 To th' worst of discontent. *Exit*.
CLOTEN
 I'll be revenged.
 His meanest garment? Well.
 (*Cym*, 2.3.149–56)

The insult gets imprinted in his mind and comically haunts him until his death, in a process that is similar to what happens to Dogberry in *Much Ado About Nothing*, who cannot forget the insult 'you are an ass'.[66] *Cymbeline* comically dramatizes a traumatic insulting effect, Cloten paradoxically fuelling the insult himself by constantly repeating and ruminating it. The scene shows that Innogen is preoccupied with the loss of her bracelet, while Cloten is obsessed with the insult that has just been inflicted on him and that remains in his heart. The text plays on this comic gap: it takes Cloten a little while to realize what has just happened to him and Innogen has already moved on to another subject with Pisanio when Cloten exclaims: 'His garment?' (2.3.137), 'His garment?' (2.3.139). Innogen's ironic defiance ('make't an action') refers to Cloten's taste for conflict in the preceding scenes and, more broadly, to the Elizabethan fashion for both duels and libel suits. Faced with indifference and irony, Cloten falls back on a childish 'I will inform your father' (2.3.152), which adds to his ridicule. Repeating the insult here comically extends its effect. Even the BBC version (directed by Elijah Moshinsky, 1982), which offers a rather dark vision of the play, brings out the comedy of the scene. Faced with Innogen sending him back to his mother's petticoats ('your mother too'), Cloten takes refuge in revenge. This insult, and the resentment deriving from it, will generate part of the plot, since Cloten will indeed 'make't an action', by dressing up as Posthumus, thus throwing the insult back to

Innogen's face in a literal way. Cloten's reacting to these words more than to others (he is also called a 'fool', 2.3.101–2) shows that the character cultivates a class consciousness, but it also suggests that this 'meanest garment' is 'material' for a rich theatrical moment.[67] Where amnesia could help Cloten, he cannot forget.[68] The character suffers from what Riley calls 'anamnesia', 'a verbal form of post-traumatic stress disorder, marked by unstoppable aural flashbacks'.[69] One can also see this reaction to insult as a form of grudge, or rancour, leading to revenge, which appears when Cloten shares his 'inner speech' with the audience:

> I would these garments were come. She said upon a time – the bitterness of which I now belch from my heart – that she held the very garment of Posthumus in more respect than my noble and natural person, together with the adornment of my qualities. With that suit upon my back will I ravish her – first kill him, and in her eyes. There shall she see my valour, which will then be a torment to her contempt. He on the ground, my speech of insultment ended on his dead body, and when my lust hath dined – which, as I say, to vex her, I will execute in the clothes that she so praised – to the court I'll knock her back, foot her home again. She hath despised me rejoicingly, and I'll be merry in my revenge.
>
> (3.5.132–46)

'The bitterness of which I now belch from my heart': the insult affects the throat, the heart and the stomach at the same time. It is no coincidence that the word 'belch' should appear here, Cloten being left with a bitter taste in his mouth and throat. Cloten smells of resentment, which Shakespeare emphasizes by playing on the double meaning of the word 'rank'. In 2.1, he laments that his high birth prevents him from duelling against lower men: 'Would he had been one of my rank!' he exclaims, leading to an ironic aside by the Second Lord: 'To have smelled like a fool' (2.1.14–16). The word 'rank' refers to social status but also to a 'strong and unpleasant smell', meaning 'rancid'

(*OED*, 4, meaning 15), which is what the Second Lord's commentary points to. The French words *rancune* and *rancœur*, like the English word 'rancour', are etymologically linked to this 'rancid' smell. The *Dictionnaire historique de la langue française* points out the following etymology: *rance* (in English 'rancid', which is one of the meanings of 'rank') comes from the Latin *rancidus*, meaning 'rotten, smelly', hence 'putrefied, foul', and figuratively 'unpleasant, unbearable'. The word derives from the rare verb *rancēre*, meaning 'to ripen, to rot'.[70] In *OED*, this etymological link is found in the word 'rancour' (classical Latin *rancēre* to be rotten or putrid). The memory of conflicts is inscribed in Cloten's own body and manifests itself from the beginning to the end of the play as an olfactory trace. Thus Cloten's first appearance on stage, after a duel with Posthumus, is accompanied by a smell signalled by the First Lord:

> Sir, I would advise you to shift a shirt. The violence of action has made you reek as a sacrifice. Where air comes out, air comes in. There's none abroad so wholesome as that you vent.
> (1.2.1–4)

The term 'reek' refers to the foul fumes given off by the scapegoat's carcass. The Lord's flattery, which seems to suggest that the air exhaled by Cloten is most delicious, cannot erase the putrefactive smell evoked by 'reek sacrifice'. When we consider that Shakespeare literally leaves Cloten's body rotting on stage – which is ironical, of course, as he had cursed Posthumus with 'The south fog rot him' (2.3.131) – Cloten becomes the embodiment of rancour. When he imagines his 'speech of insultment' on Posthumus' body, the resilience against the traumatic effect of the insult 'meanest garment' consists in the literalization of a metaphor. Cloten imagines himself triumphing over the dead body of his rival, wearing the 'meanest garment' cherished by Innogen and turning it against her in an act of rape. Cloten imagines turning verbal abuse into physical abuse.

Even if Cloten's plan fails, Innogen becomes stained by Iachimo's calumny and symbolic rape[71] and ironically becomes herself the 'meanest garment' she compared Cloten to: 'Poor I am stale,[72] a garment out of fashion' (3.4.51). Shakespeare shows the traumatic effect of words when Pisanio comments on Innogen's reaction to the calumnious and insulting letter:

> What shall I need to draw my sword? The paper
> Hath cut her throat already. No, 'tis slander,
> Whose edge is sharper than the sword, whose tongue
> Out-venoms all the worms of Nile, whose breath
> Rides on the posting winds and doth belie
> All corners of the world. Kings, queens, and states,
> Maids, matrons, nay the secrets of the grave
> This viperous slander enters. – What cheer, madam?
> (3.4.32–9)

All the images used by the Elizabethans to evoke the efficacy and materiality of words are condensed here: the point of the sword, the venom, the breath that infects to the end of the earth[73] and reaches further than the arm. All these images appear repeatedly in other plays by Shakespeare, in Elizabethan texts on the tongue, and also in their biblical and classical sources.[74] Slander reaches into the grave ('the secrets of the grave') and has a posthumous life. There is an afterlife for the slanderous word. Reading the slanderous letter about her being 'a strumpet' (3.4.21–31), Innogen, in her turn, is under the shock of insulting words and, like Cloten, ironically repeats them: 'False to his bed? What is it to be false?'; 'That's false to's bed, is it?'; 'I false?' (3.4.40; 44; 46). She keeps harping on the term 'false' (3.4.58–64) before concluding:

> I have heard I am a strumpet, and mine ear,
> Therein false struck, can take no greater wound
> Nor tent to bottom that.
> (3.4.113–15)

Nothing can heal the wounds inflicted by words. In *The Praise of a good name. The Reproch of an ill name* (1594), Charles Gibbon notes that:

> Although a good name may bee recovered agayne in time: [...] yet it wilbe long ere it bee worne out of mens mouthes and memories: yea and when the best is done, as it is hard to cure a wound so well, but that a skarre will appeare in the skinne, so you shall as hardly recover the other, but it will be a blot to the name.[75]

Innogen's linguistic wound is expressed through a surgical term ('tent'). The 'mole, cinque-spotted' Innogen has 'On her left breast' (2.2.37–8) becomes 'this stain upon her' one 'remembers' (2.4.138–9). In *Cymbeline*, the instrument of calumny is memory, as Iachimo needs to remember as many details as possible to slander Innogen. *Cymbeline* is the play in which the word 'note' appears the most often. *Cymbeline* is 'much ado about noting', as appears when Iachimo declares 'But my design – / To *note* the chamber. I will write all down' (2.2.23–4). Innogen is 'noted', that is to say stigmatized, accused, branded with a fault (*OED*, verb 2, sense 3). Each of the notes taken by Iachimo will contribute to 'noting' or accusing her.

If Cloten's imagined resilience consists in becoming an image of Posthumus, Innogen's resilience will entail becoming someone else. Only death can partially silence the trauma of abuse in Shakespeare's plays. It is literally the case in *Othello*, and symbolically true in *Much Ado About Nothing* and in *The Winter's Tale*, where Hero and Hermione must metaphorically die in order to hope to clear their tainted memory. In *Cymbeline*, this necessary – but not sufficient – passage through death is expressed in terms of forgetting. Indeed, Pisanio gives Innogen the following advice: 'You must forget to be a woman' (3.4.154); 'Nay, you must forget that rarest treasure of your cheek, / Exposing it'; 'and forget / Your laboursome and dainty trims, wherein / You made great Juno angry' (3.4.159–65). Innogen must make the choice of oblivion, erase herself by erasing any trace of femininity to which slander might cling. She must strive to forget her role, 'the woman's part' (2.5.22). By stealing her bracelet, Iachimo has 'detracted' her, robbed her of her name and replaced it with that of a whore: 'She hath bought the name of whore thus dearly', says Posthumus (2.4.128), before referring to the stain upon her that is 'as big as hell can hold' (2.4.241). The stain left by the slander is indeed unforgettable, indelible.

If Innogen suffers this detraction, the theft and the loss of her 'name', Posthumus on the other hand, wants to inscribe his name in memories: 'Every villain / Be called Posthumus Leonatus!' (5.5.223–4). It is in a paradoxical mode that Posthumus sets about inscribing his name in our memories when he discovers, with horror, Innogen's innocence. While he verbally rebuilds a temple to her glory ('The temple / Of virtue was she', 5.5.220–1), he simultaneously writes his own history and heralds his own infamy. The first scene of the play was full of praises of Posthumus, of whom we were told how unique he was (1.1.16–27). At the end of *Cymbeline*, we move from praise ('the praise of a good name') to insult ('the reproach of an ill name'):

Spit and throw stones, cast mire upon me, set
The dogs o'th' street to bay me. Every villain
Be called Posthumus Leonatus, and
Be villainy less than 'twas.

(5.5.222–5)

Posthumus changes a proper name into a *common* name that should now supplant the word 'villain' in dictionaries. The character wants to engrave the change in language itself as language is not enough to express the villainy he wants to denounce, his own. By turning his name from a proper name into a common name, Posthumus provides a new etymology, another 'root', a new memory for it. The play thus dramatizes the process by which a name is turned into an insult. The hate speech that Posthumus inflicts upon himself is also expressed in physical terms: 'spit', 'throw stone', 'cast mire', which suggests that insult may be conveyed by non-verbal means.

7

Insult beyond words

In a soliloquy that opposes words and action, Hamlet denounces the way he 'unpacks' his 'heart with words' and blames himself for falling 'a-cursing like a very drab' (*Ham*, 2.2.520–1) instead of acting. Expostulating against himself, he imagines someone who would abuse him and lists a series of verbal and non-verbal insults:

> Am I a coward?
> Who calls me villain, breaks my pate across,
> Plucks off my beard and blows it in my face,
> Tweaks me by the nose, gives me the lie i'th' throat
> As deep as to the lungs? Who does me this?
> Ha? 'Swounds, I should take it.
> (*Ham*, 2.2.506–11)

In this speech, cowardice is presented as a lack of reaction to insults of all sorts. On stage, name-calling is a verbal art, but abuse is also often conveyed by body language and by action.

Desmond Morris' *Body talk* shows that many gestures are insulting.[1] One fifth of the list of 606 gestures that he draws, from all countries, are considered as insults, most of them sexual. Insults can be conveyed by a number of gesture codes that vary from one country or culture to another. Shakespeare makes use of these insulting gestures that can be made spectacular on stage. These gestures and actions are mentioned in the scripts of the play, and thus accessible to the spectators through words. That is why I prefer the formulation 'Insult *beyond* words' to 'Insult *without* words'.

In her recent book, *Shakespeare's Body Language. Shaming Gestures and Gender Politics on the Renaissance Stage*, Miranda Fay Thomas explores some of these gestures by focusing on thumb-biting in *Romeo and Juliet*, figging in the Henriad, spitting in *Richard III* and *The Merchant of Venice* and horning in *Othello*.[2] She focuses on mechanisms of shame related to gender, but the body language that she deciphers can also be approached in terms of insults.[3] In his *Chirologia* (1644), John Bulwer notes that fingers are 'naturally apt to speak scoffes'[4] and in *The Hand on the Shakespearean Stage*, Farah Karim-Cooper studies how gestures can express a great variety of emotions.[5] The uses of thumb-biting, figging and horning in Shakespeare's plays confirm that the fingers can speak insults. If the hands can be used to convey scorn, the face can also be a vector of insult.[6] With spitting, the tongue and mouth are diverted from their natural function of speech to become a bodily sign of rejection and dejection. Miranda Fay Thomas notes that:

> In *Richard III*, we see how the action of spitting upon Richard reflects society's rejection of his disabled body; in *The Merchant of Venice*, we see how the resentment towards the Jewish moneylender is epitomized through people spitting at him in the streets.[7]

Spitting at someone's face is a physical form of insult that replaces words and reveals that one has run out of verbal ammunition, as is the case with Lady Anne, when words are not enough for her to express her hate for Richard (*R3*, 1.2.147). In his 1587 dictionary, Thomas Thomas defines *Conspŭo* as to 'spittle, to spitte against some body, to soile and raie with spittle'.[8] *Conspuer* in French comes from Latin *con-spuere*, to spit together, and means to loudly express spite and hostility, to spue. Spittle is part of the body's 'ex-crements', as is suggested in Thomas' dictionary:

> Excrēmentum, ti, n.g. Pli. The dregs or excrements of digestion made in the bodie, a fleame, choler, melancholie, urine, sweat, snivel, spitted, milke, ordure: the offal, the refuse of any thing sifted. Excrementum oris, Tacit. Spittle. Excrementum, alvi, Cels. Ordure.[9]

This definition translates the link between execration and excretion that Gaignebet and Périer drew in the article on 'L'homme et l'excretum', and that appears, for example, in Timon's symbolically spitting at his guests during the mock-banquet scene.[10] Spitting materializes the idea that insult is a means of evacuation.[11]

If non-verbal insults may be inscribed in bodily gestures, they can also be conveyed by symbolic acts. When York, the 'sturdy rebel', sits on Henry VI's 'chair of state' (*3H6*, 1.1.50–1), the symbolic usurpation of the throne constitutes an insult to the King, as Clifford notes: 'He durst not sit there had your father lived' (*3H6*, 1.1.63). When, in *Troilus and Cressida*, Achilles refuses to 'Untent his person and share the air with us' (*TC*, 2.3.165), he braves Agamemnon's authority through an 'evasion, winged thus swift with scorn' (*TC*, 2.3.112). Aeneas offends 'great Agamemnon' by not recognizing him (*TC*, 1.3.215–56). When Petruccio arrives late for his wedding in *The Taming of the Shrew*, his behaviour is interpreted as an insult, as appears when Baptista notes that 'such an injury would vex a very saint' (*TS*, 3.2.28) and the 'unreverent robes' he wears at the wedding (*TS*, 3.2.111) constitute a visual insult to the bride. When the gentlemen in *Love's Labour's Lost* intend to leave the ladies 'in the fields' so as not to break their oath, their 'welcome' is interpreted by the ladies as an insulting breach of the laws of hospitality, in a situation in which words do not compensate for an insulting act:

KING
    Fair Princess, welcome to the court of Navarre.

PRINCESS
> 'Fair' I give you back again, and 'welcome' I have not yet. The roof of this court is too high to be yours, and welcome to the wide fields too base to be mine.
>
> (*LLL*, 2.1.90–4)

In these various cases, action has an obvious insulting eloquence.[12] These acts constitute affronts, in that they are public marks of contempt. The affront is a public outrage, which is all the more offensive and effective because it is public. In this chapter I will focus on two political plays in which insults conspicuously go beyond words: *Henry V* and *King Lear*.

The insulting gifts of *Henry V*

Henry V is a play about language. It is one of the most multilingual plays in Shakespeare's corpus, and it stages a war of tongues related to the conflict between nations.[13] The whole play may have an insulting effect on the French nation, as is suggested by the fact that it took the French a few centuries to put the play on stage, Jean-Louis Benoit's 1999 version being considered as the first production of note in France. The linguistic war is perhaps best epitomized in the 'What ish my nation?' scene that takes place in the margin of the battle and shows that war rages even within the one camp. Shakespeare dramatizes the tensions between nations, in an exchange between the Welsh Fluellen and the Irish Macmorris, with Gower, the English Captain, playing the part of a sort of referee:

FLUELLEN
> Captain Macmorris, I think, look you, under your correction, there is not many of your nation –

MACMORRIS
> Of my nation? What ish my nation? Ish a villain, and a bastard and a knave, and a rascal? What ish my nation? Who talks of my nation?

FLUELLEN
> Look you, if you take the matter otherwise than is meant, Captain Macmorris, peradventure I shall think you do not use me with that affability as in discretion you ought to use me, look you, being as good a man as yourself, both in the disciplines of war, and in the derivation of my birth, and in other particularities.

MACMORRIS
> I do not know you so good a man as myself. So Chrish save me, I will cut off your head.

GOWER.
> Gentlemen both, you will mistake each other.
>
> (3.2.121–36)

This episode[14] could be regarded as another 'No abuse?' sequence, dramatizing the question of interpretation and interrogating the intentionality of words. The word 'nation' has no doubt an insulting effect on Macmorris, an effect that is counterbalanced by Fluellen's denying any abusive intention when he claims that the Irish Captain takes 'the matter otherwise than is meant'. In this context of tension between nations, the play dramatizes a series of insulting gifts. In *Henry V*, acts of giving are paradoxically turned into polite forms of abuse that make objects become offensive.

'This tun of treasure'

The 'tennis-balls' scene is one of the most memorable scenes of insult in *Henry V*. The present that is brought by the Ambassador, on behalf of the Dauphin, constitutes a diplomatic insult.

AMBASSADOR
>   Thus then, in few.
> Your highness lately sending into France
> Did claim some certain dukedoms in the right
> Of your great predecessor King Edward the Third.
> In answer of which claim the Prince our master

> Says that you savour too much of your youth
> And bids you be advised. There's naught in France
> That can be with a nimble galliard won;
> You cannot revel into dukedoms there.
> He therefore sends you, meeter for your spirit,
> This tun of treasure, and in lieu of this,
> Desires you let the dukedoms that you claim
> Hear no more of you. This the Dauphin speaks.
> KING
> What treasure, uncle?
> EXETER   Tennis-balls, my liege.
> (H5, 1.2.246–59)

With this gift, the Ambassador conveys the Dauphin's insulting answer to Henry's request, by referring to his unruly youth. The tennis-balls embody his former idle self and the 'tun of treasure' brings the King back to the days when a 'tun of man' was his 'companion' (1H4, 2.4.436). As these are the only two occurrences of the word 'tun' in the whole Shakespearean corpus, it invites us to make a connection between the two. The references to Henry's 'youth', the 'nimble galliard' and the term 'revel' pave the way for the spectacular gift that is often a moment of suspense on stage, followed by an anticlimactic effect, when we discover that the treasure is just made of tennis-balls. The sexual potential of the insult is obvious as the 'balls' may be evocative of the masculine attributes. Moreover, tennis was considered as an expensive sport reserved for idle noblemen, and thus the gift associates Henry with leisure, denying the character any kingly stature. The game is French in origin, and the word is, probably wrongly, related to the French '*tenez*' (take, receive).[15] The ironic gift is acknowledged through ironic thanks:

> We are glad the Dauphin is so pleasant with us
> His present and your pains we thank you for.
> (1.2.260–1)

The gift is received with bitter gratitude and the material balls are verbally sent back to their sender, Henry responding by transforming these insulting tennis-balls into martial weapons:

> When we have *matched* our *rackets* to these *balls*
> We will in France, by God's grace, play a *set*
> Shall strike his father's crown into the hazard.
> Tell him he hath made a *match* with such a wrangler
> That all the *courts* of France shall be disturbed
> With *chases*. And we understand him well,
> How he comes o'er us with our wilder days.
> (1.2.260–8)

Tennis becomes a metaphor for war. 'We understand him well' (1.2.267), says Henry. The gift is received as it should be, that is, as an act of provocation, the text providing several comments on it: 'he comes o'er us with our wilder days' is glossed as 'he taunts me with' by Craik.[16] Henry describes the gift as 'this mock of his' (1.2.282), the word 'mock' rebounding like a ball throughout the script:

> And tell the pleasant prince this *mock* of his
> Hath turned his balls to gun-stones, and his soul
> Shall stand sore charged for the wasteful vengeance
> That shall fly with them; for many a thousand widows
> Shall this his *mock mock* out of their dear husbands,
> *Mock* mothers from their sons, *mock* castles down,
> And some are yet ungotten and unborn
> That shall have cause to curse the Dauphin's scorn.
> (1.2.282–8)

The word 'mock' becomes a tennis-ball with which the King plays to counter the insult. He goes on by referring to the gift as a 'jest', a term ironically related to the French *geste*, meaning a heroic feat, 'A notable deed or action; an exploit' (*OED*):

> and tell the Dauphin
> His jest will savour but of shallow wit
> When thousands weep more than did laugh at it.
> (1.2.295–7)

The only martial exploit achieved by the Dauphin will be this 'jest/*geste*'.[17] Henry announces the effect the mock will have, as if the insulting gift was triggering off the war while we, as spectators, know that he has already 'resolved' (1.2.223) to wage war against France. The impact of the abusive gift reappears later in the play, when Exeter plays the part of an ambassador by paying a visit to the King and Dauphin of France. Exeter answers the insulting gift by delivering Henry's message to the Dauphin:

> Scorn and defiance, slight regard, contempt,
> And anything that may not misbecome
> The mighty sender, doth he prize you at.
> Thus says my king: an if your father's highness
> Do not, in grant of all demands at large,
> Sweeten the bitter mock you sent his majesty,
> He'll call you to so hot an answer for it
> That caves and womby vaultages of France
> Shall chide your trespass and return your mock
> In second accent of his ordinance.
>
> (2.4.117–26)

The tennis-balls resound in this sequence where we hear their 'second accent' or echo,[18] especially when the Dauphin repeats the insult:

> DAUPHIN
>   for I desire
> Nothing but odds with England. To that end,
> As matching to his youth and vanity,
> I did present him with the Paris-balls.
> EXETER
> He'll make your Paris Louvre shake for it,
> Were it the mistress-court of mighty Europe.
>
> (2.4.128–33)

Thus, war is announced through the tennis-balls, tennis no longer being the light game it used to be for Hal in *2 Henry IV* where the image of the 'tennis-court keeper' emerged in a context of bawdy bantering with Poins (*2H4*, 2.2.9–27). The intervention of mediators, the ambassadors, is typical of the international insult. This intermediary makes the insult more diplomatic and 'political' but no less assaultive. When the insult enters the international sphere, it necessarily goes through messengers. Or at least the presence of an intermediary guarantees the political and diplomatic value of the insult. Invective and insults, as practised by soldiers on the battlefield, have no place in the political sphere, where the insult must be cushioned by the presence of an intermediary. It is this intermediary who ensures that kings do not behave like ordinary men. The messenger is therefore the trace of a politicization and internationalization of insult.

After the tennis-balls, Shakespeare throws another insulting object into relief: the glove, which constitutes another paradoxically civilized form of abuse.

'Here is my glove'

The hand, the fingers and the nails are at the heart of Katherine's language lesson (*H5*, 3.4). In Jean-Louis Benoit's 1999 French production of *Henry V* performed at the Avignon Festival, with Philippe Torreton playing Henry, Katherine's lesson turned into a visually bawdy and insulting sequence, the actress thrusting up her middle finger in a gesture known as a '*doigt d'honneur*' in French, a middle-finger jerk followed by the gesture known as '*bras d'honneur*' when Katherine uttered the words 'arm', 'elbow', 'bilbow'. The hand was as abusive as the tongue, the two organs being vectors of language, oral and written. In this production, the gestures expressed all the bawdy allusions present in Shakespeare's script and were a clever way of translating difficult multilingual puns.[19]

The 'fig of Spain' (*H5*, 3.6.56–8), an obscene insulting gesture of which Pistol is so fond, also focuses the spectators' attention on the combination of the hand and the mouth.[20] Shakespeare cleverly connects the high and the low by having Katherine and Pistol share the same type of bawdy gesture.[21] Pistol 'figs' both Fluellen (3.6.66) and his kinsman, the King (4.1.61). Macmorris swears several times by his hand (3.2.89–93; 102), an oath that was, as John Kerrigan notes, 'particularly binding for the Irish'.[22] This focus on the hand paves the way for the part that will be played by an object that is associated with insult and challenge: the glove. It is in *Henry V* that the occurrences of the word 'glove' are the most numerous. The term is repeated eighteen times in the singular and once in the plural, delineating a complex circuit from 4.1 up to the end of the play. After having been insulted by Pistol, the King in disguise is insulted by Williams, who has indirectly called him a fool:

WILLIAMS
[...] Come, 'tis a foolish saying.
KING
Your reproof is something too round; I should be angry with you if the time were convenient.
WILLIAMS
Let it be a quarrel between us, if you live.
KING
I embrace it.
WILLIAMS
How shall I know thee again?
KING
Give me any gage of thine, and I will wear it in my bonnet. Then if ever thou dar'st acknowledge it I will make it my quarrel.
WILLIAMS
Here's my glove. Give me another of thine.
KING
There. [*They exchange gloves.*]

WILLIAMS
This will I also wear in my cap. If ever thou come to me and say after tomorrow 'This is my glove', by this hand, I will take thee a box on the ear.
KING
If ever I live to see it I will challenge it.
WILLIAMS
Thou dar'st as well be hanged.
KING
Well, I will do it, though I take thee in the King's company.
WILLIAMS
Keep thy word. Fare thee well.

(*H5*, 4.1.200–18)

The two men circumscribe a space for private quarrel that should remain outside the perimeter of the international battle. In *Richard II*, Bolingbroke throws down his gauntlet as a pledge (*R2*, 1.1.69–83) at a moment when, as Kerrigan notes, 'speech acts morph into action'.[23] Charles Forker explains that 'flinging it down was an act of challenge and taking it up signified acceptance'.[24] In *Henry V*, the confrontation is delayed, the gloves being put in suspension and displayed, tucked up into a belt or hat. The exchange of gloves is supposed to have a binding function, the glove being a *gage*, that is, something that en*gages*, or commits someone to doing something. The glove here is 'Something of value deposited to ensure the performance of some action' (*OED*, *gage*).[25] The gift of the glove is a way of turning a potential uncivil brawl into an official, civilized quarrel and to delay the reaction to the insult to a more 'convenient' moment. It is both the mark that an offence has been committed and the mark that the insult is integrated into codes of honour.

However, the honourable dimension of the exchange of gloves is undermined by the dramatic situation that is based on mistaken identity. A quarrel between a King and a common soldier could never have taken place, and, as Kerrigan notes, 'For Williams the quarrel is a point of honour; for the king it has shrunk into a jest'.[26] The glove that must visually be present on stage is a reminder of an insult that does not have the same impact on the two opponents. Shakespeare subverts the codes of quarrelling by introducing a comic imbalance in the process.

During the exchange with the King, Williams throws another insulting gesture into relief: the box on the ear, which was translated in French as 'un soufflet sus la joue'.[27] In a book devoted to duelling in France, François Billacois explains why the box on the ear is so dishonourable and goes against the spirit of a duel:

> To defend oneself with a sword, looking the opponent in the face, is to consider (in the double sense of the word) him, to greet and honour him, while striking him. To defend oneself with one's hand, to slap or punch him, is to remove him from one's gaze, or to close one's eyes in order to better focus one's brutal force, it is to deny him honour. It amounts to adding moral contempt to physical force. [...] And the insult is worse if the hand opens for a blow than if it closes for a punch. [...] The closed fist, in fact, a natural club, inherent in the body, not made by human industry, stuns and crushes the opponent, but at the same time reduces the attacker to the rank of a brute beast. The open hand, with a much more conscious and voluntary gesture, physically does little harm, but humiliates the other, and only the other. It proclaims in the attacker some moral superiority added to pure force which is called *authority*. The hand opens to give a blow as it opens to express a stop, a pardon, an oath, a blessing.[28]

The 'box on the ear' therefore carries a heavy symbolic weight. More than a physical assault, it is one of the worst outrages a man of honour can suffer. The box on the ear occurs several times in Shakespeare's plays, especially in *2 Henry VI*, where it is used in an unusual way to dramatize a conflict between two women, Queen Margaret and Eleanor, the Duchess of Gloucester:

> [*The Queen drops her fan.*]
> QUEEN
>   Give me my fan. What, minion, can ye not?
>   *She gives Eleanor a box on the ear.*
>   I cry you mercy, madam; was it you?
> DUCHESS
>   Was't I! Yea, I it was, proud Frenchwoman.
>   Could I come near your beauty with my nails
>   I'd set my ten commandments in your face.
>   (*2H6*, 1.3.139–43)

Beyond this parody of a challenge using the recurrent motif of the woman's nails, Williams' promise may remind the spectators of another episode in Henry's young days, when Hal is said to have struck the Lord Chief Justice. The spectators do not see this 'box on the ear' on stage, but it becomes part of the myth of Hal's rebellious and insolent youth.[29] In *2 Henry IV*, the Page announces the arrival of the Lord Chief Justice to Falstaff: 'Sir, here comes the nobleman that committed the Prince for striking him about Bardolph' (*2H4*, 1.2.56–7). Then Falstaff deflates the impact of the offensive gesture when he addresses the Lord Chief Justice:

> For the box of the ear that the Prince gave you, he gave it like a rude prince, and you took it like a sensible lord: I have checked him for it, and the young lion repents – marry, not in ashes and sackcloth, but in new silk and old sack.
>   (*2H4*, 1.2.194–8)

The 'box on the ear' that Hal gave to the Lord Chief Justice was the sign of his irreverent youth at a time when insult was an art for him. Giving the Lord a box on the ear amounted to offending the King and the father, the embodiment of authority, as appears at the end of the play, once Hal has become a King, when he addresses the Lord Chief Justice:

KING

[...] How might a prince of my great hopes forget
So great indignities you laid upon me?
What – rate, rebuke, and roughly send to prison
Th'immediate heir of England? Was this easy?
May this be washed in Lethe and forgotten?

CHIEF JUSTICE

I then did use the person of your father.
The image of his power lay then in me;
And in th' administration of his law,
Whiles I was busy for the commonwealth,
Your highness pleased to forget my place,
The majesty and power of law and justice,
The image of the king whom I presented,
And struck me in my very seat of judgement,
Whereon, as an offender to your father,
I gave bold way to my authority
And did commit you.

(2H4, 5.2.68–83)

The exchange of views between the new King and the Lord Chief Justice shows that, in matters of insults, the positions of the insulter and the insulted may change and the perspective on who is to blame may vary too. It also throws into relief the transfer of the insulting effect on another person. If you insult the Lord Chief Justice, you insult his King.

The box on the ear that Williams promises to Harry Leroy will again raise a question of authority since the contract of aggression, the oath that is taken through the exchange of gloves, cannot but be broken and will have to lead to a substitution of identities. The glove episode crops up again in 4.7 when the King deceptively questions Williams about the glove he wears in his cap:

HENRY

Soldier, why wear'st thou that glove in thy cap?

WILLIAMS

An't please your majesty, 'tis the gage of one that I should fight withal, if he be alive.

HENRY

An Englishman?

WILLIAMS

An't please your majesty, a rascal that swaggered with me last night, who, if 'a live and ever dare to challenge this glove, I have sworn to take him a box o'th' ear; or if I can see my glove in his cap, which he swore as he was a soldier he would wear if 'a lived, I will strike it out soundly.

HENRY

What think you, Captain Fluellen, is it fit this soldier keep his oath?

FLUELLEN

He is a craven and a villain else, an't please your majesty, in my conscience.

HENRY

It may be his enemy is a gentleman of great sort, quite from the answer of his degree.

FLUELLEN

Though he be as good a gentleman as the devil is, as Lucifer and Belzebub himself, it is necessary, look your grace, that he keep his vow and his oath. If he be perjured, see you now, his reputation is as arrant a villain and a jack-sauce as ever his black shoe trod upon God's ground and his earth, in my conscience, la!

HENRY

Then keep thy vow, sirrah, when thou meet'st the fellow.

WILLIAMS

So I will, my liege, as I live.

(*H5*, 4.7.119–44)

Williams keeps the memory of the abuse, while the King plays with the man and his story. Given the comic situation, the sequence both *is and is not* a scene of insult. The abuse being part of a pattern of mistaken identity, it becomes a source of comedy, the King being insulted both by Williams and by Fluellen. Henry is indeed ironically called 'rascal' by Williams and a '*jack*-sauce' by Fluellen, which is reminiscent of his companion *Jack* Falstaff. What is meant to codify the quarrel, the glove, then 'migrates from the King's hat to Fluellen's'[30] when Henry rewrites Williams' story into an episode with Alençon (4.7.151–6) and asks Fluellen: 'wear thou this favour for me and stick it in thy cap' (4.7.151–2). The King 'abuses' Williams in more than one way. The glove becomes a deceptive sign of recognition that leads Williams to give Fluellen, and not the king, a box on the ear.

> WILLIAMS
> I know this, and thus I challenge it.
> *Strikes him.*
> FLUELLEN
> 'Sblood, an arrant traitor as any's in the universal world, or in France or in England! (4.8.8–11)

The original exchange of gloves is doubled by another, which leads Williams and Fluellen to lose their landmarks and engender an erroneous quarrel, the original oath and contract being broken by the King. The moment of anagnorisis provides an interesting comment on the discrepancy between the emission and the reception of abuse:

> KING
> Give me thy glove, soldier. Look here is the fellow of it.
> 'Twas I indeed thou promised'st to strike,
> And thou hast given me most bitter terms.
> FLUELLEN
> An't please your majesty, let his neck answer for it, if there is any martial law in the world.
> KING
> How canst thou make me satisfaction?
> WILLIAMS
> All offences, my lord, come from the heart: never came any from mine that might offend your majesty.

KING
> It was our self thou didst abuse.

WILLIAMS
> Your majesty came not like yourself: you appeared to me but as a common man – witness the night, your garments, your lowliness; and what your highness suffered under that shape, I beseech you take it for your own fault and not mine, for had you been as I took you for, I made no offence; therefore I beseech your highness, pardon me.
>
> (*H5*, 4.8.40–57)

This is another 'No abuse?' sequence, in which what is presented as 'abuse' by one party is seen as being 'no offence' by the other, Shakespeare dramatizing the gap between the intention and the effect. By using the glove as a token of recognition, the playwright subverts the pattern of insult to create a comic moment. Yet, the end of the sequence dramatizes another reversal when another type of gift proves injurious to Williams. To show his pardon for Williams' abuse, the King asks Exeter to give him 'crowns':

KING
> Here, uncle Exeter, fill this glove with crowns
> And give it to this fellow. – Keep it, fellow;
> And wear it for an honour in thy cap
> Till I do challenge it. – Give him the crowns. –
> And Captain, you must needs be friends with him.

FLUELLEN
> By this day and this light, the fellow has mettle enough in his belly. – Hold, there is twelve pence for you, and I pray you to serve God, and keep you out of prawls and prabbles, and quarrels and dissensions, and I warrant you it is the better for you.

WILLIAMS
> I will none of your money.
>
> (*H5*, 4.8.58–68)

Fluellen's gift, accompanied by words of advice, has an insulting effect on Williams, whose reaction suggests that Henry's *jest* with the glove is received as an injury. Kerrigan notes that Henry has arranged for Fluellen to 'become a down-market version of himself by wearing the leek-like glove in his cap'.[31] The parallel between the glove and the leek appears indeed clearly when we study the role and circulation of the Welsh emblem in the play.

'If you can mock a leek...'

When Pistol meets Harry Le Roy on the eve of battle, he asks him to be the messenger of an insult:

> Tell him I'll knock his leek about his pate
> Upon Saint Davy's day.
>
> (*H5*, 4.1.55–6)

Pistol here wants words to 'morph into action',[32] imagining an injurious gesture that consists in turning the emblem of Wales against the Welshman Fluellen, on the Welsh national day. The action he is planning is to have an insulting impact, both on Fluellen and on the Welsh nation, the emblem being the epitome of a whole country. The spectator measures the degree of the insult when Fluellen weaves the story of the Welsh leek, showing his pride in what he calls an 'honourable badge':

FLUELLEN
> [...] If your majesty is remembered of it, the Welshmen did good service in a garden where leeks did grow, wearing leeks in their Monmouth caps, which your majesty know to this hour is an honourable badge of the service; and I do believe your majesty takes no scorn to wear the leek upon Saint Tavy's day.

KING
> I wear it for a memorable honour,
> For I am Welsh, you know, good countryman.
>
> (*H5*, 4.7.96–104)

The leek is worn with pride and honour by Fluellen, until it is replaced by the King's glove and until, like the glove, it becomes a source of dissention and conflict, in Act 5. Like the glove, the leek becomes a catalyst of insult. In 3.6, Fluellen defers the reaction to Pistol's abuse to a more convenient time, 'when time is serve' (3.6.65). In 5.1, the Welsh Captain explains why he is wearing his leek in his hat and narrates how he has had to postpone his reaction to Pistol's provocatively bidding him eat his leek:

GOWER
Nay, that's right. But why wear you your leek today? Saint Davy's day is past.

FLUELLEN
There is occasions and causes why and wherefore in all things. I will tell you ass my friend, Captain Gower. The rascally, scald, beggarly, lousy, pragging knave Pistol, which you and yourself and all the world know to be no petter than a fellow, look you now, of no merits, he is come to me and prings me pread and salt yesterday, look you, and bid me eat my leek. It was in place where I could not breed no contention with him, but I will be so bold as to wear it in my cap till I see him once again, and then I will tell him a little piece of my desires.

(*H5*, 5.1.1–13)

In this scene, the leek plays the part of the glove, an object that signals a conflictual process. In her book on Shakespeare and food, Joan Fitzpatrick notes that Fluellen 'is insulted by Pistol's suggestion that he eat the leek because the object has been demoted from noble symbol of Welsh pride to a mere vegetable'.[33] By forcing Pistol to eat the Welsh leek, Fluellen literally has him 'swallow' the insult he hurled when he reduced the leek to a mere 'eatable'.

PISTOL
Hence! I am qualmish at the smell of leek.

FLUELLEN

> I peseech you heartily, scurvy, lousy knave, at my desires, and my requests, and my petitions, to eat, look you, this leek. Because, look you, you do not love it, nor your affections and your appetites and your digestions does not agree with it, I would desire you to eat it.
>
> (*H5*, 5.1.21–7)

The sequence dramatizes the literalization of a metaphoric insult as well as a boomerang effect since Fluellen does to Pistol precisely what Pistol was planning to do to him ('bid me eat my leek'). Confronted with Pistol's disgust[34] and resistance, Fluellen offers him what he calls 'sauce' (5.1.35; 51) as encouragement, by striking and cudgelling him. The paradox of the injurious gift appears if one considers the mixture of violence and polite address in Fluellen's moment of triumph. The ironic boomerang reversal clearly appears when Fluellen declares: 'if you can mock a leek you can eat a leek' (5.1.38–9), the word 'mock' echoing the previous tennis-balls episode. After insulting Fluellen by referring to the Welsh leek in disgust ('Hence! I am qualmish at the smell of leek', 5.1.21), Pistol is literally forced to 'eat' his words. Verbal abuse is turned into physical abuse, in which one can find a suggestion of sexual humiliation, the leek being a potentially phallic symbol.[35] By calling for revenge, Pistol shows that the insult is hard to 'digest' and is going to be lodged in his throat. The *effet injure* is enhanced by the injurious gift of a 'groat' that Fluellen offers him:

FLUELLEN

> Ay, leeks is good. Hold you, there is a groat to heal your pate.

PISTOL

> Me a groat?

FLUELLEN

> Yes, verily and in truth, you shall take it, or I have another leek in my pocket which you shall eat.

PISTOL

> I take thy groat in earnest of revenge.

FLUELLEN
  If I owe you anything, I will pay you in cudgels: you shall
  be a woodmonger, and buy nothing of me but cudgels.
  God bye you, and keep you, and heal your pate. *Exit*
PISTOL
  All hell shall stir for this.
(*H5*, 5.1.59–69)

Kerrigan comments on this sequence as follows:

> Leeks, like gloves, it seems, come in pairs. The groat is a gift
> as insult, a reward that is really a punishment, in a spirit of
> beggary but also as earnest. Insult the leek again, the groat-
> pledge declares, and you know what will happen. The bond
> is tied by a threat.[36]

Pistol, whose name refers to a currency, a Spanish gold coin, is insulted by the base 'groat' he is forced to accept since he considers it is unworthy of him. He already felt abused when, misunderstanding Le Fer, he thought the French soldier was offering him 'brass' (4.4.16–20), that is another base currency. In *Henry V*, through the tennis-balls, the glove and the leek, Shakespeare develops an economy of abuse, based on gifts, exchanges and debts; the diplomatic insult finds its counterpoint in the sphere of common quarrels, the two worlds converging to show the division between and within nations. The circulation of men and goods goes together with the circulation of insults, an aspect that is also conspicuous in *King Lear*.

'Abatement of kindness': The outrages of *King Lear*

''tis worse than murder / To do upon respect such violent outrage' (2.2.213–14): the outrage that Lear is commenting upon in these lines has not been done in words but in action. Lear discovers his servant Kent (disguised as Caius) in the stocks and his reaction illustrates many of the mechanisms that characterize insult in *King Lear*. First of all, it is emblematic of the *ricochet* effects of outrage in *King Lear*: if you insult the King's servant, you insult the King. Just as Kent's verbal assault on Oswald (2.2.13–112) was a response to the latter's insulting behaviour to the King, the punishment inflicted upon Kent for his insolence rebounds onto Lear's face in all its violence. By putting Kent in the stocks, Regan and Cornwall do him wrong, but in so doing they primarily undermine the King's authority, which Lear identifies as being a 'violent outrage' that is 'worse than murder'. By its etymology, the word *outrage*, related to the Anglo-Norman and Old French *ultrage*, refers to something that goes 'beyond' (*outre* in French), a transgression. It is this transgression that constitutes an unbearable insult. Kent anticipates Lear's reaction and the transfer of insult that is taking place:

> You shall do small respect, show too bold malice
> Against the grace and person of my master,
> Stocking his messenger.
>
> (2.2.128–30)

Similarly, Gloucester refers to this *ricochet* effect when he predicts that "twill be ill taken' (2.2.157). Kent's fate does not matter; what Gloucester and Kent are concerned about is the affront made to the King. By punishing the servant, Regan and Cornwall are assaulting Lear and inflicting an outrage on him that reduces him to nothing and fills him with 'rage'. Beyond this *ricochet* effect, this non-verbal outrage is characteristic of the part that is played in *King Lear* by silent insult, insult in action and physical outrage. After hearing Kent pour out his insults on Oswald (2.2.13–112) and savouring some of the longest strings of insults in all of Shakespeare's work, one cannot help but be struck by the economy of the act that puts an end to this verbal inflation: 'Fetch forth the stocks, ho!' (2.2.124).

The 'Nothing, my lord' (1.1.87) uttered by Cordelia at the beginning of the play also cuts short verbal outbursts and excesses. However, far from being 'gracious', like Virgilia's silence in *Coriolanus* (*Cor*, 2.1.170), Cordelia's silence is odious to Lear, who seems to consider that everything that is not a compliment is an insult and that flattery is the only acceptable mode of speech. By refusing to give Lear what he wants, Cordelia plunges the play into a world where what is unspoken is more subversive and violent than what is spoken. From then on, the outrage arises not so much from words as from the absence of words, not so much from what is said as from what should have been said and is not. In *King Lear*, outrage comes from refusal, from absence, from subtraction rather than from the 'additions' that Kent speaks of when he insults Oswald (*KL*, 2.2.23). Lear's reaction also places the question of intention at the heart of the reflection on outrage. A double interpretation has been offered for the expression 'upon respect' (2.2.214), which can mean, according to R. A. Foakes, either 'upon the respect due to the King's messenger' or 'upon consideration',[37] i.e. deliberately. Lear is all the more outraged because Regan and Cornwall did it *on purpose*. Finally, the expression 'worse than murder' (2.2.213) integrates the outrage into a symbolic world of torture, which, as Caroline Spurgeon has shown, is so essential in this play.[38] The insults, wrongs and offences inflicted on Lear by his daughters are all torments that affect the symbolic body of the King and which Lear tries to resist by claiming he will be 'the pattern of all patience' and 'will say nothing' (3.2.37–8).

This section examines why the affronts suffered in this play are 'worse than murder' and shows that the whole play resonates with the word 'outrage', where one cannot fail to hear the word 'out' (a marker of exclusion and excess), the word 'rage' (meaning both rage and madness) and the word 'age': out-rage-age, three terms that are particularly significant in this play. 'Outrage' refers to excess, verbal and physical violence, but also to noise ('outcry', 'clamour' in *OED* note, noun 1.b) and fury ('to outrage' meaning 'to rage against'). I will focus on the nature of the outrages staged in *King Lear* before analyzing the mechanisms of resistance to them as they are dramatized in this play. Finally, I suggest that the whole play stages an 'outrage effect', which is all the more violent because the victim has a high self-image and is deprived of it.

Silent abuse

There are, according to Edmund, two ways of displeasing or showing 'displeasure': the 'word' and the 'countenance' (1.2.156). If the play is rich in insulting words, it is also full of silent insults, non-verbal assaults. Lear, after being a King, is confronted with Cordelia's silence, then reduced to his sole function as a father-child, when Oswald calls him 'my lady's father' (1.4.77), before ending up as naked as a worm: 'A man a worm', as Gloucester says (4.1.35). Lear's vertiginous descent, his madness, his rage, his despair are the results and manifestations of a series of affronts committed, willingly or not, by his daughters. Kent being put in the stocks concludes a long series of abuses, and heralds the physical violence Gloucester will have to endure in Act 4.

As early as 1.3, Goneril offers a kind of 'do-it-yourself guide' to insulting a King, the first tool of which consists of refusing to speak, and thus keeping silent and absent: 'I will not speak with him; say I am sick' (1.3.9), Goneril orders to Oswald. Similarly, we learn from Lear that Regan adopts the same strategy when he exclaims:

> Deny to speak with me? They are sick, they are weary,
> They have travelled all the night? – mere fetches ay,
> (2.2.277–78)

Lear sees in this absence an image of rebellion and desertion ('The images of revolt and flying off', 2.2.279). Ironically, Goneril and Regan use a strategy that is modelled on Cordelia's muteness in the opening scene. In a study of the rules of social dialogue in Shakespeare, Lynne Magnusson notes that Lear's daughters 'withhold [...] acknowledgement' of their father and King by refusing to speak to him.[39] By leaving Lear's questions unanswered ('Who put my man i'the stocks?', 2.2.371; 377; 387), Shakespeare highlights this tactic of silence, which consists in keeping Lear at a distance, putting him off side, excluding him. There is an 'out' in Lear's 'out-rage'. Lear summarizes this exclusion, saying: ''tis Goneril [...] kicked the poor King her father' (3.6.46–8).

Goneril's instructions to Oswald also emphasize the theatrical dimension of the offences against Lear, which are literally staged. There are physical ways of displaying insolence, as Kent suggests when he describes Oswald as 'the very fellow which of late / Displayed so saucily against your highness' (2.2.230–31). Goneril in fact asks Oswald to put on the mask of insolence by engaging in a kind of pantomime: 'If you come slack of former services / You shall do well' (1.3.9–11); 'Put on what weary negligence you please' (1.3.13), 'And let his knights have colder looks among you' (1.3.23). Goneril becomes a stage director here, anxious to produce her effect: 'I'd have it come to question' (1.3.14); 'I would breed from hence occasions, and I shall, / That I may speak' (Q. 1.3.25–6). Like the servants in *Romeo and Juliet* who want to start a quarrel with a thumb-biting gesture (*RJ*, 1.1), Goneril uses her servant's behaviour to broach a quarrel with her father.

The next scene shows that Oswald follows the instructions to the letter. When Lear calls him, Oswald leaves the stage with an insulting 'So please you' (1.4.46) that specifically does *not please* Lear. Oswald brazenly meets the King's glance, to which Lear responds: 'Do you bandy looks with me, you rascal?' (1.4.82). Silence, absence, glances and smiles: these are the original outrages in *King Lear*. So, it is not fortuitous that Kent, when Cornwall asks him about Oswald – 'Why dost thou call him knave? What is his fault?' (2.2.87) –, should reply 'His countenance likes me not' (2.2.88). In *Shakespeare and Violence*, R. A. Foakes writes about the 'climate of violence' at court and reads Kent's response as an indication of a world where Lear has instilled a taste for gratuitous violence in everyone.[40] According to Goneril, insult answers insult: 'By day and night he wrongs me. Every hour / He flashes into one gross crime or other / That sets us all at odds' (1.3.4–6);

'[he] upbraids us / On every trifle' (1.3.7). Kent's words ('his countenance likes me not') also suggest that it is Oswald's face, look and attitude that constitute the insult. It is indeed through his 'countenance' that Oswald insults Lear and Kent. The use of the verb 'like' to mean 'please' is revealing in a world where Lear has established the wrong equivalence between pleasing and loving, in the first scene. If we choose to hear this 'like' as a 'like' rather than a 'please', then the text suggests that Oswald, by his attitude and existence, is himself the insult, and that the aggression comes from him and not from Kent.

Shakespeare literalizes the *affront* by drawing the viewer's attention to Goneril's 'forehead', or *front* in French. When Lear finally sees his daughter, he first notices her frowning:

> How now, daughter? What makes that frontlet on?
> Methinks you are too much of late i'the frown.
>
> (*KL*, 1.4.180–1)

The terms 'frontlet' and 'frown' show that Goneril embodies the af*front*. The word 'frontlet' may refer to a band with which Goneril shows some alleged headache, but it can also be considered as a metaphor for a wrinkled forehead, a metaphor confirmed by the word 'frown' that follows. For Lear, the headache is merely a pretext and some outrageous deceptive excuse.

After adopting a strategy of evasion, Regan and Goneril finally come to words. Imitating Cordelia once again, Goneril adopts a straightforward speech, which Lear again receives as insulting. There are no abusive words in Goneril's speech, just a few references to her father's age. Yet every one of her words amputates Lear of the members of his court, until it is reduced to only the Fool. When, like a child, Lear comes to tell Regan about his pain, he lists the outrages done to him as follows:

> She hath abated me of half my train,
> Looked black upon me, struck me with her tongue
> Most serpent-like, upon the very heart.
>
> (2.2.348–50)

Outrage is approached in physical terms ('abated', 'struck') that find their spectacular expression in the outrages done to Kent's body first, and to Gloucester's a little later. The English term 'injuries', used several times in the play (2.2.493; 3.1.17; 3.3.11), reflects this intersection of the symbolic and physical dimensions of aggression that causes both harm and insult.

Resistance to abuse

The play stages mechanisms of resistance to abuse epitomized by such words as 'endure' or 'patience'. Ironically, it is these mechanisms of resistance and avoidance that make the destructive enterprise 'worse than murder' by prolonging the torture.

The first mechanism of resistance is to deny the outrage, by questioning its reality. The absence of words opens the door to a euphemistic reception of the insult. In the Folio version, at the moment when Lear receives Cordelia's 'Nothing, my lord' (1.1.87), he tries to soften its offensive impact with the question 'Nothing?' (1.1.88). The Lear played by Laurence Olivier in Michael Elliott's film (1983) first pretends to hear nothing when he hears Cordelia's 'Nothing', tilting his head in a gesture that suggests he has not heard. With the question 'Nothing?' Lear both creates and denies the insult. Lear formulates this strategy of avoidance when he responds to the concerns of the Third Knight who notices a 'great abatement of kindness' (1.4.58):

> Thou but rememberest of mine own conception. I have perceived a most faint neglect of late, which I have rather blamed as mine own jealous curiosity than as a very pretence and purpose of unkindness. I will look further into't.
> (1.4.65–69)

Lear euphemizes the outrage by taking responsibility for it and postponing his reaction, Shakespeare here showing again that the outrage or insult exists only if you acknowledge it, only if you receive it as such.

The same mechanism of resistance appears when Lear discovers Kent in the stocks. Before acknowledging the violence of the outrage against him with the hyperbolic ''tis worse than murder' (2.2.213), Lear attempts to avoid it:

LEAR
   What's he that hath so much thy place mistook
   To set thee here?
KENT
                              It is both he and she,
   Your son and daughter.
LEAR
   No.
KENT
   Yes.
LEAR
   No, I say.
KENT
   I say, Yea.
(q) LEAR
   No, no, they would not.
KENT
   Yes, they have. (q)
LEAR
   By Jupiter, I swear no.
KENT
   By Juno, I swear ay.
LEAR
                              They durst not do't:
   They could not, would not do't: [...]
                              (2.2.202–13)

After first using humour as a shield by asking Kent if he is making a pastime of his shame ('Mak'st thou this shame thy pastime?', 2.2.197), Lear attempts to deny the outrage done to him.

Faced with Regan and Cornwall's insulting absence, Lear uses the same euphemistic technique by imagining that his guests are indeed suffering. 'No, but not yet, maybe he is not well' (2.2.294), he says, finding excuses for his hosts, until the sight of Kent in the stocks makes him regain his lucidity: 'this act persuades me / That this remotion of the Duke and her / Is practice only' (2.2.302–4). Once again, insult and deception ('practice') overlap.

Lear protects himself from insult by denying it when he ironically lists the offences that Regan has not (yet) done to him:

> No, Regan, thou shalt never have my curse.
> [...]
>   'Tis not in thee
> To grudge my pleasures, to cut off my train,
> To bandy hasty words, to scant my sizes
> And, in conclusion, to oppose the bolt
> Against my coming in.
>
>   (2.2.359–66)

As long as one denies the outrage, as long as one does not recognize it, the outrage does not exist. It is a matter of reception. This appears very clearly when Lear comments on Regan taking Goneril by the hand, which he sees as a sign of abuse:

LEAR
 O, Regan, will you take her by the hand?
GONERIL
 Why not by the hand, sir? How have I offended?
 All's not offence that indiscretion finds
 And dotage terms so.
       (*KL*, 2.2.383–6)

Goneril's words both deny and constitute the insult as she questions the presence of an offence ('How have I offended?')

while reducing her kingly father to the status of an old fool. According to her, Lear takes things ill and likes to see offence where there is none, which is confirmed when Regan describes her father as 'being apt to have his ear *abused*' (2.2.497). The word 'abused' means 'deceived', but it may also mean 'insulted' here. In *Lear*, outrage is described by Regan as 'the injuries that they [wilful men] themselves procure' (2.2.493).

There is another way for Lear to respond to abuse: the trial. By organizing, in 3.6 of the Quarto version, the imaginary trial of his daughters, the King seeks redress for the 'injury', i.e. for the injustices, wrongs and damage done to him. This is in vain, since the court lets the accused escape: 'False justicer, why hast thou let her 'scape?' (3.6.55).

There is yet another way of warding off insult: execration, the art of cursing, which Kenneth Gross has devoted a chapter to (*'King Lear* and the Register of Curse') in his book *Shakespeare's Noise*.[41] The expression 'violent outrage' finds its explicit manifestation in the outbursts of rage, in the verbal excesses that Lear indulges in. The storm scene is like the literalization of the 'out-rage', the outward sign of the inner devastation suffered by Lear. Lear is 'enraged' at the outrages done to him. 'The king is in high rage', says Gloucester (2.2.485), while Cordelia speaks of 'his ungoverned rage' (4.4.19). The term 'rage' here refers to both fury and madness. The fury ('rage', 3.2.1) of the elements is of course the outward manifestation of Lear's fury, but what rages outside also shows the 'out-r-age' that devastates the King. Lear's imprecations are merely a longer version of Gloucester's exclamation 'O cruel! O you gods' (3.7.69) when his eyes are gouged out.

Insult as subtraction

It may be surprising to associate two extremes of outrage, Cordelia's seemingly innocent 'nothing' and Gloucester's enucleation. Beyond the fact that these extremes both lead to nothingness, to emptiness (lack of words, lack of eyes), their joint analysis confirms that outrage exists only as an effect. Indeed, it is striking that Cordelia's innocent 'nothing' creates far more damage than Gloucester's plight, which is reinterpreted and becomes a punishment rather than an outrage, when Edgar says: 'The dark and vicious place where thee he got / Cost him his eyes' (5.3.170–1).

Only what is recognized as such is an insult. By juxtaposing the scene of insult between Kent and Oswald and the scene in which Lear discovers Kent, Shakespeare expresses the gap between the word of insult and the effect of insult, and between the inefficiency of saying and the efficiency of doing. With Kent and Oswald, we attend an insulting scene that has no effect, since at no point is Oswald truly outraged by Kent's verbal aggression. On the contrary, when Lear discovers Kent, the insulting effect occurs without any word of insult being uttered. *King Lear* stages the *insulting effect*, or the outrage effect as described by Larguèche, the destructive effect of the insult or affront that is 'worse than murder', because it calls into question and removes the very identity of the victim, leading him to loss of self and madness. Several critics, including Stanley Cavell, William Zak and, more recently, Ewan Fernie,[42] have described the sense of shame that pervades the play and takes hold of Lear, but also of Gloucester, who refers to the marker of shame through the word 'blush' (1.1.9), or the character of Edgar, whose disguise reveals the shame he feels. In *Shame in Shakespeare*, Fernie describes *King Lear* as 'a play of shame',[43] and we would like to explore how shame is articulated with insults. Larguèche analyzed the insulting effect in psychoanalytical terms that shed light on the trauma experienced by Lear. According to her, the insulting *effect* comes from the fact that the insulted person is exposed to the eyes of a third party 'under a negative image, by someone else, without being prepared for it'.[44] This 'exposure of oneself under a negative image'[45] leads to a feeling of shame. Larguèche notes that it is 'the tyrannical importance given to the image one offers of oneself'[46] that produces shame. Thus, 'what the insulted person would feel in the eyes of the third party would be a "social anxiety", an anxiety about the loss of esteem, which itself depends on [...] the "tyrannical importance given to the image one offers of oneself".[47] In the eyes of the insulted, the 'negative image' in which he is 'exposed' leads to disappointing the ego ideal. From this perspective, Kent's role is to maintain a certain self-esteem in the King. Thus, when Regan puts Kent in those stocks, the affront to Lear is all the greater because Kent was the last guarantee of his existence as a King. Lear is no longer a King, and the fact that he is told so in deed provokes a feeling of shame, a social as well as a narcissistic anguish. According to Larguèche:

> The unmasking to which the insulted person is subjected would consist of a real exposure, an exhibition, but precisely of the 'negative' side of himself, of what should remain hidden, the 'backside', thus resulting in his 'losing face'.[48]

This exposure or *mise à nu* in French is exactly what the Fool's comment expresses: 'thou gav'st them the rod and putt'st down thine own breeches' (1.4.164–5), an idea that crops up again in Gloucester's comparing a man to a worm (4.1.35) and in the play's evocation of nakedness (3.4.103–7). Both an infantile image and an expression of a world being turned upside-down, this image of Lear pulling down his breeches appears to be the emblem of the outrageous effect as we have just described it. All the affronts made to Lear contribute to revealing, to exhibiting his 'backside', his impotence. The symbolic castration suffered by Gloucester, when Cornwall and Regan pluck out his beard and then gouge out his eyes, seems to be the physical expression of the castration, the symbolic reduction or subtraction suffered by Lear throughout the play, especially when his daughters cut the number of his followers. The men Lear is deprived of are like the manly hairs Regan plucks out of Gloucester's chin. The term 'abuse' used nine times in the play[49] and the word 'ravish', which Gloucester uses when he says 'These hairs which thou dost ravish from my chin' (3.7.38), confirm the idea that what the play is about is '*violent* outrage' indeed.

'O you kind gods! / Cure this great breach in his abused nature' (4.7.14–15); 'I am mightily abused' (4.7.53), 'Do not abuse me' (4.7.77): Lear uses the word 'abuse' three times when he rediscovers Cordelia in Act 4. The recurrence of the word 'abuse' signals that *King Lear* is a story of insult and that at the source of this story of insult there is an error of interpretation and judgement. Lear has 'abused' himself by misunderstanding Cordelia's silence. The Fool explores the limits of outrage, the boundaries between insult and free speech. The role of the Fool is twofold when it comes to apprehending the outrages suffered by Lear: he both reveals and attenuates them. By teaching differences 'between a bitter fool and a sweet one' (1.4.134–5), the Fool reminds Lear of his former splendour, thus emphasizing his decline: 'Thou wast a pretty fellow when thou hadst no need to care for her frowning' (1.4.182–3). But if he emphasizes insults through his comments, the Fool is also a soothing presence who welcomes Lear into his world of Fools. On the heath, only the Fool remains to try to alleviate the King's suffering: 'None but the fool, who labours to outjest / His heart-struck injuries' (3.1.16–17). When the 'poor fool' disappears (5.3.304), whether it is the Fool or Cordelia, all sources of consolation disappear with him.

Epilogue: Shakespeare's theatre of insult

Shakespeare's drama is a theatre of insult.
Insults are at the centre of the crises dramatized in Shakespeare's plays, whether they constitute abuse, creating a 'world of hurt' in word or in action, or whether they are, in William B. Irvine's term, 'un-sults'.[1] From an excess of words to a lack of words, from ludic flyting to trauma, from mechanisms of rebellion to strategies of control, insults often lie at the heart of Shakespeare's dramatic art and challenge our contemporary sensibilities. Insults in Shakespeare's plays epitomize the ambivalence of the tongue as a source of pleasure and pain.

Beyond a cabinet of curiosities

Shakespearean insults are often considered as entertaining words that one can use out of context, mostly for fun. For example, a workshop organized at the 2016 World Shakespeare Congress in Stratford-London included a Shakespeare Karaoke that invited attendants to read strings of insults. Such a choice showed the theatrical potential of words of abuse that seem to be the perfect means to have people 'stand up for Shakespeare'. However, it was also emblematic of an approach to insults that mainly considers them as ludic objects. The same kind of approach can be found in the series of anthologies of Shakespeare's insults (Insults for Doctors, Insults for Lawyers, Insults for Teachers, etc.);[2] on insult mugs, fridge magnets, cushions, tablecloths, diaries, face-masks, socks, bandages, playing cards and calendars; and in the Shakespearean insults generator that is accessible on the Internet.[3] These examples evidence the pleasure that Shakespearean insults can generate, but they also constitute an approach to insults that leaves aside their instability and complexity, epitomized by the initial question raised in this book: 'No abuse?'

The aim of this book was to go beyond insults as a cabinet of linguistic curiosities to suggest that an in-depth understanding of Shakespearean insults in their dramatic and socio-historical contexts may illuminate not only words but also whole scenes and plays. Thus the volume has shown that many of Shakespeare's plays can be identified as *plays of insult*: from *Romeo and Juliet* and its pivotal 'villain' sequence to *King Lear*, the action of which originates in an abusive 'Nothing'; from *Much Ado About Nothing* and its devastating aborted marriage scene, to *Henry V*'s insulting gifts, the seventeen plays focused on in this book can all be regarded as plays *of* insults and plays *about* insults. While insult is destructive in some contexts, in others Shakespeare presents it as a great source of creativity and recreation, a speech game that can become a metadramatic device. The book has also showed the ways in which Shakespeare often combines several modes of insults in the same play, thus suggesting how words can both kill and please, and be a source of comedy and tragedy at the same time.

The main objective of this book has been to consider Shakespeare's art of insult in all its complexity, and to invite readers to revisit Shakespeare's plays from a perspective that interrogates the articulation of words and deeds. Focusing on some memorable scenes of insult, abusive mouths and insulting effects in the plays, the book will, I hope, shift how readers and spectators understand and read both Shakespeare's insults and plays.

Insults and the life of words

On stage, insults are given a voice and body. Thus gestures that accompany the emission or reception of insults are of key significance, whether actors follow convention or interpret them in novel ways. A raised fist or hand, a pointed finger, foaming at the mouth, or a reddened face can be the physical signals of abuse or, at least of the feelings it expresses, such as anger or despair. In *Passions of the Minde* (1601), Thomas Wright links language and passions, noting that certain types of language betray certain passions. By insulting, often accompanied by the physical symptoms of anger, one externalizes an emotion, which explains the spectacular dimension of this speech act.[4] Wright associates insult with anger when he mentions gaming:

> Play pregnantly proveth passions, for pride, choller, and covetousnes commonly wait upon great gamesters: some when they leese, ire and choler so inflameth them, that you would take them rather for bedlams than reasonable creatures; they sweare, curse, and crie, every word spoken against them, sufficeth to pick a quarrell, or deserveth (in their judgements) a buffet.[5]

The author also establishes equivalences between certain passions and certain types of voice:

> men in ire and wrath, shewe by their pronuntiation, the flame which lodgeth in their breasts. Wherefore Cato gave counsell, that souldiers, in the warre, should terrifie their enemies with vehement voyces and cries.[6]

But insult is not just an expression of anger. Wright sees insult in a different light when he argues that mockery is one of the manifestations of envy or pride:

> Certaine men entertain their company with scoffing, nipping, gibing and quipping: they think to have wonne a great

victorie, if in discovering some others defect, they can make the company laugh merrily: they will seeme to make much of you, but to the embracements of scorpions follow stinging tailes. This scoffing proceedeth from some, of meere simplicitie and foolishnes, as common jesters and therefore wise men weigh not such folies: others jeasts for recreation without harme, with no other intention, but onely to be merry: but those which especially ought to bee marked, and their company eschewed, so quip and nip, that they principally pretend to discredite, or shame those persons at whom they jeast: and this scoffing manner is most malitious, and it proceedeth from pride and envie.[7]

Wright distinguishes two categories of mockery: one that amuses and the other that hurts. The mocker is associated with the image of the scorpion, the word that stings. A certain type of mockery is associated with play and laughter but above all with spectacle. The mockery can work only if there is an audience that can show the success of a good word with their laughter. The playful and spectacular aspect of verbal attacks is explicitly underlined here. Insult is the spectacle of the word. Wright describes the ambivalence of insults that are an expression of violence but also a manifestation of conviviality and playfulness. With insults, the spectators waver between tears and laughter. Sometimes pale, sometimes red with anger, the insulter may show his emotion by biting his lips or giving murderous looks. The Elizabethan actor who played the insult must have been tempted to overdo it, showing the excesses of language through physical excesses. Shakespeare sometimes points to the physical effects of verbal violence in his plays. In *2 Henry VI*, we are given a glimpse of the performance of this verbal violence, when Suffolk delineates a phenomenology of cursing:

> Could curses kill, as doth the mandrake's groan
> I would invent as bitter searching terms,
> As curst, as harsh and horrible to hear,
> Delivered strongly through my fixed teeth,

With full as many signs of deadly hate,
As lean-faced Envy in her loathsome cave.
My tongue should stumble in mine earnest words,
Mine eyes should sparkle like the beaten flint,
My hair be fixed an end, as one distract;
Ay, every joint should seem to curse and ban.
(2H6, 3.2.310–19)

The insulter, by his or her excesses, resembles a madman[8] or mad woman who cannot be controlled.

On stage, all the nuances of insults may be performed by the actor or actress. The actor's splutters can be part of the physical and theatrical language of insult and may suggest that one is literally spitting one's words in the other's face. During a performance of *The Merchant of Venice* by the Royal Shakespeare Company in 1993, directed by David Thacker, the actor playing Gratiano (Mark Lockyer) conspicuously sputtered as he hurled insults at Shylock. Whether this physical sign was intended or not, natural or artificial, it expressed the hatred contained in these insults and became the anatomical expression of the abuse suffered by Shylock. An insulting gesture incorporated into the staging can become essential to the performance and interpretation of a play. For example, in Sam Mendes' 1993 production of *The Tempest*, Ariel (Simon Russell Beale) spat in Prospero's face (Alec McCowen) before leaving him, at the end of the play, a choice that completely changed the spectator's view of their relationship. Through this act and the insult it constituted, the farewell scene between Ariel and Prospero called for a reinterpretation of the entire play.

A director can also play on the discrepancies between sound and image, between the insulting words we hear and the smile that accompanies them. The BBC version of *Troilus and Cressida* plays on these discrepancies between sound and image when it shows Thersites cursing the whole of humanity while doing his laundry. The insult also takes shape in the theatre through the actor's voice. An insult can be whispered or shouted, which also implies a variety of movements and proxemic choices. Sometimes this vocal dimension of the insult is imposed by the text. In *Much Ado About Nothing*, as in the BBC version, Benedick must speak his insults to Claudio in a tone of confidence and secrecy that corresponds to the duelling mode. A controlled insult does not have the same effect on the spectator as a thunderous insult. The playwright gives indications as to the way the insults should be performed. For example, the text of *Henry V* indicates a discrepancy between tone and content, when Fluellen insults and humiliates Pistol in a most courteous manner, telling him 'God pless you Anchient Pistol, you scurvy lousy knave, God pless you!' (*H5*, 5.1.17–18). The mixture of polite addresses and insults forces the actor to insult courteously, with the potential for comedy entailed by this paradoxical tone. While Shakespeare plays on the comic discrepancy between the tone and the content of the insult, he also knows how to intensify the insult by integrating it into an apocalyptic atmosphere, as is the case in *King Lear* where the sound of curses finds its natural counterpart in the din of thunder.

Lingua, quo tendis?

'Tongue, where are you going?'[9]: such is the essential question that Shakespeare's theatre raises through its art of insults, a question that is extremely relevant in today's society. This question illustrates the ambivalence of the tongue in which the same word can be abusive or not and in which any word may prove offensive in a specific context. In Shakespeare's plays an 'if' can be a treasonous word causing Hastings' beheading in *Richard III* (3.4.73–5) and then become, according to Touchstone, 'the only peacemaker' (*AYL*, 5.4.101). There can be much vice or 'much virtue' in an 'if' (*AYL*, 5.4.101).

Our contemporary society is obsessed with and suffers from the offensive impact that words can have. The web has obviously become the playground of evil tongues and an easy medium for abuse, mockery, slander, verbal humiliation or hateful speech. In February 2019 in France, a group of journalists that went under the pseudonym 'LOL' on social networks was denounced for having harassed mainly female colleagues through that faceless, anonymous medium. The collective abuse, which took women as targets, was supposed to make the group 'laugh out loud'; it was supposed to be 'no abuse'. In fact, it seems that these words had a significant impact of various kinds. Contemporary politics has to deal with the way words must, may or can be controlled to avoid outrageous torrents of linguistic injuries left unpunished while preserving freedom of speech. Words have probably never had such an extensive, global power as they have today, at a time when they circulate quicker and at a wider scale than they ever have. In the all-virtual digital world, the power of words has never been so real, and words definitely act. In Shakespeare's period, the world was smaller; words' wings did not carry them as fast and far as they do today but Shakespeare's world was obsessed with the insulting impact of words too. Some of his plays, such as *Othello*, *The Merchant of Venice* or *The Taming of the Shrew*, and some of their sequences or productions can be offensive to our modern sensitivities. There is some potential insulting Shakespeare in Shakespeare's insults. When I work on Shakespeare's insults with my students now, I realize that words that seemed to be no abuse a few years ago have now become abuse. I remember a time when sharing the anti-Falstaffian insults was, to me at least, a benign pleasure; now I feel these anti-fat words may hurt. The insulting effect depends on the tongue that speaks but also on the ear that hears and on the circumstances of hearing. A seemingly innocuous word may cause a lot of harm. Praise may be a vector of abuse. Silence may hurt. Shakespeare's theatre offers much food for thought on this essential instability, unpredictability and reversibility of words. When Falstaff is confronted with the newly kinged Hal at the end of *2 Henry IV*, he brutally discovers that the circumstances of enunciation have changed. When he was speaking to Hal, words did not hurt; now that Hal is the King, the context has changed and words are to be received differently.

'I know thee not, old man' (5.5.46): here are probably some of the most insulting words in the whole Shakespearean corpus. Hearing these words, Falstaff protects himself by pretending it is still part of the game. Refusing to hear, he declares to his companions: 'This that *you* heard was but a colour' (*2H4*, 5.5.84–5). Yet the insulting effect will resurface in *Henry V*, and kill him. 'No abuse?' Yes, abuse, after all.

NOTES

Introduction

1 'Abutor' in Thomas Cooper, *Thesaurus Linguae Romanae et Britannicae* [1565] (London, 1578, STC (2nd ed.) / 5688). See the same entry in Thomas Thomas, *Dictionarium Linguae Latinae et Anglicanae* (London, 1587, STC (2nd ed.) / 24008).

2 George Puttenham, *The Arte of English Poesie* (London, 1589, STC (2nd ed.) / 20519.5), 150.

3 John Florio, *A World of Words. Words or Most Copious, and Exact Dictionarie in Italian and English* (London, 1598, STC (2nd ed.) / 11098).

4 The *Oxford English Dictionary Online* will be referred to as *OED* throughout the book.

5 *OED*, Abuse, 5.

6 Ibid., 7.

7 See J. McLaverty, 'No abuse: The Prince and Falstaff in the tavern scenes of *Henry IV*', *Shakespeare Survey* 34 (1981): 105–10, 106–7.

8 Ibid., 105.

9 Évelyne Larguèche, *L'effet injure. De la pragmatique à la psychanalyse*, coll. 'Voix nouvelles en psychanalyse' (Paris: PUF, 1983). Lynne Magnusson describes the pragmatic approach as: 'the discipline that studies how communication works within social contexts', in *Shakespeare and Social Dialogue, Dramatic Language and Elizabethan Letters* (Cambridge: Cambridge University Press, 1999), 143.

10 See Claude Paradin, *Devises Heroïques* [1557], Introduction by Alison Saunders (Aldershot: Scolar Press, 1989), 109–10.

11 See the English version, Claude Paradin, *The Heroicall Devises of M. Claudius Paradin* (London, 1591, STC (2nd ed.) / 19183), 137–8.

12 George Wither, *A Collection of Emblemes* [1635], Introduction by Michael Bath (Aldershot: Scolar Press, 1989), Book 1, 42.

13 Mikhail Bakhtin, *Rabelais and His World* [1965], trans. Hélène Iswolsky (Bloomington and Indianapolis: Indiana University Press, 1984), 16.

14 Thomas, *Dictionarium*, 'Insulto'.

15 Florio, *A World of Words*, 'Insultare'.

16 Richard Perceval, *Dictionary in Spanish and English* (London, 1599, STC (2nd ed.) / 19620), 'Insultár'.

17 Randle Cotgrave, *A Dictionary of the French and English Tongues* (London, 1611, STC (2nd ed.) / 5830), 'Insulter'.

18 Claude Hollyband, *Dictionary French and English* (London, 1593, STC (2nd ed.) / 6737), 'Injure'.

19 Cotgrave, 'S'entr'injurier', 'injurier'.

20 On thumb-biting, see Miranda Fay Thomas, *Shakespeare's Body Language. Shaming Gestures and Gender Politics on the Renaissance Stage* (London and New York: Bloomsbury. The Arden Shakespeare, 2020), Chapter 1, 23–43. See also, Nathalie Vienne-Guerrin, *Shakespeare's Insults: A Pragmatic Dictionary* (London and New York: Bloomsbury. The Arden Shakespeare, 2016), 403–7. On this scene, see Chapter 3 of this book.

21 John Langshaw Austin, *How to Do Things with Words* (Oxford: Oxford University Press, 1962).

22 Pierre Guiraud, *Les Gros mots* (Paris: PUF, 1975), 34.

23 Ibid., 35.

24 On spitting, see Thomas, *Shakespeare's Body Language*, Chapters 3 and 4, 71–113.

25 Évelyne Larguèche, *Injure et sexualité. Le corps du délit* (Paris: PUF, 1997), 95.

26 Ibid., 95.

27 Ibid., 78.

28 Ibid., 109.

29 Ibid., 136.
30 This idea is explored in the collection of essays edited by Didier Girard and Jonathan Pollock, *Invectives, Quand le corps reprend la parole* (Perpignan: Presses Universitaires de Perpignan, 2006).
31 Pierre Bourdieu, *Language and Symbolic Power* (Cambridge: Polity Press, 1992), 105.
32 Ibid., 105–6.
33 Ibid., 107.
34 Ibid., 109.
35 Ibid., 116.
36 Ibid., 72.
37 Judith Butler, *Excitable Speech. A Politics of the Performative* (New York: Routledge, 1997), 4–5.
38 Jean-Jacques Lecercle and Denise Riley, *The Force of Language* (Houndmills: Palgrave, 2004), 47. Another version of Denise Riley's chapter on 'bad words' was published under the title 'Malediction' in her monograph, *Impersonal Passion. Language as Affect* (Durham and London: Duke University Press, 2005), 9–27.
39 William B. Irvine, *A Slap in the Face. Why Insults Hurt – And Why They Should Not* (Oxford: Oxford University Press, 2013), 96.
40 *Much Ado About Nothing*, ed. Claire McEachern. The Arden Shakespeare, Third Series (London and New York: Bloomsbury, 2007), 303.
41 Kenneth Gross, *Shakespeare's Noise* (Chicago and London: The University of Chicago Press, 2001), 1; 209 (note 1).
42 All references to the Bible are taken from *The Geneva Bible: A Facsimile of the 1560 Edition*. With an introduction by Lloyd E. Berry (Madison: University of Wisconsin Press, 1969). To have a broader panorama of the tongue, see Nathalie Vienne-Guerrin, *The Unruly Tongue in Early Modern England. Three Treatises* (Lanham: Fairleigh Dickinson University Press, 2012).
43 See Nathalie Vienne-Guerrin, 'Le miel et le fiel: des excès de bouche dans *Timon of Athens*', in *Shakespeare et l'excès*, Actes

du Congrès 2007 de la Société Française Shakespeare, ed. Pierre Kapitaniak and Jean-Michel Déprats, 206–22. https://journals.openedition.org/shakespeare/1038 (accessed 20 July 2021).

44 Russ McDonald, *Shakespeare and the Arts of Language* (Oxford: Oxford University Press, 2001), Chapter 8, 'Words effectual, Speech Unable', 164–92.

45 See Andreas H. Jucker and Irma Taavitsainen, 'Diachronic Speech Act Analysis. Insults from Flyting to Flaming', *Journal of Historical Pragmatics* 1, no. 1 (2000): 67–95, 84–7.

46 See Vienne-Guerrin, *The Unruly Tongue*, xxii.

47 Desiderius Erasmus, *Lingua*, trans. Elaine Fantham, in *Collected Works of Erasmus* 29 (Toronto: University of Toronto Press, 1989), 249–412, 365 (LB IV 722D / ASD IV-1 330). Quoted by Carla Mazzio, 'Sins of the Tongue,' in David Hillman and Carla Mazzio, eds, *The Body in Parts. Fantasies of Corporeality in Early Modern Europe* (New York and London: Routledge, 1997), 52–79, 53.

48 Thomas Adams, 'The Taming of the Tongue', in *The Sacrifice of Thankefulnesse A Sermon Preached at Pauls Crosse* [...] (London, 1616, STC (snd ed.) / 125), 22. In *The Works of Thomas Adams*, vol. 3 (Eureka: Tanski Publications, 1998), 10–22, 10, the word is spelt 'insubjectable'. Quoted by Mazzio, 54.

49 Priscilla Bawcutt, 'The Art of Flyting', *Scottish Literary Journal* 10, no. 2 (1983): 5–24, 8.

50 See *William Dunbar: The Complete Works*, ed. John Conlee (Kalamazoo: Medieval Institute Publications, Western Michigan University, 2004), Poem 83, 181–98.

51 Tom Scott, *Dunbar, A Critical Exposition of the Poems* (Edinburgh, London: Oliver and Boyd, 1966), 175.

52 Margaret Galway, 'Flyting in Shakspere's [sic] Comedies', *The Shakespeare Association Bulletin* 10, no. 4 (October 1935): 183–91.

53 On 'heroic flyting', see Ward Parks, 'Flyting, Sounding, Debate. Three Verbal Contest Genres', *Poetics Today* 7, no. 3 (1986): 439–54; 'Flyting and Fighting: Pathways in the Realization of the Epic Contest', *Neophilologus* 70 (1986): 292–306; 'The Flyting Speech in Traditional Heroic Narrative', *Neophilologus* 71 (1987): 285–95; 'The Flyting Contract and

Adversarial Patterning in the Alliterative *Morte Arthure*', in *Traditions and Innovations, Essays on British Literature of the Middle Ages and the Renaissance*, ed. David G. Allen and Robert A. White (Newark: University of Delaware Press, 1990), 59–74; *Verbal Dueling in Heroic Narrative, the Homeric and Old English Traditions* (Princeton: Princeton University Press, 1990).

54 Johan Huizinga, *Homo Ludens. A Study of the Play-Element in Culture* (New York: Angelico Press, reprint of the first edition published by Routledge and Kegan Paul [1949], 2006), 84.

55 W. H. Auden, *The Dyer's Hand and Other Essays* (London: Faber and Faber, 1963), 383.

56 See Jerome Neu, *Sticks and Stones. The Philosophy of Insults* (Oxford: Oxford University Press, 2008), in which Chapter 3 focuses on 'Insult in play and ritual' (57–81) and Chapter 5 focuses on the 'language of abuse', and notably on 'Shakespearean thoughts in insults' (113–35), esp. 121–3.

57 Larguèche, *Injure et sexualité*, 95.

58 See Bridget Escolme, *Emotional Excess on the Shakespearean Stage: Passion's Slaves* (London: Bloomsbury, 2013), 9.

59 Keir Elam, *Shakespeare's Universe of Discourse. Language-Games in the Comedies* (Cambridge: Cambridge University Press, 1984), 9.

60 Keith Allan and Kate Burridge, *Forbidden Words, Taboo and the Censuring of Language* (Cambridge: Cambridge University Press, 2006), 86–7.

61 Geoffrey Hughes, *An Encyclopedia of Swearing. The Social History of Oaths, Profanity, Foul Language, and Ethnic Slurs in the English-Speaking World* (Armonk, NY: M.E. Sharpe, 2006), 176–7.

62 Irvine, *A Slap in the Face*, Chapter 3, 71–89, '*un-sults*', 89.

63 Frank Warnke, 'Amorous Agon, Erotic Flyting: Some Play-motifs in the Literature of Love', in *Auctor Ludens: Essays on Play in Literature*, ed. Gerald Guinness and Andrew Hurley (Philadelphia: J. Benjamin, 1986), 99–112.

64 Parks, Walter Ward. *Verbal Dueling in Heroic Narrative, the Homeric and Old English Traditions* (Princeton: Princeton University Press, 1990), 162.

65 Huizinga, *Homo Ludens*, 84.

Chapter 1

1. Galway, 'Flyting', 183–91.
2. C. S. Lewis, *Studies in Words* (Cambridge: Cambridge at the University Press, 1960), 21–3.
3. See Laroque, François, 'Shakespeare's "Battle of Carnival and Lent". The Falstaff Scenes reconsidered' (*1 & 2 Henry IV*), in *Shakespeare and Carnival, after Bakhtin*, ed. Ronald Knowles (Houndmills: Macmillan, 1998), 83–96; see Nathalie Vienne-Guerrin, 'Les jeux de l'injure dans *Henry IV*', in *Shakespeare et le Jeu*, ed. Pierre Kapitaniak, Société Française Shakespeare, 2005, 185–99. https://journals.openedition.org/shakespeare/713 (accessed 20 July 2021). See Pieter Bruegel's *The Battle of Carnival and Lent* (1559).
4. Elam, *Shakespeare's Universe of Discourse*, 311.
5. *The Seconde Tome of Homelyes* (London, 1563, STC (2nd ed.) / 13664), 'An Homyly against Gluttonie and Dronkennes', 103^v–112^r, 110^{rv}.
6. See Michel Jeanneret, *A Feast of Words: Banquets and Table Talk in the Renaissance*, trans. Jeremy Whiteley and Emma Hughes (Chicago: The University of Chicago Press; Cambridge: Polity Press, 1991). In French, *Des Mets et des Mots. Banquets et propos de tables à la Renaissance* (Paris: Corti, 1987).
7. See Jonathan Hall, 'The Evacuations of Falstaff', in *Shakespeare and Carnival. After Bakhtin*, ed. Ronald Knowles (Houndmills: Macmillan, 1998), 123–51; Nathalie Vienne-Guerrin, '"Castalian King Urinal Hector of Greece": la "langue latrine" dans *The Merry Wives of Windsor*', in *Langue et Altérité dans la culture de la Renaissance / Language and Otherness in Renaissance Culture*, ed. Ann Lecercle and Yan Brailowsky (Nanterre: Presses Universitaires de Paris Ouest, 2008), 15–29. See Rosemary Kegl, '"The adoption of abominable terms": The Insults That Shape Windsor's Middle Class', *English Literary History* 61 (1994): 253–78.
8. See Chapter 7 of this book.
9. See Jeanneret, *Des Mots et des Mets*.

10 Puttenham, *The Arte of English Poesie*, 201–6.
11 See *King Henry IV Part 1*, ed. A. R. Humphreys, Arden Edition (London and New York: Routledge, 1960), 104.
12 See Georges Vigarello, *The Metamorphoses of Fat. A History of Obesity*, trans. C. Jon Delogu (New York: Columbia University Press, 2013).
13 The expression is oxymoronic as the 'ruffians' of the Morality Plays were usually young.
14 The word 'ruffian' refers to the Devil of the Morality Plays. Moreover, when Hal tells Falstaff that 'These lies are like their father that begets them, gross as a mountain, open, palpable' (2.4.218–19), he compares him to the Devil who proverbially was the father of lies. Etymologically, the word 'devil' (from the Latin *diabolus* and the Greek *diabolos*) refers to calumny.
15 See Bakhtin, *Rabelais and His World*, 192–3: 'What is the thematic content of the oaths? It is mainly the rending of the human body. Swearing was mostly done in the name of the members and the organs of the divine body: the Lord's body, his head, blood, wounds, bowels; or in name of the relics of saints and martyrs – feet, hands, fingers – which were preserved in churches. The most improper and sinful oaths were those invoking the body of the Lord and its various parts, and these were precisely oaths most frequently used.'
16 See Stephen Hawes, *The Co[n]vercyon of Swerers* (London, 1509, STC (2nd ed.) / 12943), a poem in which Christ says: 'Beholde your servauntes how they do tere me / By cruell othes now upon every syde / Aboute the worlde launcynge my woundes wyde' (Aii^v).
17 Eight out of the eleven occurrences in the whole Shakespearean corpus. On Swearing in Shakespeare's plays, see Ashley Montague, *The Anatomy of Swearing* [1967] (Philadelphia: University of Pennsylvania Press, 2001), Chapter 8: 'Swearing in Shakespeare', 136–53; Geoffrey Hughes, *Swearing. A Social History of Foul Language, Oaths and Profanity in English* (Oxford: Blackwell, 1991), 108–19; Melissa Mohr, *Holy Sh*t. A Brief History of Swearing* (Oxford: Oxford University Press, 2013), 166–9.

18 I borrow the expression from Bruce R. Smith in *The Acoustic World of Early Modern England. Attending to the O-Factor* (Chicago and London: The University of Chicago Press, 1999), Chapter 3, 49–95.

19 Bakhtin, *Rabelais and His World*, 411.

20 See Eric Partridge, *Shakespeare's Bawdy* (London and New York: Routledge, 1947).

21 On *copia*, see McDonald, *Shakespeare and the Arts of Language*, 27–9.

22 Puttenham, *The Arte of English Poesie*, 159–61, 159. On this figure of lying, see Andrew Hadfield, *Lying in Early Modern English Culture. From the Oath of Supremacy to the Oath of Allegiance* (Cambridge: Cambridge University Press, 2017), 190.

23 Bakhtin, *Rabelais and His World*, 16; 165 & ff; 248–9; 409; 415–21; 432; 459 & ff.

24 On Bardolph's nose, see Ariane M. Balizet, '"Amend Thy Face": Contagion and Disgust in the Henriad', in *Contagion and the Shakespearean Stage*, ed. Darryl Chalk and Mary Floyd-Wilson (Cham: Palgrave Macmillan, 2019), 127–45.

25 Larguèche, *L'effet injure*, 69–95.

26 See Jonathan Sawday's *The Body Emblazoned. Dissection and the Human Body in Renaissance Culture* (London and New York: Routledge, 1995).

27 Bakhtin, *Rabelais and His World*, 432.

28 Neil Rhodes, *Elizabethan Grotesque* (London, Boston and Henley: Routledge & Kegan, 1980), 22. According to Rhodes, Shakespeare demonstrates the influence of Thomas Nashe whose satirical texts and notably his quarrel with Harvey in *Have With You to Saffron Walden*, are teeming with that type of insult. Rhodes also notes that 'These unsavoury similes are the staple of the low style in Elizabethan comic prose and hence of the grotesque' (101).

29 Patricia Parker, *Shakespeare from the Margins, Language, Culture, Context* (Chicago: The University of Chicago Press, 1996).

30 See 'You whoreson cur!' (2.1.39), 'You dog!' (2.1.49), 'You cur!' (2.1.51), 'O thou damned cur!' (2.1.83), 'you whoreson

indistinguishable cur' (5.1.27–8). The canine metaphor is developed when Achilles calls him 'Thou core of envy' (5.1.4) and when Patroclus calls him 'thou damnable box of envy' (5.1.24). According to Della Porta, the dog, with his fangs, represents envy. See Giambattista della Porta, *De Humane Physionomonia* [1586] (Paris: Aux Amateurs de Livres, 1990), 264: 'Invidi ad canes'.

31 On railing, see Maria Teresa Micaela Prendergast, *Railing, Reviling, and Invective in English Literary Culture, 1588–1617: The Anti-Poetics of Theater and Print* (Burlington, VT: Ashgate, 2012), 1–48.

32 On Homer's Thersites, see Nancy Worman, *Abusive Mouths in Classical Athens* (Cambridge: Cambridge University Press: 2008), where Thersites is described as a 'quintessential low-status abuser' (53), an embodiment of 'grudge' and 'envy' (166, note 43).

33 Only Ajax refuses to grant him the licence of the Fool: 'I shall cut out your tongue' (*TC*, 2.1.107).

34 In *Troilus and Cressida* warlike action appears as a form of consumption, notably in the dialogue between Achilles and Hector in 4.5. See David Hillman, 'The Gastric Epic: *Troilus and Cressida*', *Shakespeare Quarterly* 48, no. 3 (1997): 295–313.

35 'Strikes him' (*TC*, 2.1.11), 'Beats him' (*TC*, 2.1.39; 51).

36 Irvine, *A Slap in the Face*, 63.

37 'The plague of Greece upon thee!' (2.1.11), 'A red murrain o'thy jade's tricks!' (2.1.18), 'I would thou didst itch from head to foot. An I had the scratching of thee, I would make thee the loathsomest scab in Greece' (2.1.25–7), 'thou core of envy' (5.1.4), 'thou crusty batch of nature' (5.1.5), 'Now, the rotten diseases of the south, guts-griping, ruptures, catarrhs, loads o' gravel i'th' back, lethargies, cold palsies, raw eyes, dirt-rotten livers, wheezing lungs, bladders full of imposthume, sciaticas, limekilns i'th' palm, incurable bone-ache and the rivelled fee-simple of the tetter, take and take again such preposterous discoveries!' (5.1.17–23).

38 'Thou mongrel beef-witted lord' (2.1.11–12), 'Thou sodden-witted lord, thou hast no more brain than I have in my elbows;

an asinico may tutor thee. Thou scurvy valiant ass' (2.1.42–4), 'Lo, lo, lo, lo, what modicums of wit he utters! His evasions have ears thus long. I have bobbed his brain more than he has beat my bones. I will buy nine sparrows for a penny, and his pia mater is not worth the ninth part of a sparrow' (2.1.66–70), 'This Ajax [...] has not so much wit [...] as will stop the eye of Helen's needle' (2.1.74–8), 'A great deal of your wit, too, lies in your sinews, or else there be liars' (2.1.96–7), '(Ajax. I shall cut out your tongue.) Thersites. 'Tis no matter. I shall speak as much wit as thou afterwards' (2.1.107–9), 'Let me carry another [letter] to his horse, for that's the more capable creature' (3.3.307–8).

39 See Sawday, *The Body Emblazoned*.

40 See also 'Fragment' (*TC*, 5.1.8).

41 Homer, *Iliad*. Books 1–12, trans. A. T. Murray, rev. William F. Wyatt (Loeb Classical Library, Cambridge, MA: Harvard University Press, 1999), Book 2, lines 198–277, 74–81.

42 T. McAlindon, 'Language, Style and Meaning in *Troilus and Cressida*', *PMLA* 84, no. 1 (1969): 29–43, 38.

43 Puttenham, *The Arte of English Poesie*, 216.

44 See *TC*, 1.2.177–8: 'I'll tell you them all by their names as they pass by'.

45 John Harington, *A New Discourse of a Stale Subject Called the Metamorphosis of Ajax* [1596], ed. Elizabeth Story Donno (New York: Columbia University Press, 1962).

46 For more on 'Ajax' as an insult, see Vienne-Guerrin, *Dictionary*, 7–8.

47 Worman, *Abusive Mouths in Classical Athens*.

48 The figure of Actaeon is regularly associated with flattery. See Nathalie Vienne-Guerrin, '*Coriolanus* or the "Arraignment of an Unruly Tongue"', in Coriolan *de William Shakespeare. Langages, Interprétations, Politique(s)*, ed. Richard Hillman (Tours: Presses universitaires François-Rabelais, 2007), 133–53, 139–42.

49 See Vienne-Guerrin, *The Unruly Tongue*.

50 On reciprocal consumption, see Daniel W. Ross, '"What a number of men eats Timon": Consumption in *Timon of Athens*',

Iowa State Journal of Research 59, no. 3 (February, 1985): 273–84.

51 See C. H. Hobday, 'Why the Sweets Melted: A Study in Shakespeare's Imagery', *Shakespeare Quarterly* 16, no. 1 (Winter 1965): 3–17.

52 Robert C. Elliott, *The Power of Satire: Magic, Ritual, Art* (Princeton: Princeton University Press, 1960), 156.

53 Elliott, *The Power of Satire*, 159.

54 Richard Fly, *Shakespeare's Mediated World* (Amherst: University of Massachusetts Press, 1976), 119–42.

55 *The Riverside Shakespeare*, General and textual editors, G. Blakemore Evans, with the assistance of J. J. M. Tobin, 2nd ed. (Boston, NY: Houghton Mifflin Company, 1997), 1491.

56 On Shakespeare and hate, see Peter Kishore Saval, *Shakespeare in Hate. Emotions, Passions, Selfhood* (London: Routledge, 2016).

57 Claude Gaignebet and Marie-Claude Perier, 'L'homme et l'excretum: de l'exécré à l'excrété', in *Histoire des Mœurs*, ed. Jean Poirier, vol. 1 (Paris: La Pléiade, 1990), 831–93.

58 On the meaning of gargoyles to express the sins of the tongue, see Éric Beaumatin and Michel Garcia, eds, *L'Invective au Moyen Âge, Atalaya, Revue Française d'Études Médiévales Hispaniques* 5 (1994) (Paris: Presses de la Sorbonne Nouvelle, 1995), 262.

59 Nathalie Vienne-Guerrin, '*Coriolanus* or the "Arraignment of an Unruly Tongue"', 140.

60 See Clifford Davidson, '*Timon of Athens*: The Iconography of False Friendship', *The Huntington Library Quarterly* 43, no. 3 (Summer 1980): 181–200.

61 See Plutarch's 'How to tell a flatterer from a friend' ('Quomodo adulator ab amico internoscatur'), in *Moralia* 1, trans. Frank Cole Babbitt (Loeb Classical Library, Cambridge, MA: Harvard; London: Heinemann, 1927, repr. 1949), 263–395 (48E–74E).

62 Geffrey Whitney, *A Choice of Emblemes* [1586], introduction John Manning (Aldershot: Scolar Press, 1989), 147.

63 Elliott, *The Power of Satire*, 159.

64 Harold Fisch, 'Shakespeare and the Language of Gesture', *Shakespeare Studies* XIX (1987): 239–51, 246.

65 Gross, *Shakespeare's Noise*, '*King Lear* and The Register of Curse', 161–92, 163: 'By an eerie, punning logic, both curses and those who curse join the ranks of the persons whom the Elizabethans called "cursitors"'.

66 About 'dirae', see Puttenham, *The Arte of English Poesie*, Chapter XXIX, 46.

67 A crux: 'sour words' is 'four words' in F.

68 John Jowett, ed., *The Life of Timon of Athens* (Oxford: Oxford University Press, 2004), 315.

69 See *Aesop's Fables*, trans. Laura Gibbs (Oxford: Oxford World's Classics, 2002); 'Fable of the Satyr and his Guest', 173–4. See Whitney, *A Choice of Emblemes*, 160 ('Bilingues Cavendi').

70 Lindsay Watson, *Arae. The Curse Poetry of Antiquity* (Leeds: Francis Cairns, 1991).

Chapter 2

1 Warnke, 'Amorous Agon'.

2 Baldassare Castiglione, *The Courtyer*, originally published in 1528, trans. Sir T. Toby (London, 1561, STC (2nd. ed. / 4778)), Book 2, that partly focuses on 'merie Jestes and Pranckes', Tiii^v.

3 Ibid., Tiii^v–Tiv^r.

4 On repartee, see Irvine, *A Slap in the Face*, 9.

5 Castiglione, *The Courtyer*, Book 2, Tiii^v.

6 On this pun on 'suitor' and 'shooter', see *LLL*, 4.1.107–27.

7 C. L. Barber, *Shakespeare's Festive Comedy, A Study of Dramatic Form and Its Relation to Social Custom* (Princeton, NJ: Princeton University Press, 1972 [1959]), 6–7.

8 Ibid.

9 Warnke, 'Amorous Agon', 99. The italics are original.

10 On 'Double Talk', see McDonald, *Shakespeare and the Arts of Language*, Chapter 7, 137–63.

11   Warnke, 'Amorous Agon', 106.
12   Skiles Howard, *The Politics of Courtly Dancing in Early Modern England* (Amherst: University of Massachusetts Press, 1998), 86–7.
13   See Keith Allan and Kate Burridge, *Euphemism and Dysphemism, Language Used as Shield and Weapon* (New York, Oxford: Oxford University Press, 1991).
14   William Lyly, *A Shorte Introduction of Latin Grammar* (London, 1558, STC (2nd ed.) / 15613.3.), Civ^v. See *Much Ado About Nothing*, ed. McEachern, 257.
15   On civility and courtesy, see Anna Bryson, *From Courtesy to Civility. Changing Codes of Conduct in Early Modern England* (Oxford Clarendon Press: Oxford University Press, 1998).
16   Giovanni Della Casa, *Galateo* (London, 1576, STC (2nd ed.) / 4738), 25.
17   For a linguistic study on courtesy and Shakespeare, see Bianca Dell Villano, *Using the Devil with Courtesy: Shakespeare and the Language of (Im)Politeness* (Bern: Peter Lang, 2018).
18   Elliot Krieger, *A Marxist Study of Shakespeare's Comedies* (London and Basingstoke: The MacMillan Press, 1979), 40.
19   Barber, *Shakespeare's Festive Comedy*, 248–57 (Chapter on *Twelfth Night* entitled 'Liberty testing courtesy').
20   Della Casa, *Galateo*, 84.
21   See Gross, *Shakespeare's Noise*.
22   On this 'noise' on screen, see Nathalie Vienne-Guerrin, '"The noise they make" in *A Midsummer Night's Dream* on Screen', in *Shakespeare on Screen*: A Midsummer Night's Dream, ed. Sarah Hatchuel and Nathalie Vienne-Guerrin (Rouen: Publications de l'Université de Rouen, 2004), 87–99.
23   Galway, 'Flyting', 185.
24   Patricia Parker, 'Rude mechanicals', in *Subject and Object in Renaissance Culture*, ed. Margreta de Grazia, Maureen Quilligan, and Peter Stallybrass (Cambridge: Cambridge University Press, 1996), 43–82; Parker, *Shakespeare from the Margins*, Chapter 3, '"Rude mechanicals": *A Midsummer Night's Dream* and Shakespearean Joinery', 83–115.

25 Della Casa, *Galateo*, 62–3.
26 Ibid., 64.
27 Ibid., 65.
28 Castiglione, *The Courtyer*, Book 3, Ii ii^v.
29 Ibid., Ii iii^v.

Chapter 3

1 See François Billacois, *Le Duel dans la société française des XVIè et XVIIè siècles* (Paris: Éditions de l'École des Hautes Études en Sciences Sociales, 1986), 49. Billacois notes that Elizabeth presided over one of these trials in 1571. One finds an aborted trial by combat at the beginning of *Richard II*.

2 James I, A Publication of His Maties Edict and Severe Censure Against Private Combats and Combatants (London, 1613, STC (2nd ed.) / 8498.5.). See Francis Bacon, *The Charge of Francis Bacon Against duels* (London, 1614).

3 Benjamin Jonson, *The Alchemist*, in *The Cambridge Edition of the Works of Ben Jonson*, ed. David Bevington, Martin Butler and Ian Donaldson (Cambridge: Cambridge University Press, 2012), vol. 3, 626, 2.6.66–9.

4 William Segar [Richard Jones], *The Booke of Honour and Armes* (London, 1590, STC (2nd ed.) / 22163).

5 Silver George, *Paradoxes of Defense* (London, 1599, STC (2nd ed.) / 22554).

6 Giacomo Di Grassi, *His True Arte of Defence* (London, 1594, STC (2nd ed.) / 12190).

7 Vincentio Saviolo, *His Practise, in two Bookes* (London, 1595, STC (2nd. ed.) / 21789).

8 Billacois, *Le Duel dans la société française*, 21.

9 *Romeo and Juliet*, ed. René Weis, Arden Shakespeare, Third Series (London: Bloomsbury, 2012), 124.

10 Thomas, *Shakespeare's Body Language*. Chapter 1, 'Thumb-biting: Performing Toxic Masculinity in *Romeo and Juliet*', 23–43.

11 *Romeo and Juliet*, ed. Jill L. Levenson (Oxford: Oxford University Press, 2000), 146, note 39.
12 Vienne-Guerrin, *Dictionary*, 270–2.
13 Saviolo, *His Practise,* B2^r.
14 Saviolo, *His Practise*, 'Address to the Reader', B2^r.
15 Cotgrave, *A Dictionary of the French and English Tongues*, Kkk^r.
16 Hughes, *An Encyclopedia of Swearing*, 39.
17 About this gesture, see N. Vienne-Guerrin, *Dictionary*, 186–8; Miranday Fay Thomas, *Shakespeare's Body Language*, Chapter 2, 'Figging: Spanish Anxieties and *Ancient* Grudges in Pistol's *Henriad*', 45–69.
18 Saviolo, *His Practise*, B2^v.
19 Ibid.
20 Markku Peltonen, *The Duel in Early Modern England. Civility, Politeness and Honour* (Cambridge: Cambridge University Press, 2003), 48.
21 Saviolo, *His Practise*, 12^{rv} (or sig. E3^{rv}). Pages are numbered in several ways in this book.
22 Ibid., O3^v–O4^r.
23 Ibid., O3^v.
24 Ibid., P2^r.
25 Ibid., P3^r.
26 Ibid.
27 Ibid., P3^v.
28 Ibid., P2^v.
29 See Samuel Rowlands' poem on the 'Odious quarreller', in *Looke to It: For, Ile Stabbe ye* (London, 1604, STC (2nd ed.) / 21398), D3^r.
30 Saviolo, *His Practise*, R3^v.
31 Ibid., R3^v–R4^r.
32 Ibid., R4^r.
33 Segar, *The Booke of Honor and Armes*, 18.
34 Peltonen, *The Duel in Early Modern England,* 47–8, quoting from Simon Robson, *The Courte of Civill Courtesie* (London, 1577, STC (2nd ed.) / 21134.5), 24.

35 See Vienne-Guerrin, *Dictionary*, 270–2.
36 Saviolo, *His Practise*, R4ᵛ–Sʳ.
37 On lying as an insult, see Hadfield, *Lying in Early Modern English Culture*, 185.
38 Saviolo, *His Practise*, Sʳ–Sᵛ.
39 Ibid., Sᵛ.
40 Ibid., V4ᵛ.
41 'That he that will parte two that are fighting, must go between them both, having great regarde that he neither hindreth one more than the other; nor suffereth the one more to endanger his enemie than the other' (Saviolo, *His Practise*, R2ʳ).
42 Saviolo, *His Practise*, Z4ʳ.
43 *As You Like It*, ed. Juliet Dusinberre, The Arden Shakespeare, Third Series (London: Thomson Learning, 2006), 337.
44 Saviolo, *His Practise*, Sᵛ.
45 Ibid., S2ʳ.
46 Ibid., S2ᵛ–T4ᵛ.
47 On the parody of duelling manuals, see Hadfield, *Lying in Early Modern Culture*, 210–11.
48 Saviolo, *His Practise*, S2ʳ. These categories of lies are also enumerated in the first book of Segar's *Booke of Honor and Armes*, 5–12.
49 Saviolo, *His Practise*, Cc3ʳ⁻ᵛ.
50 Ibid., Ff1ᵛ–Gg3ʳ.
51 John Northbrooke, *A Treatise Wherein Dicing, Dauncing, Vaine Plaies or Enterludes with Other Idle Pastimes, etc. Commonly Used on the Sabboth Day, Are Reprooved, by the Authoritie of the Worde of God and Auncient Writers* (London, 1577, STC (2nd ed.) / 18670), in the address to the 'Christian and Faithful Reader', n.p.
52 Joseph Swetnam, *The Schoole of the Noble and Worthy Science of Defence* (London, 1617, STC (2nd ed.) / 23543), 6.
53 Swetnam, *The Schoole*, 9–10.
54 Saviolo, *His Practise*, Xᵛ.
55 Ibid., X2ᵛ.

56 On 'thou' as an insult, see Vienne-Guerrin, *Dictionary*, 401–3. On 'you' and 'thou', see Penelope Freedman, *You and Thou in Shakespeare: A Practical Guide for Actors, Directors, Students and Teachers*, Arden Performance Companions (London: Bloomsbury, 2021).

Chapter 4

1   Ian Maclean, *Interpretation and Meaning in the Renaissance* (Cambridge: Cambridge University Press, 1992), 186–7.

2   Laura Gowing, 'Language, Power and the Law: Women's Slander Litigation in Early Modern London', in *Women, Crime and the Courts in Early Modern England*, ed. Jenny Kermode and Garthine Walker (London: UCL Press, 1995), Chapter 2, 26–47, 29.

3   Maclean, *Interpretation and Meaning*, 187.

4   W. S. Holdsworth, 'Defamation in the Sixteenth and Seventeenth Centuries', *The Law Quarterly Review*, vol. XL, (July, 1924): 302–15, 302.

5   See *Stuart Royal Proclamations, Vol I, Royal Proclamations of King James I 1603–1625*, ed. James F. Larkin (Oxford: At the Clarendon Press, 1973), xv; xvii.

6   Before 1660, *Common Law* did not make a distinction between written and oral forms of defamation. However, J. H. Baker notes that: 'Written defamation (libel) was, nevertheless, treated in a special way by the criminal law, where neither publication nor untruth were required to be shown. The Star Chamber, in particular, sometimes punished libel with "sharp sentences". This special treatment may account for the doctrine that words which were not actionable if merely spoken might become actionable if disseminated in writing; and that truth might not be a defence even to a civil action for libel.' J. H. Baker, *An Introduction to English Legal History* (London: Butterworths, 1990), 506–7.

7   F. G. Emmison, *Elizabethan Life: Disorder*, Essex Record Office Publication, no. 56 (Chelmsford: Essex County Council, 1970), 71–9.

8   Gowing, 'Language, power and the law', 32.
9   Ibid.
10 Emmison (*Elizabethan Life: Disorder*, 66) refers to Michael Dalton, the author of *The Countrey Justice, Containing the Practice of the Justices of Peace Out of Their Sessions: Gathered for the Better Help of Such Justices of Peace as Have Not Been Much Conversant in the Studie of the Lawes of the Realme* (6th ed.1643). Mentioned by J. A. Sharpe, *Defamation and Sexual Slander in Early Modern England: The Church Courts at York* (Borthwick Papers 58, 1980), 32.
11 Emmison, *Elizabethan Life: Disorder*, 66. He notes that 'A later ballad, with a sketch of the victim sentenced to both pillory and gallows' is illustrated in F. G. Emmison, *Archives and Local History* (London: Methuen, 1965), 83.
12 Sharpe, *Defamation and Sexual Slander...*
13 *OED*, 'note', v.2, 3.
14 *Much Ado About Nothing*, ed. McEachern, 202, note 23. See *OED*, 'stale', n.3.
15 See 'I am an ass indeed: you may prove it by my long ears' (*CE*, 4.4.30–1).
16 See *Much Ado About Nothing*, ed. A. R. Humphreys, Arden (London: Methuen, 1981), 190: 'Dogberry appears unwittingly to achieve a pun. *Years* could be a variant of *ears*, as in the phrase "as long as donkeys' *years*". Craik (p. 309) cites the Interlude *Misogonus*, I. ii. 63–4 (c. 1570), where the Fool says, "Nothinge greves me but my *yeares* be so longe / my master will take me for balames asse".'
17 J. A. Sharpe, '"Such Disagreement betwyx Neighbours": Litigation and Human Relations in Early Modern England', in *Disputes and Settlements. Law and Human Relations in the West*, ed. John Bossy (Cambridge: Cambridge University Press, 1983), 167–87, 171.
18 S. F. C. Milsom, *Historical foundations of the Common Law* (London: Butterworths, 1981), 380.
19 Quoted and translated by R. H. Helmholz in 'Canonical Defamation in Medieval England', *The American Journal of Legal History* XV (1971): 255–68, 256.

20 Helmholz, 'Canonical Defamation … ', 256.
21 Ibid., 258.
22 Ibid., 258–9.
23 Ibid., 260.
24 *Statutes of the Realm*, a new edition in 12 Vols of the Statutes from 1235 to 1713 (London: Dawsons of Pall Mall, 1810–1828), I, 101. Available online: https://babel.hathitrust.org/cgi/pt?id=pst.000017915496&view=1up&seq=281&skin=2021 (Accessed 23 July 2021).
25 Helmholz, 'Canonical Defamation … ', 264.
26 Ibid., 266.
27 In 1442.
28 Helmholz, 'Canonical Defamation … ', 268. See also C. H. S. Fifoot, *History and Sources of the Common Law Tort and Contract* (London: Steevens and Sons Limited, 1949), 127: 'If defamation were a sin, the sinner must do penance, but the victim could not be allowed to make a profit'.
29 Helmholz, 'Canonical Defamation … ', 268.
30 Baker, *An Introduction*, 495.
31 Ibid., 501.
32 Ibid., 498.
33 Ibid., 498.
34 Ibid., 499.
35 Ibid., 500.
36 F. G. Emmison, *Elizabethan Life: Morals and Church Courts*. Essex Record Office Publications, no. 63. (Chelmsford: Essex County Council, 1973), 48. Emmison is referring to Richard Burn, *Ecclesiastical Law* (London, ed. of 1773), i, 476–84.
37 Emmison, *Elizabethan Life: Morals and Church Courts*, 48.
38 Baker, *An Introduction*, 500.
39 John C. Lassiter, 'Defamation of Peers: The Rise and Decline of the Action for *Scandalum Magnatum*, 1497–1773', *The American Journal of Legal History*, XXII (1978): 216–36.
40 William Sheppard, *Action upon the Case for Slander* (London, 1662, Wing / S3173A), 5.

41 William Blackstone, *Commentaries on the Laws of England Book the Third* (Oxford: Clarendon Press, 1768), vol. 3, Chap. 8, 123, quoted by Lassiter, 'Defamation of Peers... ', 216.

42 Lassiter, 'Defamation of Peers... ', 217.

43 Ibid., 218.

44 Ibid.

45 Ibid.

46 Lawrence Stone, *The Crisis of the Aristocracy, 1558–1641* (Oxford: At the Clarendon Press, 1965).

47 Lassiter, 'Defamation of Peers... ', 220.

48 For example, 'base lord' or 'base fellow'.

49 Lassiter, 'Defamation of Peers... ', 220.

50 Stone, *The Crisis of the Aristocracy*, 240–2. Quoted by J. A. Sharpe in '"Such Disagreement Betwyx Neighbours"... ', 168.

51 From 1574 to 1592. See Baker, *An Introduction*, 501.

52 John March, *Actions for Slaunder* (London, 1647, Wing / M571), 9.

53 Sharpe, '"Such Disagreement Betwyx Neighbours"... ', 178.

54 R. H. Helmholz, *Select Cases on Defamation to 1600* (London: Selden Society, 1985), Introduction, p. xlvi.

55 Baker, *An Introduction*, 501.

56 Sharpe, '"Such Disagreement Betwyx Neighbours"... ', 172.

57 March, *Actions for Slaunder*, 2.

58 See Vienne-Guerrin, *The Unruly Tongue*.

59 See *The Geneva Bible*: 'I Thoght, I wil take hede to my waies, that I sinne not with my to[n]gue: I wil kepe my mouth brideled, while the wicked is in my sight' (Psal. XXXIX, ver. 1).

60 March, *Actions for Slaunder*, 9–10.

61 Ibid., 10.

62 Ibid., 3.

63 Baker, *An Introduction*, 501.

64 See John H. Baker and S. F. C. Milsom, *Sources of English Legal History, Private law to 1750* (London: Butterworths,

1986), 637. The reference to this case is Anon. (1575) LI MS. Maynard 77, 339 (C. P.).

65 Quoted by Baker and Milsom, *Sources*, 639.
66 See Baker, *An Introduction*, 502. The case reference is Poe v. Mondford (1598) Cro. Eliz. 620.
67 On this, see Baker and Milsom, *Sources*, 643, where many examples can be found.
68 Baker, *An Introduction*, 502.
69 Lucio is the voice of many: 'Some say' … ; 'other some' … (3.1.354–5); 'They say' (3.1.367); 'Some report … ' (3.1.371); 'Say that I said so' (3.1.442).
70 'Wencher or doer' (Partridge).
71 David Cressy, *Dangerous Talk. Scandalous, Seditious, and Treasonable Speech in Pre-Modern England* (Oxford and New York: Oxford University Press, 2010), Chapter 2, 'Abusive Words', 17–38, 'Scandalum Magnatum', 29–33, 29.
72 Cressy, *Dangerous Talk*, 29.
73 Lindsay M. Kaplan, 'Slander for Slander in *Measure for Measure*', in *Renaissance Drama*, New Series XXI, *Disorder and the Drama*, 1990, 23–54.

Chapter 5

1 Sermon 59 by Thomas Adams, in *The Works of Thomas Adams*, vol. 3, 10–22.
2 Ronald B. Bond, ed., *Certain Sermons or Homilies (1547) and A Homily against Disobedience and Wilful Rebellion (1570), A Critical Edition* (Toronto: University of Toronto Press, 1987), 190–201. This homily is attributed to Hugh Latimer.
3 Short work in verse by Stephen Hawes (London, 1509, STC (2nd ed.) / 12943).
4 Thomas Becon, London, 1543 (STC (2nd ed.) / 1730.5).
5 Edmond Bicknoll, London, 1579 (STC (2nd ed.) / 3049).

6 Jean de Marconville, translation, with a foreword by T. S. (London, 1592, STC (2nd ed.) / 17313). See Vienne-Guerrin, *The Unruly Tongue*.

7 William Perkins (Cambridge, 1593, STC (2nd ed.) / 19688). See Vienne-Guerrin, *The Unruly Tongue*.

8 George Webbe (London, 1619, STC (2nd ed.) / 25156). See Vienne-Guerrin, *The Unruly Tongue*.

9 About slander, see M. Lindsay Kaplan, *The Culture of Slander in Early Modern England* (Cambridge: Cambridge University Press, 1997); Ina Habermann, *Staging Slander and Gender in Early Modern England* (Aldershot: Ashgate, 2003).

10 See David Bevington, '"Why Should Calamity Be Full of Words?" The Efficacy of Cursing *in Richard III*', *Iowa State Journal of Research* 56 (1981): 9–21.

11 W. H. Clemen, *A Commentary on Shakespeare's* Richard III (London: Methuen, 1957), 58.

12 Ibid., 58.

13 A. P. Rossiter, *Angel with Horns. Five Lectures on Shakespeare* (London and New York: Longman, 1961), 'The Unity of *Richard III*', 1–22.

14 Alice Lotvin Birney, *Satiric Catharsis in Shakespeare* (Berkeley, LA, London: University of California Press, 1973), 'The Satiric curser Against Richard III', 20–46.

15 Shirley Carr Mason, '"Foul Wrinkled Witch": Superstition, Scepticism and Margaret of Anjou in Shakespeare's *Richard III*', *Cahiers Élisabéthains* 52 (October 1997): 25–37, 27.

16 Adams, 'The Taming of the Tongue', 17.

17 Thomas Heywood, *Gynaikeion* (London, 1624, STC (2nd ed.) / 13326), 236–40, quoted by Lisa Jardine in *Still Harping on Daughters: Women and Drama in the Age of Shakespeare* (New York and London: Harvester Wheatsheaf, 1983), 137, n. 66.

18 'Foul wrinkled witch' (1.3.163), 'Have done thy charm, thou hateful withered hag' (1.3.214).

19 See Alciat's emblem entitled 'Maledicentia', *Les Emblèmes* [1551] (Paris: Klincksieck, 1997), 59. In it, one sees Archilochus' tomb, and a cloud of wasps above it. The motto is

'Archiloci tumulo insculptas de marmore vespas / Esse ferunt, linguae certa sigila malae' (It is said that the wasps that are engraved in Archilochus' marble tomb are the certain signs of a malicious tongue). In *Poetaster*, Jonson conjures up the traditional image of the bard, when, replying to his detractors, he writes: 'I could do worse, / Arm'd with Archilocus fury, write Iambics, / Should make the desperate lashers hang themselves. / Rime 'hem to death, as they do Irish rats / In drumming tunes.' Ben Jonson, *Poetaster*, ed. Tom Cain (Manchester: Manchester University Press, 1995), 'Apological Dialogue', ll. 147–51, 269.

20 Rowlands, *Looke to It, for Ile Stabbe ye*, C2^r.

21 Bicknoll cites the example of a mother cursing her daughter and saying: 'The Dyvel take thee: or the Dyvel flye upon thee'. He then exposes the consequence of this malediction: 'And the self same houre her daughter fel madde, and was possessed of a dyvel'. *A Swoord agaynst Swearyng*, 44^r.

22 See Watson, *Arae*, 13.

23 Ann Lecercle speaks of 'bodily emission' in 'Corps, regard, parole: Basilisk and Antichrist in *Richard III*', in *Le Tyran. Shakespeare contre Richard III*, ed. Dominique Goy-Blanquet and Richard Marienstras (Amiens: Presses de l'UFR Clerc Université Picardie, 1990), 27–50, 42.

24 See Thomas, *Shakespeare's Body Language*, Chapter 'Spitting at Richard: Taming the Beast in *Richard III*', 71–91.

25 George Puttenham, *The Arte of English Poesie*, Book 1, Chapter XXIV, 37.

26 Puttenham, *The Arte of English Poesie*, Book 1, Chapter XXIV, 46.

27 Ovid concludes his *Invective against Ibis* with an end that is not an end. See *Ovid His Invective against Ibis*, trans. Thomas Underdown (London, 1569, STC (2nd ed.) / 18949).

28 In his Preface to Larguèche's *L'effet Injure*, viii. Quoted by Ann Lecercle, 'Corps, regard, parole ... ', 41.

29 C. L. Barber and Richard P. Wheeler, *The Whole Journey, Shakespeare's Power of Development* (Berkeley, Los Angeles and London: University of California Press, 1986), Chapter IV, 'Savage Play and the Web of Curses in *Richard III*', 86–124.

30 Anne calls him 'this fiend' (1.2.34), 'devil' (1.2.45; 73), 'thou dreadful minister of hell' (1.2.46), 'foul devil' (1.2. 50), 'devilish slave' (1.2.91), she evokes his 'hell-governed arm' (1.2.67). Margaret also calls him aside 'devil!' (1.3.117), 'thou cacodemon' (1.3.143), then loud and clear 'the son of hell' (1.3.229), 'the devil' (1.3.297). Richard is also called 'a hell-hound' (4.4.48), 'That foul defacer of God's handiwork' (4.4.53), 'hell's black intelligencer' (4.4.71), 'the devil' (4.4.418). The Duchess compares him to 'vice' (2.2.28).

31 In this play, the word 'dog', that is mainly applied to Richard, expresses ferociousness and is linked with the image of the fangs. Richard is called 'dog', 'hound' and 'cur'. See 1.3.215, 1.3.288, 4.4.47–58, 4.4.78.

32 1.2.19, 1.3.241, 4.4.81. The image of the spider refers to a creature that weaves its web and spreads its venom.

33 4.1.54. In *3H6*, Richard associates himself with this image when he declares: 'I'll slay more gazers than the basilisk' (3.2.187). About the word 'basilisk', see Ann Lecercle, 'Corps, regard, parole … '.

34 See 3.2.10, 27, 28, 32, 72; 3.4.81, 4.5.2, 5.2.7. The image of the 'hog' or the 'boar' is associated with Richard in this play. The 'white boar' is Richard's emblem. The other characters thus return his blazon against him.

35 1.3.227. See 'this foul swine' (5.2.10).

36 1.2.104. Anne plays on the word 'hog' which evokes Richard's coat of arms.

37 1.2.19, 1.2.150, 1.3.245, 4.4.81, 4.4.145. See *3H6*, 2.2.135–8. In the whole Shakespearean corpus, only Timon (*Tim*, 4.3.370) and Cloten (*Cym*, 4.2.90) are compared with toads as well.

38 See Kenneth Muir, *Macbeth*, Arden edition (London: Routledge, 1964), 106 (note).

39 'creeping venomed thing' (1.2.20), 'poisonous bunch-backed toad' (1.3.245), 'His venom tooth' (1.3.290), 'deadly venom' (4.1.61).

40 'Marry' and 'By Saint Paul' are his favourite oaths. They can be considered as 'mild oaths', compared with 'Zounds' that is the object of censure.

41 To swear by Christ's body, wounds or blood amounts to crucifying him again. See notably Hawes, *The Co[n]vercyon of Swerers* (1509).

42 Bond, ed., *Certain Sermons and Homilies*, 191. See also in the anonymous *The Anathomie of Sinne* (London, 1603, STC (2nd ed.) / 12465.5), the chapter that is entitled 'Malediction what', F8^{rv}: 'The contrarie to malediction is benediction or blessing, when wee wish well to all men, yea unto our enemies. Blesse them that curse, Do good to them that hate'.

43 Anon., *Anathomy of Sinne*, F8^{rv}.

44 See Chapter 4 of this book.

45 See Vienne-Guerrin, *The Unruly Tongue*, xxxiv–vi.

46 See Florio, *A World of Words*, 'Gareggiatore: a striver, contender, brauler, scoulder, or chatter' and 'Gracchione, Gracchiatore. a chatter, a cackler, a railer, a prater, a tatler'. See also John Florio, *Queen Anna's New World of Words* (London, 1611, STC (2nd ed.) / 11099), 'Gracchióne. a chatter, a pratler, a babler, a tatler. Also a railer, a scold'.

47 On the rewriting of the figure of the shrew, see Nathalie Vienne-Guerrin, 'La réécriture de la "Mégère" dans le théâtre de Shakespeare', in *Réécritures*, ed. Jean-Pierre Maquerlot (Rouen: Publication de l'Université de Rouen, 2000), 77–92.

48 Martin Ingram, '"Scolding women cucked or washed": A Crisis in Gender Relations in Early Modern England?', in *Women, Crime and the Courts*, eds. Jenny Kermode and Garthine Walker (Chapel Hill and London: The University of North Carolina Press, 1994), 48–80, 51. Ingram questions most of the conclusions formulated by D. E. Underdown in 'The Taming of the Scold: The Enforcement of Patriarchal Authority in Early Modern England', in *Order and Disorder in Early Modern England*, ed. Anthony Fletcher and John Stevenson (Cambridge: Cambridge University Press, 1985), 116–39. See also Lynda E. Boose's seminal study, 'Scolding Brides and Bridling Scolds: Taming the Woman's Unruly Member', *Shakespeare Quarterly* 41, no. 2 (1991): 179–213.

49 Cressy, *Dangerous Talk*, 'Insult and Scolding', 19–23, 19. On the topic of scolding, see Sandy Bardsley, *Venomous*

Tongues: Speech and Gender in Late Medieval England (Philadelphia: University of Pennsylvania Press, 2006).

50 Ingram, '"Scolding women... "', 51.
51 See Kirilka Stavreva, *Words Like Daggers. Violent Female Speech in Early Modern England* (Lincoln and London: University of Nebraska Press, 2015).
52 Underdown, 'The Taming of the Scold... ', 120.
53 Ingram, '"Scolding women... "', 53.
54 Reginal Scot, *The Discovery of Witchcraft* (London, 1584, STC (2nd ed.) / 21864), Book I, Chapter III, 7. Quoted by Barbara Rosen in *Witchcraft in England, 1558–1618* (Amherst: The University of Massachusetts Press [1969] 1991), 174.
55 Ingram, '"Scolding women... "', 53. For more detail on types of punishment, see Emmison, *Elizabethan Life: Morals and Church Courts*, Chap. 9, 'Trial and Punishment', 281–315.
56 Ingram, '"Scolding women... "', 58.
57 Ibid.
58 This implied a stronger humiliation. See Boose, 'Scolding Brides... ', 187.
59 William Sheppard, *An Epitome of All the Common & Statute Laws of This Nation* (London, 1656, Wing / S3184), Chap. 144, 893. Quoted by Boose, 'Scolding Brides... ', 186.
60 Boose, 'Scolding Brides... ', 185. About this stool, see John Webster Spargo, *Juridical Folklore in England, Illustrated by the Cucking-Stool* (Durham, NC: Duke University Press, 1944).
61 Underdown, 'The Taming of the Scold... ', 129.
62 'A Homilie Agaynst Contention and Brawlynge', in Bond, ed., *Certain Sermons and Homilies*, 200.
63 Ingram, '"Scolding women... "', 68.
64 See E. P. Thompson, 'Rough Music: Le charivari anglais', *Annales (Économies, Sociétés, Civilisations)* 27, no. 2 (Janvier–Juin 1972): 285–312.
65 Underdown, 'The Taming of the Scold... ', 127.
66 Boose, 'Scolding Brides... ', 189.
67 Ibid.

68 François Laroque, *Shakespeare's Festive World* (Cambridge: Cambridge University Press, 1991), 211.

69 Wayne A. Rebhorn, 'Petruchio's "Rope Tricks": *The Taming of the Shrew* and the Renaissance Discourse of Rhetoric', *Modern Philology* 92, no. 3 (February 1995): 294–327.

70 See Vienne-Guerrin, '"He'll rail in his rope/robe tricks": l'injure comme feu d'artifices dans *The Taming of the Shrew*', *Sillages Critiques* 10 (2009), https://journals.openedition.org/sillagescritiques/1807 (accessed 23 July 2021).

71 In Camille Wells Slights, 'The Raw and the Cooked in *The Taming of the Shrew*', *Journal of English and Germanic Philology* 88 (1989): 168–89. Reproduced in *Shakespeare Criticism Yearbook*, 1989, vol. 13, 3–11, it is noted that *The Taming of the Shrew* 'is a world of objects' (4).

72 Slights, 'The Raw and the Cooked...', 3.

Chapter 6

1 Larguèche, *L'effet injure*, 144.

2 Deborah Willis, '"The Gnawing Vulture": Revenge, Trauma Theory, and *Titus Andronicus*', *Shakespeare Quarterly* 53, no. 1 (Spring 2002): 21–52, 25.

3 Thomas P. Anderson, *Performing Early Modern Trauma from Shakespeare to Milton* (Aldershot: Ashgate, 2006), 3–4.

4 Patricia A. Cahill, *Unto the Breach: Martial Formations, Historical Trauma, and the Early Modern Stage* (Oxford: Oxford University Press, 2008), 9.

5 Catherine Silverstone, *Shakespeare, Trauma and Contemporary Performance* (New York: Routledge, 2011).

6 Silverstone, *Shakespeare, Trauma...*, 2.

7 Ibid., 21.

8 Denise Riley, *Impersonal Passion...*, 14.

9 Robert C. Evans, 'Ophelia and Trauma Theory in Shakespeare's *Hamlet*', in Robert C. Evans, ed., *Critical Insights*: Hamlet (Amenia, NY: Grey House Publishing, 2019), 40–55.

10 Evans, 'Ophelia and Trauma Theory ... ', 40.
11 Ronnie Janoff-Bulman, *Shattered Assumptions: Towards a New Psychology of Trauma* (New York: Free Press; Toronto: Maxwell Macmillan Canada; New York: Maxwell Macmillan International, 1992).
12 Evans, 'Ophelia and Trauma Theory ... ', 42.
13 Shoshana Ringel and Jerrold R. Brandell, eds, *Trauma. Contemporary Directions in Trauma Theory, Research, and Practice* (New York: Columbia University Press, 2020).
14 Gert Buelens, Sam Durrant and Robert Eaglestone, eds, *The Future of Trauma Theory. Contemporary Literary Cultural Criticism* (London and New York: Routledge, 2014).
15 Butler, *Excitable Speech*, 6.
16 Ibid., 10
17 Ibid. Butler quotes Shoshana Felman's book, *The Literary Speech Act: Don Juan with J. L. Austin, or Seduction in Two Languages*, trans. Catherine Porter (Ithaca: Cornell University Press, 1983), 96.
18 Butler, *Excitable Speech*, 10. On intentionality, see Jonathan Culpeper, *Impoliteness. Using Language to Cause Offence* (Cambridge: Cambridge University Press, 2011), Chapter 2: 'Understanding Impoliteness II: Intentionality and Emotions', 48–70.
19 Claude Paradin, *Devises Heroïques*, 109–10.
20 *The Courtiers Academie*, originally written in Italian by Count Haniball Romei, a gentleman of Ferrara, and translated into English by I.K. (London, 1598, STC (2nd ed.) / 21311), 152.
21 *Henry V*, ed. Gary Taylor (Oxford: Oxford university Press, 1982), 254.
22 *King Henry IV Part 2*, ed. A. R. Humphreys (Routledge: London and New York, Arden, 1966), 24, quoting J. Hunter's 1871 edition.
23 Riley, *Impersonal Passion*, Chapter on 'Malediction', 11–12. An earlier version of this chapter was published in Lecercle and Riley, *The Force of Language*, 'Bad words', 46–62.
24 See, among others, Madeleine Doran, 'Good Name in *Othello*', *Studies in English Literature, 1500–1900* 7, no. 2 (Spring

1967): 195–217; Joyce H. Sexton, *The Slandered Woman in Shakespeare* (Victoria: English Literary Studies of the University of Victoria, no. 12, 1978), 50–61; Arthur L. Jr. Little, 'The Primal Scene of Racism in *Othello*: An Essence That's Not Seen', *Shakespeare Quarterly* 43, no. 3 (1993): 304–24; Kenneth Gross, 'Slander and Skepticism in *Othello*', *ELH* 56, no. 4 (Winter 1989): 819–52; Kenneth Gross, 'Denigration and Hallucination in *Othello*', in *Shakespeare's Noise* (Chicago and London: The University of Chicago Press, 2001), 102–30.

25 On 'whore' in *Othello*, see Kay Stanton, *Shakespeare's Whores. Erotics, Politics and Poetics* (New York: Palgrave Macmillan, 2014), 34–40; Lisa Jardine, '"Why should he call her whore?" Defamation and Desdemona's Case', in *Addressing Frank Kermode: Essays in Criticism and Interpretation*, ed. Margaret Tudeau-Clayton and Martin Warner (Urbana: University of Illinois Press, 1991), 124–53.

26 *Othello*, edited by E. A. J. Honigmann [1997], rev. edition, The Arden Shakespeare, Third Series (London, Oxford: Bloomsbury, 2016), 283.

27 Janoff-Bulman, *Shattered Assumptions*, 6–12.

28 Riley, *Impersonal Passion*, 12.

29 Ibid., 15.

30 Nathalie Vienne-Guerrin, '"Sicilia is a so-forth": La Rumeur dans *The Winter's Tale*', in *A Sad Tale's Best for Winter: Approches critiques du* Conte d'hiver *de Shakespeare*, ed. Yan Brailowsky, Anny Crunelle-Vanrigh and Jean-Michel Déprats (Paris: Presses Universitaires Paris Ouest, 2011), 149–63.

31 Lecercle and Riley, *The Force of Language*, Chapter 2 ('Bad Words'), 47; or Riley, *Impersonal Passion*, 10.

32 Riley, *Impersonal Passion*, 10.

33 Ibid., 13–14.

34 Ibid., 12; 16.

35 Ibid., 17.

36 See Stanton, *Shakespeare's 'Whores'*, Introduction, 1.

37 Riley, *Impersonal Passion*, 21.

38 Ibid., 17.

39 Ibid., 18. On this ambivalence, see Jean-Jacques Lecercle, *The Violence of Language* (Routledge: London and New York, 1990), Chapter 3 'A Theory of the Remainder', 103–9 ('Language Speaks, I Speak Language').

40 Évelyne Larguèche, *L'Injure à fleur de peau* (Paris: L'Harmattan, 1993), 10 and 157.

41 See Évelyne Larguèche, *Espèces de… Les Lois de l'effet injure* (Chambéry: Université de Savoie: Éditions du Laboratoire Langages, Littératures, Sociétés, 2009); Nathalie Vienne-Guerrin, '"Base Phrygian Turk!" Injures et "espèces de…": Analyse microscopique d'un étrange spécimen shakespearien', *LISA* VI, no. 3 (2008): 80–91. http://lisa.revues.org/377. (Accessed 10 July 2021).

42 See Riley's formulation in her book entitled *Impersonal Passion*.

43 Riley, *Impersonal Passion*, 9.

44 On spitting in *The Merchant of Venice*, see Thomas, *Shakespeare's Body Language*, Chapter 4, 93–113.

45 Riley, *Impersonal Passion*, 11.

46 Ibid., 14.

47 Ibid.

48 Denise Riley, '"A Voice without a Mouth": Inner Speech', in Lecercle and Riley, *The Force of Language*, 7–45 (Chapter 1).

49 Butler, *Excitable Speech*, 36.

50 See, for example, Webbe, *The Araignement of an Unruly Tongue* (1619), in Vienne-Guerrin, *The Unruly Tongue*, 18–20.

51 Butler, *Excitable Speech*, 1–41 ('Linguistic Vulnerability').

52 Samuel Beckett, 'Texts for Nothing', XIII, in *Collected Shorter Prose 1945–1980* (London: John Calder, 1984), 152. Quoted by Lecercle and Riley, *The Force of Language*, 171.

53 Lecercle and Riley, *The Force of Language*, 7.

54 John Baret, *An Alveary or Triple Dictionary, in English, Latin and French* (London, 1574, STC (2nd ed.) / 1410.).

55 Larguèche, *L'injure à fleur de peau*, 68.

56 Riley, *Impersonal Passion*, 17.

57 Belarius evokes the same kind of reversal of values when he compares the life he has with his sons to that led by dung beetles, which is happier than the life of eagles: 'The sharded beetle in a safer hold / Than is the full-winged eagle' (3.3.20–1). Valerie Wayne refers to the Aesopic fable of 'The Eagle and the Dung Beetle', in *Cymbeline*, ed. Valerie Wayne, The Arden Shakespeare, Third Series (London and New York: Bloomsbury, 2017), 244.

58 In *Renaissance Clothing and the Materials of Memory* (Cambridge: Cambridge University Press, 2000), Ann Rosalind Jones and Peter Stallybrass note (200–1) that it is relevant to have the Folio 1 version in mind to read 'heires' instead of, or together with, 'haires', suggesting that Posthumus' meanest garment is more precious than all the heirs Cloten could engender. As Innogen is answering Cloten who has just said that from an ignoble union can only emerge 'brats and beggary' (2.3.119), this reading seems all the more attractive.

59 'And that she should love this fellow and refuse me!' (1.2.18).

60 *Cymbeline*, ed. Martin Butler (Cambridge: Cambridge University Press, 2005), 129.

61 In 'Worn Worlds: clothes and identity on the Renaissance stage', Peter Stallybrass explains the paradox of a term that means both freedom and servitude: 'To oversimplify, livery in a *household* was a mark of servitude whereas livery in a *guild* was a mark of freedom', in *Subject and Object in Renaissance Culture*, ed. Margreta de Grazia, Maureen Quilligan and Peter Stallybrass (Cambridge: Cambridge University Press, 1996), Chapter 10, 289–320, 289.

62 Ros King, Cymbeline, *Constructions of Britain* (Aldershot: Ashgate, 2005), 26.

63 Jones and Stallybrass, *Renaissance Clothing*, 201.

64 Ibid. See also Stallybrass, 'Worn Worlds', 309–10.

65 Jones and Stallybrass, *Renaissance Clothing*, 38.

66 See chapter 4 in this book.

67 See Lina Perkins Wilder, *Shakespeare's Memory Theatre. Recollection, Properties, and Character* (Cambridge: Cambridge University Press, 2010), 1.

68 See Riley's expression, *Impersonal Passion*, 9.
69 Ibid., 14.
70 *Dictionnaire Historique de la Langue Française*, ed. Alain Rey (Paris: Dictionnaire Le Robert, 1993).
71 See the references to Philomel and Tereus (*Cym*, 2.2.45–6) and to Tarquin (*Cym*, 2.2.12).
72 On 'stale', see Harington, *A New Discourse of a Stale Subject*. See Vienne-Guerrin, 'Castalian King Urinal Hector of Greece … '.
73 See 'If her breath were as terrible as her terminations, there were no living near her, she would infect to the north star' (*MA*, 2.1.233–4).
74 See Vienne-Guerrin, *The Unruly Tongue*, xvii–lii.
75 Charles Gibbon, *The Praise of a Good Name. The Reproch of an Ill Name* (London, 1594, STC (2nd ed.) / 11819), 29.

Chapter 7

1 Desmond Morris, *Bodytalk. A World Guide to Gestures* (London: Jonathan Cape, 1994).
2 Thomas, *Shakespeare's Body Language*, Chapters 1 to 5.
3 See Vienne-Guerrin, *Dictionary*, 'Fig/Fico', 184–8; 'Thumb-biting', 403–7; 'Horn', 236–8.
4 John Bulwer, *Chirologia, or, the Naturall Language of the Hand* (London, 1644, Wing / B5466), 182; quoted by Desmond Morris, *Gestures, Their Origins and Distribution* (London: Jonathan Cape, 1979), 121.
5 Farah Karim-Cooper, *The Hand on the Shakespearean Stage. Gesture, Touch and the Spectacle of Dismemberment* (London and New York: Bloomsbury Arden Shakespeare, 2016), 73.
6 See Vienne-Guerrin, *Dictionary*, 'Face', 179–83. On the expressivity of the face, see *Shakespeare and the Power of the Face*, ed. James A. Knapp (London and New York: Routledge, 2015).
7 Thomas, *Shakespeare's Body Language*, 72.

8   Thomas, *Dictionarium*, 'Conspŭo'.
9   Ibid., 'Excrēmentum'.
10   See Chapter 2 in this book.
11   See Vienne-Guerrin, '"Castalian King Urinal"... '.
12   See David Bevington, *Action Is Eloquence. Shakespeare's Language of Gesture* (Cambridge, MA: Harvard UP, 1984).
13   See Nathalie Vienne-Guerrin, '"Couple a gorge!": La guerre des langues dans *Henry V* de Shakespeare', in *Langues Dominantes/Langues Dominées*, ed. Laurence Villard and Nicolas Ballier (Rouen: PURH, 2008), 165–80.
14   Vienne-Guerrin, *Dictionary*, 299–301 ('nation').
15   For more on 'tennis-balls', see Vienne-Guerrin, *Dictionary*, 397–8.
16   *King Henry V*, ed. T. W. Craik [1995], The Arden Shakespeare, Third Series (London: Thomson Learning, 2005), 149.
17   About jesting, see Chris Holcomb, *Mirth Making. The Rhetorical Discourse on Jesting in Early Modern England* (Columbia: University of South Carolina Press, 2001).
18   *King Henry V*, ed. Craik, 196.
19   On this production, see Janice Valls-Russell, *Cahiers Élisabéthains* 57 (April 2000): 132–4.
20   On 'fico' or the 'fig of Spain', see Vienne-Guerrin, *Dictionary*, 386–8; Thomas, *Shakespeare's Body Language*, Chapter 2, 'Figging: Spanish Anxieties and *Ancient* Grudges in Pistol's Henriad', 45–69.
21   On the connection between Katherine and Pistol, see Thomas, *Shakespeare's Body Language*, 52–3.
22   John Kerrigan, *Shakespeare's Binding Language* (Oxford: Oxford University Press, 2016), Chapter 9 ('Oaths, Threats, and *Henry V*'), 239; 520 (note 11).
23   Kerrigan, *Shakespeare's Binding Language*, 213.
24   *King Richard II*, ed. Charles Forker, The Arden Shakespeare, Third Series (London: Thomson Learning, 2002), 184–5.
25   On the pledge, or gage, see Kerrigan, *Shakespeare's Binding Language*, 224; 246.

26 Kerrigan, *Shakespeare's Binding Language*, 246.
27 See L. H., *A Dictionary French and English* (London, 1571, STC 2nd ed. /6832), Hollyband and Cotgrave: 'Soufflet: m. A paire of bellowes; also, a box, cuffe, or whirret on th'eare'. See Don Diègue's reaction to the disgraceful gesture in Corneille's *Le Cid* (Act 1, scenes 3 and 4).
28 Billacois, *Le Duel dans la société française*, 328–9. My translation.
29 On the variant versions of the story of Hal's striking the Justice, see *King Henry IV Part 2*, ed. James C. Bulman, The Arden Shakespeare, Third Series (London and New York: Bloomsbury, 2016), 189; 398.
30 Kerrigan, *Shakespeare's Binding Language*, 247.
31 Ibid.
32 Ibid., 213.
33 Joan Fitzpatrick, *Food in Shakespeare: Early Modern Dietaries and the Plays* (Aldershot and Burlington, VT: Ashgate, 2007), 37–44 ('*Henry 5*: Figs and Leeks'), 41.
34 On leek as a source of disgust, see Colleen E. Kennedy, '"Qualmish at the smell of leek". Overcoming Disgust and Creating the Nation-state in *Henry V*', in *Disgust in Early Modern English Literature*, ed. Natalie K. Eschenbaum and Barbara Correll (London: Routledge, 2016), 124–41.
35 Gordon Williams, *A Dictionary of Sexual Language and Imagery in Shakespearean and Stuart Literature*, in 3 vol. (London: The Athlone Press, 1994), vol. 2, 795–6.
36 Kerrigan, *Shakespeare's Binding Language*, 250.
37 *King Lear*, ed. R. A. Foakes, The Arden Shakespeare, Third Series (London: Thomson Learning, 1997), 240.
38 Caroline Spurgeon, *Shakespeare's Imagery and What It Tells Us* (Cambridge: Cambridge University Press, 1965), 338–43.
39 Magnusson, *Shakespeare and Social Dialogue*, 142–53, 142.
40 R. A. Foakes, *Shakespeare and Violence* (Cambridge: Cambridge University Press, 2003), 142–8, 145.
41 Gross, *Shakespeare's Noise*, 161–92.

42 Stanley Cavell, *Disowning Knowledge in Six Plays of Shakespeare* (Cambridge: Cambridge University Press, 1987); William F. Zak, *Sovereign Shame. A Study of* King Lear (Lewisburg: Bucknell University Press, 1984); Ewan Fernie, *Shame in Shakespeare* (London and New York: Routledge, 2002).

43 Fernie, *Shame in Shakespeare*, 174.

44 Larguèche, *L'effet injure*, 119.

45 Ibid.

46 Ibid., 120. Larguèche is quoting Sigmund Freud, *Malaise dans la Civilisation* (Paris: Presses Universitaires de France, 1976), 81.

47 Larguèche, *L'effet injure*, 120, quoting Freud, *Malaise dans la Civilisation*, 81.

48 Larguèche, *L'effet injure*, 122. On 'Face and offence', see Culpeper, *Impoliteness*, Chapter 1.3, 24–31.

49 1.3.21; 2.2.147; 2.2.497; 3.7.90; 4.1.24; 4.7.15; 4.7.53; 4.7.77; 5.1.11.

Epilogue

1 Irvine, *A Slap in the Face*, 89; 93.

2 See, for example, Rex Gibson's *Shakespeare's Language, a Handbook for Teachers* (Cambridge: Cambridge University Press, 1997), which integrates worksheets on insults (135–7), one of which is entitled 'Insults: make up your own!'; Wayne F. Hill and Cynthia J. Öttchen, *Shakespeare's Insults, Educating Your Wit* [1991] (Cambridge: Mainsail Press, 1993); Barry Kraft, *Create over 100,000 of Your Own Shakespearean Insults* (New York: Smithmark Publishers, 1998); Sarah Royal and Jillian Hofer, *Thou Spleeny Swag-Bellied Miscreant: Create Your Own Shakespearean Insults* (Philadelphia: Running Press, 2014); *The Little Book of Shakespeare's Insults, the Bard's Best Barbs* (London: Welbeck Publishing, 2021); Patricia Crouch, *The Shakespeare Insults Coloring Book* (London: Gumdrop Press, 2020).

3 https://www.playingwithplays.com/shakespeare-insult-generator/ (Accessed 20 July 2021). See also Barry Kraft, *Shakespeare Insult Generator: Mix and Match More than 150,000 Insults in the Bard's Own Words* (San Francisco: Chronicle Books, 2014).

4 In *Action Is Eloquence*, 89–90, Bevington summarizes the main codes that govern the representation of anger.

5 Thomas Wright, *The Passions of the Minde* [1601] (Hildesheim: Georg Olms Verlag, 1973), 197–8.

6 Ibid., 212.

7 Ibid., 176.

8 On signs that are common to anger and madness, see John Davies, *Microcosmos* (Oxford, 1603, STC (2nd ed.) / 6333), 186–7. Quoted by Bevington, *Action Is Eloquence*, 92.

9 See Paradin, *Devises Heroïques*, 109–10; Erasmus, *Adages* II. i. 1 to II. vi. 100, vol. 33, trans. R.A.B. Mynors (Toronto: University of Toronto Press, 1991), Adage 39 ('Lingua quo vadis? Tongue, whither wouldst thou?'), II. ii. 39 / LB II. 460 C-D, 93.

BIBLIOGRAPHY OF WORK CITED

Adams, Thomas. 'The Taming of the Tongue'. In *The Sacrifice of Thankefulnesse A Sermon Preached at Pauls Crosse* [...]. London, 1616, STC (2nd ed.) / 125.
Adams, Thomas. 'The Taming of the Tongue'. In *The Works of Thomas Adams*, reprinted from the series of Standard Divines by James Nichol. With a memoir of the author by Joseph Angus, in three volumes, 1861–6, vol. 3, 10–22. Eureka: Tanski Publications, 1998.
Aesop. *Aesop's Fables*, translated by Laura Gibbs. Oxford: Oxford World's Classics, 2002.
Alciati, Andreae (Alciat). *Les Emblèmes* [1551]. Paris: Klincksieck, 1997.
Allan, Keith and Kate Burridge. *Euphemism and Dysphemism, Language Used as Shield and Weapon*. New York and Oxford: Oxford University Press, 1991.
Allan, Keith and Kate Burridge. *Forbidden Words, Taboo and the Censuring of Language*. Cambridge: Cambridge University Press, 2006.
Anderson, Thomas P. *Performing Early Modern Trauma from Shakespeare to Milton*. Aldershot: Ashgate, 2006.
Anonymous. *The Anathomie of Sinne*. London, 1603, STC (2nd ed.) / 12465.5.
Auden, W. H. *The Dyer's Hand and Other Essays*. London: Faber and Faber, 1963.
Austin, John Langshaw. *How to Do Things with Words*. Oxford: Oxford University Press, 1962.
Bacon, Francis. *The Charge of Francis Bacon against duels*. London, 1614, STC (2nd ed.) / 1125.
Baker, John H. and S. F. C. Milsom. *Sources of English Legal History, Private law to 1750*. London: Butterworths, 1986.
Baker, John H. *An Introduction to English Legal History*. London: Butterworths, 1990.

Bakhtin, Mikhail. *Rabelais and His World*. 1965, translated by Hélène Iswolsky. Bloomington and Indianapolis: Indiana University Press, 1984.

Balizet, Ariane M. '"Amend Thy Face:" Contagion and Disgust in the Henriad'. In *Contagion and the Shakespearean Stage*, edited by Darryl Chalk and Mary Floyd-Wilson, 127–45. Cham: Palgrave Macmillan, 2019.

Barber, C. L. and Richard P. Wheeler. *The Whole Journey, Shakespeare's Power of Development*. Berkeley, Los Angeles and London: University of California Press, 1986.

Barber, C. L. *Shakespeare's Festive Comedy, a Study of Dramatic Form and Its Relation to Social Custom*. 1959. Princeton, New Jersey: Princeton University Press, 1972.

Bardsley, Sandy. *Venomous Tongues: Speech and Gender in Late Medieval England*. Philadelphia: University of Pennsylvania Press, 2006.

Baret, John. *An Alveary or Triple Dictionary, in English, Latin and French*. London, 1574, STC (2nd ed.) / 1410.

Bawcutt, Priscilla. 'The Art of Flyting'. *Scottish Literary Journal* 10, no. 2 (1983): 5–24.

Beaumatin, Éric and Michel Garcia, eds. *L'Invective au Moyen Âge. Atalaya, Revue Française d'Études Médiévales Hispaniques* 5 (1994). Paris: Presses de la Sorbonne Nouvelle, 1995.

Beckett, Samuel. 'Texts for Nothing', XIII. In *Collected Shorter Prose 1945–1980*. London: John Calder, 1984.

Becon, Thomas. *An Invectyve Agenst the Moost Wicked & Detestable Vyce of Swearing*. London, 1543, STC (2nd ed.) / 1730.5.

Bevington, David. '"Why Should Calamity be Full of Words?" The Efficacy of Cursing in *Richard III*'. *Iowa State Journal of Research* 56 (1981): 9–21.

Bevington, David. *Action Is Eloquence. Shakespeare's Language of Gesture*. Cambridge, MA: Harvard University Press, 1984.

Bicknoll, Edmond. *A Swoord agaynst Swearyng*. London, 1579, STC (2nd ed.) / 3049.

Billacois, François. *Le Duel dans la société française des XVIè et XVIIè siècles*. Paris: Éditions de l'École des Hautes Études en Sciences Sociales, 1986.

Birney, Alice Lotvin. *Satiric Catharsis in Shakespeare*. Berkeley, Los Angeles and London: University of California Press, 1973.

Blackstone, William. *Commentaries on the Laws of England*, vol. 3. Oxford: Clarendon Press, 1768.
Bond, Ronald B., ed. *Certain Sermons or Homilies (1547) and a Homily against disobedience and Wilful Rebellion (1570), A Critical Edition*. Toronto: University of Toronto Press, 1987.
Boose, Lynda E. 'Scolding Brides and Bridling Scolds: Taming the Woman's Unruly Member', *Shakespeare Quarterly* 42, no. 2 (1991): 179–213.
Bourdieu, Pierre. *Language and Symbolic Power*. Cambridge: Polity Press, 1992.
Bryson, Anna. *From Courtesy to Civility. Changing Codes of Conduct in Early Modern England*. Oxford Clarendon Press: Oxford University Press, 1998.
Buelens, Gert, Sam Durrant and Robert Eaglestone, eds. *The Future of Trauma Theory. Contemporary Literary Cultural Criticism*. London and New York: Routledge, 2014.
Bulwer, John. *Chirologia, or, the Naturall Language of the Hand*. London, 1644, Wing / B5466.
Butler, Judith. *Excitable Speech. A Politics of the Performative*. New York: Routledge, 1997.
Cahill, Patricia A. *Unto the Breach: Martial Formations, Historical Trauma, and the Early Modern Stage*. Oxford: Oxford University Press, 2008.
Castiglione, Baldassare. *The Courtyer*, originally published in 1528, translated by Sir T. Toby. London, 1561, STC (2nd ed.) / 4778.
Cavell, Stanley. *Disowning Knowledge in Six Plays of Shakespeare*. Cambridge: Cambridge University Press, 1987.
Charles Gibbon. *The Praise of a Good Name. The Reproch of an Ill Name*. London, 1594, STC (2nd ed.) / 11819.
Clemen, W. H. *A Commentary on Shakespeare's* Richard III. London: Methuen, 1957.
Cooper, Thomas. *Thesaurus Linguae Romanae et Britannicae*. London, 1578, STC (2nd ed.) / 5688.
Cotgrave, Randle. *A Dictionary of the French and English Tongues*. London, 1611, STC (2nd ed.) / 5830.
Cressy, David. *Dangerous Talk. Scandalous, Seditious, and Treasonable Speech in Pre-Modern England*. Oxford and New York: Oxford University Press, 2010.
Crouch, Patricia. *The Shakespeare Insults Coloring Book*. London: Gumdrop Press, 2020.

Culpeper, Jonathan. *Impoliteness. Using Language to Cause Offence*. Cambridge: Cambridge University Press, 2011.
Davidson, Clifford. '*Timon of Athens*: The Iconography of False Friendship'. *The Huntington Library Quarterly* 43, no. 3 (Summer 1980): 181–200.
Davies, John. *Microcosmos*. Oxford, 1603, STC (2nd ed.) / 6333.
Dell Villano, Bianca. *Using the Devil with Courtesy: Shakespeare and the Language of (Im)Politeness*. Bern: Peter Lang, 2018.
Della Casa, Giovanni. *Galateo*. London, 1576, STC (2nd ed.) / 4738.
Della Porta, Giambattista. *De Humane Physionomonia*. 1586. Paris: Aux Amateurs de Livres, 1990.
Di Grassi, Giacomo. *His True Arte of Defence*. London, 1594, STC (2nd ed.) / 12190.
Doran, Madeleine. 'Good Name in *Othello*'. *Studies in English Literature, 1500–1900* 7, no. 2 (Spring 1967): 195–217.
Dunbar, William. 'The Flyting of Dunbar and Kennedy'. In *William Dunbar: The Complete Works*, edited by John Conlee. Kalamazoo: Medieval Institute Publications, Western Michigan University, 2004, Poem 83, 181–98.
Elam, Keir. *Shakespeare's Universe of Discourse. Language-Games in the Comedies*. Cambridge: Cambridge University Press, 1984.
Elliott, Robert C. *The Power of Satire: Magic, Ritual, Art*. Princeton: Princeton University Press, 1960.
Emmison, F. G. *Archives and Local History*. London: Methuen, 1965.
Emmison, F. G. *Elizabethan Life: Disorder*. Essex Record Office Publication, no. 56. Chelmsford: Essex County Council, 1970.
Emmison, F. G. *Elizabethan Life: Morals and Church Courts*. Essex Record Office Publications, no. 63. Chelmsford: Essex County Council, 1973.
Erasmus, Desiderius. *Adages* II. i. 1 to II. vi. 100, vol. 33, translated by R.A.B. Mynors. Toronto: University of Toronto Press, 1991.
Erasmus, Desiderius. *Lingua*, translated by Elaine Fantham. In *Collected Works of Erasmus* 29, 249–412. Toronto: University of Toronto Press, 1989.
Escolme, Bridget. *Emotional Excess on the Shakespearean Stage: Passion's Slaves*. London: Bloomsbury, 2013.
Evans, Robert C. 'Ophelia and trauma Theory in Shakespeare's *Hamlet*'. In *Critical Insights:* Hamlet, edited by Robert C. Evans, 40–55. Amenia, NY: Grey House Publishing, 2019.

Felman, Shoshana. *The Literary Speech Act: Don Juan with J. L. Austin, or Seduction in Two Languages*, translated by Catherine Porter. Ithaca: Cornell University Press, 1983.
Fernie, Ewan. *Shame in Shakespeare*. London and New York: Routledge, 2002.
Fifoot, C. H. S. *History and Sources of the Common Law Tort and Contract*. London: Steevens and Sons Limited, 1949.
Fisch, Harold. 'Shakespeare and the Language of Gesture'. *Shakespeare Studies* XIX (1987): 239–51.
Fitzpatrick, Joan. *Food in Shakespeare: Early Modern Dietaries and the Plays*. Aldershot and Burlington, VT: Ashgate, 2007.
Florio, John. *A World of Words or Most Copious, and Exact Dictionarie in Italian and English*. London, 1598, STC (2nd ed.) / 11098.
Florio, John. *Queen Anna's New World of Words*. London, 1611, STC (2nd ed.) / 11099.
Fly, Richard. *Shakespeare's Mediated World*. Amherst: University of Massachusetts Press, 1976.
Foakes, R. A. *Shakespeare and Violence*. Cambridge: Cambridge University Press, 2003.
Freedman, Penelope. *You and Thou in Shakespeare: A Practical Guide for Actors, Directors, Students and Teachers*. Arden Performance Companions. London: Bloomsbury, 2021.
Freud, Sigmund. *Malaise dans la Civilisation*. Paris: Presses Universitaires de France, 1976.
Gaignebet, Claude and Marie-Claude Périer. 'L'homme et l'excretum: de l'excécré à l'excrété'. In *Histoire des Mœurs*, edited by Jean Poirier, Vol. 1, 831–93. Paris: La Pléiade, 1990.
Galway, Margaret. 'Flyting in Shakspere's [sic] Comedies'. *The Shakespeare Association Bulletin* 10, no. 4 (October, 1935): 183–91.
The Geneva Bible: A Facsimile of the 1560 Edition. With an introduction by Lloyd E. Berry Madison: University of Wisconsin Press, 1969.
Gibson, Rex. *Shakespeare's Language, a Handbook for Teachers*. Cambridge: Cambridge University Press, 1997.
Girard, Didier and Jonathan Pollock, eds. *Invectives, Quand le corps reprend la parole*. Perpignan: Presses Universitaires de Perpignan, 2006.
Gowing, Laura. 'Language, Power and the Law: Women's Slander Litigation in Early Modern London'. In *Women, Crime and the*

Courts in Early Modern England, edited by Jenny Kermode and Garthine Walker, 26–47. London: UCL Press, 1994.

Gross, Kenneth. 'Slander and Skepticism in *Othello*'. *ELH* 56, no. 4 (Winter 1989): 819–52.

Gross, Kenneth. *Shakespeare's Noise*. Chicago and London: The University of Chicago Press, 2001.

Guiraud, Pierre. *Les Gros mots*. Paris: PUF, 1975.

Habermann, Ina. *Staging Slander and Gender in Early Modern England*. Aldershot: Ashgate, 2003.

H. L., *A Dictionary French and English*. London, 1571, STC (2nd ed.) / 6832.

Hadfield, Andrew. *Lying in Early Modern English Culture. From the Oath of Supremacy to the Oath of Allegiance*. Cambridge: Cambridge University Press, 2017.

Hall, Jonathan. 'The Evacuations of Falstaff'. In *Shakespeare and Carnival. After Bakhtin*, edited by Ronald Knowles, 123–51. Houndmills: Macmillan, 1998.

Harington, John. *A New Discourse of a Stale Subject Called the Metamorphosis of Ajax* [1596], edited by Elizabeth Story Donno. New York: Columbia University Press, 1962.

Hawes, Stephen. *The Co[n]vercyon of Swerers*. London, 1509, STC (2nd ed.) / 12943.

Helmholz, R. H. 'Canonical Defamation in Medieval England'. *The American Journal of Legal History* XV (1971): 255–68.

Helmholz, R. H. *Select Cases on Defamation to 1600*. London: Selden Society, 1985.

Heywood, Thomas. *Gynaikeion*. London, 1624, STC (2nd ed.) / 13326.

Hill, Wayne F. and Cynthia J. Öttchen, *Shakespeare's Insults: Educating Your Wit* [1991]. Cambridge: Mainsail Press, 1993.

Hillman, David. 'The Gastric Epic: *Troilus and Cressida*'. *Shakespeare Quarterly* 48, no. 3 (1997): 295–313.

Hobday, C. H. 'Why the Sweets Melted: A Study in Shakespeare's Imagery'. *Shakespeare Quarterly* 16, no. 1 (Winter 1965): 3–17.

Holcomb, Chris. *Mirth Making. The Rhetorical Discourse on Jesting in Early Modern England*. Columbia: University of South Carolina Press, 2001.

Holdsworth, W. S. 'Defamation in the Sixteenth and Seventeenth Centuries'. *The Law Quarterly Review* XL (July, 1924): 302–15.

Hollyband, Claude. *Dictionary French and English*. London, 1593, STC (2nd ed.) / 6737.

Homer. *Iliad*. Books 1–12, translated by A. T. Murray, revised by William F. Wyatt. Loeb Classical Library. Cambridge, MA: Harvard University Press, 1999.

Howard, Skiles. *The Politics of Courtly Dancing in Early Modern England*. Amherst: University of Massachusetts Press, 1998.

Hughes, Geoffrey. *An Encyclopedia of Swearing. The Social History of Oaths, Profanity, Foul Language, and Ethnic Slurs in the English-Speaking World*. Armonk, NY: M.E. Sharpe, 2006.

Hughes, Geoffrey. *Swearing. A Social History of Foul Language, Oaths and Profanity in English*. Oxford: Blackwell, 1991.

Huizinga, Johan. *Homo Ludens. A Study of the Play-Element in Culture*. 1949. New York: Angelico Press, reprint of the first edition published by Routledge and Kegan Paul, 2006.

Ingram, Martin. '"Scolding Women Cucked or Washed": A Crisis in Gender Relations in Early Modern England?'. In *Women, Crime and the Courts*, edited by Jenny Kermode and Garthine Walker, 48–80. Chapel Hill and London: The University of North Carolina Press, 1994.

Irvine, William B. *A Slap in the Face. Why Insults Hurt – And Why They Should Not*. Oxford: Oxford University Press, 2013.

James I. *A Publication of His Maties Edict and Severe Censure against Private Combats and Combatants*. London, 1613, STC (2nd ed.) / 8498.5.

Janoff-Bulman, Ronnie. *Shattered Assumptions: Towards a New Psychology of Trauma*. New York: Free Press; Toronto: Maxwell Macmillan Canada; New York: Maxwell Macmillan International, 1992.

Jardine, Lisa. *Still Harping on Daughters: Women and Drama in the Age of Shakespeare*. New York and London: Harvester Wheatsheaf, 1983.

Jardine, Lisa. '"Why should he call her whore?" Defamation and Desdemona's Case'. In *Addressing Frank Kermode: Essays in Criticism and Interpretation*, edited by Margaret Tudeau-Clayton and Martin Warner, 124–53. Urbana: University of Illinois Press, 1991.

Jeanneret, Michel. *A Feast of Words: Banquets and Table Talk in the Renaissance*, translated by Jeremy Whiteley and Emma Hughes. Chicago: The university of Chicago Press, 1991.

Jeanneret, Michel. *Des Mets et des Mots, Banquets et Propos de Table à la Renaissance*. Paris: Corti, 1987.

Jones, Ann Rosalind and Peter Stallybrass. *Renaissance Clothing and the Materials of Memory*. Cambridge: Cambridge University Press, 2000.

Jonson, Benjamin. *Poetaster*, edited by Tom Cain. Manchester: Manchester University Press, 1995.

Jonson, Benjamin. *The Alchemist*. In *The Cambridge Edition of the Works of Ben Jonson*, edited by David Bevington, Martin Butler and Ian Donaldson. Cambridge: Cambridge University Press, 2012, Vol. 3.

Jucker, Andreas H. and Irma Taavitsainen. 'Diachronic Speech Act Analysis. Insults from Flyting to Flaming'. *Journal of Historical Pragmatics* 1, no. 1 (2000): 67–95.

Kaplan, Lindsay M. 'Slander for Slander in *Measure for Measure*'. *Renaissance Drama*, New Series 21 (1990): 23–54.

Kaplan, M. Lindsay. *The Culture of Slander in Early Modern England*. Cambridge: Cambridge UP, 1997.

Karim-Cooper, Farah. *The Hand on the Shakespearean Stage. Gesture, Touch and the Spectacle of Dismemberment*. London and New York: Bloomsbury Arden Shakespeare, 2016.

Kegl, Rosemary. '"The Adoption of Abominable Terms": The Insults That Shape Windsor's Middle Class'. *English Literary History* 61 (1994): 253–78.

Kennedy, Colleen E. '"Qualmish at the Smell of Leek". Overcoming Disgust and Creating the Nation-state in *Henry V*'. In *Disgust in Early Modern English Literature*, edited by Natalie K. Eschenbaum and Barbara Correll, 124–41. London: Routledge, 2016.

Kerrigan, John. *Shakespeare's Binding Language*. Oxford: Oxford University Press, 2016.

King, Ros. Cymbeline. *Constructions of Britain*. Aldershot: Ashgate, 2005.

Knapp, James A., ed. *Shakespeare and the Power of the Face*. London and New York: Routledge, 2015.

Kraft, Barry. *Thy Father Is a Gorbellied Codpiece! Create over 100,000 of Your Own Shakespearean Insults*. New York: Smithmark Publishers, 1998.

Kraft, Barry. *Shakespeare Insult Generator: Mix and Match More than 150,000 Insults in the Bard's Own Words*. San Francisco: Chronicle Books, 2014.

Krieger, Elliot. *A Marxist Study of Shakespeare's Comedies*. London and Basingstoke: The Macmillan Press, 1979.

Larguèche, Évelyne. *Espèces de… Les Lois de l'effet injure*. Chambéry: Université de Savoie: Éditions du Laboratoire Langages, Littératures, Sociétés, 2009.
Larguèche, Évelyne. *Injure et sexualité. Le corps du délit*. Paris: PUF, 1997.
Larguèche, Évelyne. *L'effet injure. De la pragmatique à la psychanalyse*. Coll. 'Voix nouvelles en psychanalyse'. Paris: PUF, 1983.
Larguèche, Évelyne. *L'Injure à fleur de peau*. Paris: L'Harmattan, 1993.
Larkin, James F, ed. *Stuart Royal Proclamations, Vol I, Royal Proclamations of King James I 1603–1625*. Oxford: At the Clarendon Press, 1973.
Laroque, François. 'Shakespeare's "Battle of Carnival and Lent". The Falstaff Scenes Reconsidered' (*1 & 2 Henry IV*). In *Shakespeare and Carnival, after Bakhtin*, edited by Ronald Knowles, 83–96. Houndmills: Macmillan, 1998.
Lassiter, John C. 'Defamation of Peers: The Rise and Decline of the Action for *Scandalum Magnatum*, 1497–1773'. *The American Journal of Legal History* XXII (1978): 216–36.
Lecercle, Ann. 'Corps, Regard, Parole: Basilisk and Antichrist in *Richard III*'. In *Le Tyran. Shakespeare contre Richard III*, edited by Dominique Goy-Blanquet and Richard Marienstras, 27–50. Amiens: Presses de l'UFR Clerc Université Picardie, 1990.
Lecercle, Jean-Jacques and Denise Riley. *The Force of Language*. Houndmills: Palgrave, 2004.
Lecercle, Jean-Jacques. *The Violence of Language*. London and New York: Routledge, 1990.
Lewis, C. S. *Studies in Words*. Cambridge: Cambridge at the University Press, 1960.
Little, Arthur L. Jr. 'The Primal Scene of Racism in *Othello*: An Essence That's Not Seen'. *Shakespeare Quarterly* 43, no. 3 (1993): 304–24.
The Little Book of Shakespeare's Insults, The Bard's Best Barbs. London: Welbeck Publishing, 2021.
Lyly, William. *A Shorte Introduction of Latin Grammar*. London, 1558, STC (2nd ed.) / 15613.3.
Maclean, Ian. *Interpretation and Meaning in the Renaissance*. Cambridge: Cambridge University Press, 1992.
Magnusson, Lynne. *Shakespeare and Social Dialogue. Dramatic Language and Elizabethan Letters*. Cambridge: Cambridge University Press, 1999.

March, John. *Actions for Slaunder*. London, 1647, Wing / M571.
Marconville, Jean de. *A Treatise of the Good and Evil Tongue*, translation, with a foreword by T. S. London, 1592, STC (2nd ed.) / 17313.
Mason, Shirley Carr. '"Foul Wrinkled Witch": Superstition, Scepticism and Margaret of Anjou in Shakespeare's *Richard III*'. *Cahiers Élisabéthains* 52 (October 1997): 25–37.
Mazzio, Carla. 'Sins of the Tongue'. In *The Body in Parts. Fantasies of Corporeality in Early Modern Europe*, edited by David Hillman and Carla Mazzio, 52–79. New York and London: Routledge, 1997.
McAlindon, Thomas. 'Language, Style and Meaning in *Troilus and Cressida*'. *PMLA* 84, no. 1 (1969): 29–43.
McDonald, Russ. *Shakespeare and the Arts of Language*. Oxford: Oxford University Press, 2001.
McLaverty, Joseph. 'No Abuse: The Prince and Falstaff in the Tavern Scenes of *Henry IV*'. *Shakespeare Survey* 34 (1981): 105–10.
Milsom, S. F. C. *Historical Foundations of the Common Law*. London: Butterworths, 1981.
Mohr, Melissa. *Holy Sh*t. A Brief History of Swearing*. Oxford: Oxford University Press, 2013.
Montague, Ashley. *The Anatomy of Swearing*. 1967. Philadelphia: University of Pennsylvania Press, 2001.
Morris, Desmond. *Bodytalk. A World Guide to Gestures*. London: Jonathan Cape, 1994.
Morris, Desmond. *Gestures, Their Origins and Distribution*. London: Jonathan Cape, 1979.
Neu, Jerome. *Sticks and Stones. The Philosophy of Insults*. Oxford: Oxford University Press, 2008.
Northbrooke, John. *A Treatise Wherein Dicing, Dauncing, Vaine Plaies or Enterludes with Other Idle Pastimes, etc. Commonly Used on the Sabboth day, Are Reprooved, by the Authoritie of the Worde of God and Auncient Writers*. London, 1577, STC (2nd ed.) / 18670.
Ovid. *Ovid His Invective against Ibis*, translated by Thomas Underdown. London, 1569, STC (2nd ed.) / 18949.
Oxford English Dictionary on line. Oxford University Press, 2021.
Paradin, Claude. *Devises Heroïques*. 1557. Introduction by Alison Saunders. Aldershot: Scolar Press, 1989.

Paradin, Claude. *The Heroicall Devises of M. Claudius Paradin*. London, 1591, STC (2nd ed.) / 19183.
Parker, Patricia. 'Rude Mechanicals'. In *Subject and Object in Renaissance Culture*, edited by Margreta de Grazia, Maureen Quilligan, and Peter Stallybrass, 43–82. Cambridge: Cambridge University Press, 1996.
Parker, Patricia. *Shakespeare from the Margins, Language, Culture, Context*. Chicago: The University of Chicago Press, 1996.
Parks, Walter Ward. 'Flyting and Fighting: Pathways in the Realization of the Epic Contest'. *Neophilologus* 70 (1986): 292–306.
Parks, Walter Ward. 'Flyting, Sounding, Debate. Three Verbal Contest Genres'. *Poetics Today* 7, no. 3 (1986): 439–54.
Parks, Walter Ward. 'The Flyting Speech in Traditional Heroic Narrative'. *Neophilologus* 71 (1987): 285–95.
Parks, Walter Ward. 'The Flyting Contract and Adversarial Patterning in the Alliterative *Morte Arthure*'. In *Traditions and Innovations, Essays on British Literature of the Middle Ages and the Renaissance*, edited by David G. Allen and Robert A. White, 59–74. Newark: University of Delaware Press, 1990.
Parks, Walter Ward. *Verbal Dueling in Heroic Narrative, the Homeric and Old English Traditions*. Princeton: Princeton University Press, 1990.
Partridge, Eric. *Shakespeare's Bawdy*. London and New York: Routledge, 1947.
Peltonen, Markku. *The Duel in Early Modern England. Civility, Politeness and Honour*. Cambridge: Cambridge University Press, 2003.
Perceval, Richard. *Dictionary in Spanish and English*. London, 1599, STC (2nd ed.) / 19620.
Perkins, William. *A Direction for the Government of the Tongue According to God's Worde*. Cambridge, 1593, STC (2nd ed.) / 19688.
Plutarch. 'How to Tell a Flatterer from a Friend' ('Quomodo adulator ab amico internoscatur'). In *Moralia* 1, translated by Frank Cole Babbitt, 263–395 (48E–74E). Loeb Classical Library. Cambridge, MA: Harvard; London: Heinemann, 1927 (repr. 1949).
Prendergast, Maria Teresa Micaela. *Railing, Reviling, and Invective in English Literary Culture, 1588–1617: The Anti-Poetics of Theater and Print*. Burlington, VT: Ashgate, 2012.

Puttenham, George. *The Arte of English Poesie*. London, 1589, STC (2nd ed.) / 20519.5.

Rebhorn, Wayne A. 'Petruchio's "Rope Tricks": *The Taming of the Shrew* and the Renaissance Discourse of Rhetoric', *Modern Philology* 92, no. 3 (February 1995): 294–327.

Rey, Alain, ed. *Dictionnaire Historique de la Langue Française*, edited by Alain Rey. Paris: Dictionnaire Le Robert, 1993.

Rhodes, Neil. *Elizabethan Grotesque*. London, Boston and Henley: Routledge & Kegan, 1980.

Riley, Denise. '"A Voice without a Mouth": Inner Speech'. In *The Force of Language*, edited by Jean-Jacques Lecercle and Denise Riley, 7–45. Houndmills: Palgrave, 2004.

Riley, Denise. *Impersonal Passion. Language as Affect*. Durham and London: Duke University Press, 2005.

Ringel, Shoshana and Jerrold R. Brandell, eds. *Trauma. Contemporary Directions in Trauma Theory, Research, and Practice*. New York: Columbia University Press 2020.

Robson, Simon [R. S.]. *The Courte of Civill Courtesie* (London, 1577), STC (2nd ed.) / 21134.5.

Romei, Haniball. *The Courtiers Academie*, originally written in Italian by Count Haniball Romei, a gentleman of Ferrara, and translated into English by I. K. London, 1598, STC (2nd ed.) / 21311.

Rosen, Barbara. *Witchcraft in England, 1558–1618*. 1969. Amherst: The University of Massachusetts Press, 1991.

Ross, Daniel W. '"What a number of men eats Timon": Consumption in *Timon of Athens*'. *Iowa State Journal of Research* 59, no. 3 (February 1985): 273–84.

Rossiter, A. P. *Angel with Horns. Five lectures on Shakespeare*. London and New York: Longman, 1961.

Rowlands, Samuel. *Looke to It: For, Ile Stabbe ye*. London, 1604, STC (2nd ed.) / 21398.

Royal Sarah and Jillian Hofer. *Thou Spleeny Swag-Bellied Miscreant: Create Your Own Shakespearean Insults*. Philadelphia: Running Press, 2014.

Saval, Peter Kishore. *Shakespeare in Hate. Emotions, Passions, Selfhood*. London: Routledge, 2016.

Saviolo, Vincentio. *His Practise, in Two Bookes*. London, 1595, STC (2nd. ed.) / 21789.

Sawday, Jonathan. *The Body Emblazoned. Dissection and the Human Body in Renaissance Culture*. London and New York: Routledge, 1995.

Scot, Reginal. *The Discovery of Witchcraft*. London, 1584, STC (2nd ed.) / 21864.
Scott, Tom. *Dunbar, a Critical Exposition of the Poems*. Edinburgh, London: Oliver and Boyd, 1966.
The Seconde Tome of Homelyes of Such Matters as Were Promised and Intituled in the Former Part of Homelyes. London, 1563, STC (2nd ed.) / 13664.
Segar, William [Richard Jones]. *The Booke of Honour and Armes*, London, 1590, STC (2nd ed.) / 22163.
Sexton, Joyce H. *The Slandered Woman in Shakespeare*. Victoria: English Literary Studies of the University of Victoria, no. 12, 1978.
Shakespeare, William and Thomas Middleton. *Timon of Athens*, edited by Anthony B. Dawson and Gretchen E. Minton. The Arden Shakespeare, Third Series. London: Methuen Drama, 2008.
Shakespeare, William. *All's Well That Ends Well*, edited by Suzanne Gossett and Helen Wilcox. The Arden Shakespeare, Third Series. London and New York: Bloomsbury, 2019.
Shakespeare, William. *Antony and Cleopatra*, edited by John Wilders. The Arden Shakespeare, Third Series. London: Bloomsbury, 1995.
Shakespeare, William. *As You Like It*, edited by Juliet Dusinberre. The Arden Shakespeare, Third Series. London: Thomson Learning, 2006.
Shakespeare, William. *The Comedy of Errors*, edited by Kent Cartwright. The Arden Shakespeare, Third Series. London: Bloomsbury, 2016.
Shakespeare, William. *Cymbeline*, edited by Martin Butler. Cambridge: Cambridge University Press, 2005.
Shakespeare, William. *Cymbeline*, edited by Valerie Wayne. The Arden Shakespeare, Third Series. London and New York: Bloomsbury, 2017.
Shakespeare, William. *Hamlet*, edited by Ann Thompson and Neil Taylor. The Arden Shakespeare, Third Series. London: Thomson Learning, 2006.
Shakespeare, William. *Henry V*, edited by Gary Taylor. Oxford: Oxford University Press, 1982.
Shakespeare, William. *King Henry IV Part 1*, edited by Arthur Raleigh Humphreys. Arden Edition. London and New York: Routledge, 1960.

Shakespeare, William. *King Henry IV Part 1*, edited by David Scott Kastan. The Arden Shakespeare, Third Series. London: Thomson Learning, 2002.

Shakespeare, William. *King Henry IV Part 2*, edited by Arthur Raleigh Humphreys. Routledge: London and New York, Arden, 1966.

Shakespeare, William. *King Henry IV Part 2*, edited by James C. Bulman. The Arden Shakespeare, Third Series. London and New York: Bloomsbury, 2016.

Shakespeare, William. *King Henry V*, edited by Thomas Wallace Craik. 1995. The Arden Shakespeare, Third Series. London: Thomson Learning, 2005.

Shakespeare, William. *King John*, edited by Jesse M. Lander and J. J. M. Tobin. The Arden Shakespeare, Third Series. London: Bloomsbury, 2018.

Shakespeare, William. *King Lear*, edited by R. A. Foakes. 1997. The Arden Shakespeare, Third Series. London: Thomson Learning, 2005.

Shakespeare, William. *King Richard II*, edited by Charles R. Forker. The Arden Shakespeare, Third Series. London: Thomson Learning, 2002.

Shakespeare, William. *King Richard III*, edited by James R. Siemons. The Arden Shakespeare, Third Series. London and New York: Bloomsbury, 2009.

Shakespeare, William. *The Life of Timon of Athens*, edited by John Jowett. Oxford: Oxford University Press, 2004.

Shakespeare, William. *Love's Labour's Lost*, edited by H. R. Woudhuysen. The Arden Shakespeare, Third Series. London: Methuen Drama, 1998.

Shakespeare, William. *Macbeth*, edited by Kenneth Muir. Arden Shakespeare. London: Routledge, 1964.

Shakespeare, William. *Measure for Measure*, edited by A. A. Braunmuller and Robert N. Watson. The Arden Shakespeare, Third Series. London and New York: Bloomsbury, 2020.

Shakespeare, William. *The Merchant of Venice*, edited by John Drakakis. The Arden Shakespeare, Third Series. London and New York: Bloomsbury, 2010.

Shakespeare, William. *A Midsummer Night's Dream*, edited by Sukanta Chaudhuri. The Arden Shakespeare, Third Series. London: Bloomsbury, 2017.

Shakespeare, William. *Much Ado about Nothing*, edited by Arthur Raleigh Humphreys. Arden. London: Methuen, 1981.

Shakespeare, William. *Much Ado about Nothing*, edited by Claire McEachern. The Arden Shakespeare, Third Series. London and New York: Bloomsbury, 2007.
Shakespeare, William. *Othello*, edited by E. A. J. Honigmann, revised with a new introduction by Ayanna Thompson. The Arden Shakespeare, Third Series. London and New York: Bloomsbury, 2016.
Shakespeare, William. *Romeo and Juliet*, edited by Jill L. Levenson. Oxford: Oxford University Press, 2000.
Shakespeare, William. *Romeo and Juliet*, edited by René Weis. The Arden Shakespeare, Third Series. London: Bloomsbury, 2012.
Shakespeare, William. *The Riverside Shakespeare*, 2nd ed. Boston, general and textual editor G. Blakemore Evans (with J. J. M. Tobin). New York: Houghton Mifflin Company, 1997.
Shakespeare, William. *The Taming of the Shrew*, edited by Barbara Hodgdon. The Arden Shakespeare, Third Series. London: Methuen, 2010.
Shakespeare, William. *Titus Andronicus*, edited by Jonathan Bate. The Arden Shakespeare, Third Series. London and New York: Routledge, 1995.
Shakespeare, William. *Troilus and Cressida*, edited by David Bevington. 1998. The Arden Shakespeare, Third Series. London: Thomson Learning, 2006.
Shakespeare, William. *Twelfth Night or What You Will*, edited by Keir Elam. The Arden Shakespeare, Third Series. London: Methuen Drama, 2008.
Sharpe, J. A. '"Such Disagreement betwyx Neighbours": Litigation and Human Relations in Early Modern England'. In *Disputes and Settlements. Law and Human Relations in the West*, edited by John Bossy, 167–87. Cambridge: Cambridge University Press, 1983.
Sharpe, J. A. *Defamation and Sexual Slander in Early Modern England: The Church Courts at York. Borthwick Papers* 58. York: University of York: Borthwick Institute of Historical Research, 1980.
Sheppard, William. *Action upon the Case for Slander*. London, 1662, Wing / S3173A.
Sheppard, William. *An Epitome of all the Common & Statute Laws of This Nation*. London, 1656, Wing / S3184.
Silver, George. *Paradoxes of Defense*, London, 1599, STC (2nd ed.) / 22554.
Silverstone, Catherine. *Shakespeare, Trauma and Contemporary Performance*. New York: Routledge, 2011.

Slights, Camille Wells. 'The Raw and the Cooked in *The Taming of the Shrew*'. *Journal of English and Germanic Philology* 88 (1989): 168–89.

Smith, Bruce R. *The Acoustic World of Early Modern England. Attending to the O-Factor*. Chicago and London: The University of Chicago Press, 1999.

Spargo, John Webster. *Juridical Folklore in England, Illustrated by the Cucking-Stool*. Durham, NC: Duke University Press, 1944.

Spurgeon, Caroline. *Shakespeare's Imagery and What It Tells Us*. Cambridge: Cambridge University Press, 1965.

Stallybrass, Peter. 'Worn Worlds: Clothes and Identity on the Renaissance Stage'. In *Subject and Object in Renaissance Culture*, edited by Margreta de Grazia, Maureen Quilligan, and Peter Stallybrass, 289–320. Cambridge: Cambridge University Press, 1996.

Stanton, Kay. *Shakespeare's Whores. Erotics, Politics and Poetics*. New York: Palgrave Macmillan, 2014.

The Statutes of the Realm: Printed by Command of His Majesty King George the Third, in Pursuance of an Address of the House of Commons of Great Britain. From Original Records and Authentic Manuscripts. A new edition in 12 vols. of the statutes from 1235 to 1713. London: Dawsons of Pall Mall, 1810–28.

Stavreva, Kirilka. *Words Like Daggers. Violent Female Speech in Early Modern England*. Lincoln and London: University of Nebraska Press, 2015.

Stone, Lawrence. *The Crisis of the Aristocracy, 1558–1641*. Oxford: At the Clarendon Press, 1965.

Swetnam, Joseph. *The Schoole of the Noble and Worthy Science of Defence*. London, 1617, STC (2nd ed.) / 23543.

Thomas, Miranda Fay. *Shakespeare's Body Language. Shaming Gestures and Gender Politics on the Renaissance Stage*. The Arden Shakespeare. London and New York: Bloomsbury, 2020.

Thomas, Thomas. *Dictionarium Linguae Latinae et Anglicanae*. London, 1587, STC (2nd ed.) / 24008.

Thompson, E. P. 'Rough Music: Le charivari anglais', *Annales (Économies, Sociétés, Civilisations)*, 27, n°2, (Janvier-Juin 1972): 285–312.

Underdown, D. E. 'The Taming of the Scold: The Enforcement of Patriarchal Authority in Early Modern England'. In *Order and Disorder in Early Modern England*, edited by Anthony Fletcher and John Stevenson, 116–39. Cambridge: Cambridge University Press, 1985.

Valls-Russell, Janice. 'Review of *Henry V*, directed by Jean-Louis Benoit for Théâtre de l'Aquarium, Papal Court, Avignon Theatre Festival, Avignon, 16 July 1999'. *Cahiers Élisabéthains* 57 (April 2000): 132–4.

Vienne-Guerrin, Nathalie. '"Base Phrygian Turk!": Injures et "espèces de … ": analyse microscopique d'un étrange spécimen shakespearien'. *LISA* VI, no. 3 (2008): 80–91. http://lisa.revues.org/377 (Accessed 10 July 2021).

Vienne-Guerrin, Nathalie. '"Castalian King Urinal Hector of Greece": la "langue latrine" dans *The Merry Wives of Windsor*'. In *Langue et Altérité dans la culture de la Renaissance / Language and Otherness in Renaissance Culture*, edited by Ann Lecercle and Yan Brailowsky, 15–29. Nanterre: Presses Universitaires de Paris Ouest, 2008.

Vienne-Guerrin, Nathalie. '*Coriolanus* or the "Arraignment of an Unruly Tongue"'. Coriolan *de William Shakespeare. Langages, Interprétations, Politique(s)*, edited by Richard Hillman, 133–53. Tours: Presses universitaires François-Rabelais, 2007.

Vienne-Guerrin, Nathalie. '"Couple a gorge!": La guerre des langues dans *Henry V* de Shakespeare'. In *Langues Dominantes/Langues Dominées*, edited by Laurence Villard and Nicolas Ballier, 165–80. Rouen: PURH, 2008.

Vienne-Guerrin, Nathalie. 'Des mauvaises langues dans *Richard III*'. *XVII-XVIII. Revue de la Société d'études anglo-américaines des XVIIe et XVIIIe siècles* 49 (November 1999): 55–76.

Vienne-Guerrin, Nathalie. '"He'll rail in his rope/robe tricks": l'injure comme feu d'artifices dans *The Taming of the Shrew*'. In *L'artifice*, edited by Élisabeth Angel-Perez and Pierre Iselin, *Sillages Critiques* 10, 2009.

Vienne-Guerrin, Nathalie. '"His meanest Garment": la mémoire du mot dans *Cymbeline*', edited by Christophe Hausermann, 167–81. *Proceedings of the 2013 Société Française Shakespeare Conference*, 2013.

Vienne-Guerrin, Nathalie. '"Killing courtesy": *Le Songe* ou la courtoisie mise en pièce(s)'. *XVII-XVIII. Revue de la Société d'études anglo-américaines des XVIIe et XVIIIe siècles* 55 (2002): 27–49.

Vienne-Guerrin, Nathalie. 'L'anatomie de l'insulte dans *1 Henry IV*'. *Bulletin de la Société de Stylistique Anglaise* 17 (1996): 21–35.

Vienne-Guerrin, Nathalie. 'L'injure et la guerre dans *Troilus and Cressida*'. *Bulletin de la Société de Stylistique Anglaise* 22 (2001): 21–36.

Vienne-Guerrin, Nathalie. 'La réécriture de la Mégère dans le théâtre de Shakespeare'. In *Réécritures*, edited by Jean-Pierre Maquerlot, 77–92. Rouen: Publications de l'Université de Rouen, 2000.

Vienne-Guerrin, Nathalie. 'La réécriture des codes de duel dans l'injure Shakespearienne'. In *Réécritures*, edited by Jean-Pierre Maquerlot, 37–53. Rouen: Publications de l'Université de Rouen, 2000.

Vienne-Guerrin, Nathalie. 'Le miel et le fiel: des excès de bouche dans *Timon of Athens*'. In *Shakespeare et l'excès*, edited by Pierre Kapitaniak and Jean-Michel Déprats, 206–22. Proceedings of Société Française Shakespeare Conference, 2007.

Vienne-Guerrin, Nathalie. 'Les jeux de l'injure dans *Henry IV*'. In *Shakespeare et le Jeu*, edited by Pierre Kapitaniak, 185–99. Proceedings of the Société Française Shakespeare Conference, 2005.

Vienne-Guerrin, Nathalie. '"The noise they make" in *A Midsummer Night's Dream* on screen'. In *Shakespeare on Screen: A Midsummer Night's Dream*, edited by Sarah Hatchuel and Nathalie Vienne-Guerrin, 87–99. Rouen: Publications de l'Université de Rouen, 2004.

Vienne-Guerrin, Nathalie. '"Sicilia is a so-forth": La Rumeur dans *The Winter's Tale*'. In *A Sad Tale's Best for Winter: Approches critiques du Conte d'hiver de Shakespeare*, edited by Yan Brailowsky, Anny Crunelle-Vanrigh and Jean-Michel Déprats, 149–63. Paris: Presses Universitaires Paris Ouest, 2011.

Vienne-Guerrin, Nathalie. *Shakespeare's Insults: A Pragmatic Dictionary*. London and New York: Bloomsbury. The Arden Shakespeare, 2016.

Vienne-Guerrin, Nathalie. '"'tis worse than murder": *King Lear* ou les derniers outrages'. In *'The true blank of thine eye', Approches Critiques de* King Lear, edited by Pascale Drouet and Pierre Iselin, 265–78. Paris: Presses Universitaires de la Sorbonne, 2009.

Vienne-Guerrin, Nathalie. *The Unruly Tongue in Early Modern England. Three Treatises*. Lanham: Fairleigh Dickinson University Press, 2012.

Vienne-Guerrin, Nathalie. '"You have rated me": The Insults of *The Merchant of Venice*'. *Literaria Pragensia* 23, issue 45,

Memory, Conflict & Commerce in Early Modern Europe, edited by Martin Procházka, Paola Spinozzi and Rui Carvalho Homem (September 2013): 82–97.

Vigarello, Georges. *The Metamorphoses of Fat. A History of Obesity*, translated by C. Jon Delogu. New York: Columbia University Press, 2013.

Warnke, Frank. 'Amorous Agon, Erotic Flyting: Some Play-motifs in the Literature of Love'. In *Auctor Ludens: Essays on Play in Literature*, edited by Gerald Guinness and Andrew Hurley, 99–112. Philadelphia: J. Benjamin, 1986.

Watson, Lindsay. *Arae. The Curse Poetry of Antiquity*. Leeds: Francis Cairns, 1991.

Webbe, George. *The Araignement of an Unruly Tongue*. London, 1619, STC (2nd ed.) / 25156.

Whitney, Geffrey. *A Choice of Emblemes*. 1586. Introduction by John Manning. Aldershot: Scolar Press, 1989.

Wilder, Lina Perkins. *Shakespeare's Memory Theatre. Recollection, Properties, and Character*. Cambridge: Cambridge University Press, 2010.

Williams, Gordon. *A Dictionary of Sexual Language and Imagery in Shakespearean and Stuart Literature*, 3 vol. London: The Athlone Press, 1994.

Willis, Deborah. '"The Gnawing Vulture": Revenge, Trauma Theory, and *Titus Andronicus*'. *Shakespeare Quarterly* 53, no. 1 (Spring 2002): 21–52.

Wither, George. *A Collection of Emblemes*. 1635. Introduction by Michael Bath. Aldershot: Scolar Press, 1989.

Worman, Nancy. *Abusive Mouths in Classical Athens*. Cambridge: Cambridge University Press, 2008.

Zak, William F. *Sovereign Shame. A Study of King Lear*. Lewisburg: Bucknell University Press, 1984.

DETAILED OUTLINE

Introduction: 'No abuse?' 1
The insulting effect: To do or not to do things with words 3
'Foul wind' and 'poniards' 10
The Shakespearean flyting or the phony war 13

1 The spectacular rhetoric of insult 19
   1 Henry IV or 'gormandizing' abuse 19
      'Unsavoury similes' 21
      'Breathe a while and then to it again' 24
      Bardolph's ambivalent nose 27
   Troilus and Cressida or rank abuse 29
      'Come in and rail' 29
      Telling 'what thou art by inches' 32
      'I'll decline the whole question' 34
   Timon of Athens and execration 39
      'He pours it out' 39
      'Multiplying bans' 42
      'Let … language end' 45

2 The 'merry war': Insult as a love game 49
   The 'skirmishes of wit' in *Much Ado About Nothing* 50
      An art of repartee 50
      'I jest not' 59

'Killing courtesy' in *A Midsummer Night's Dream* 61
   'If you were civil …' 62
   'As this their jangling I esteem a sport' 66
   'If we offend …' 71
   'Odious savours sweet' 78

3 'Quarrelling by the book': Insult and duelling codes 81
   'Do you quarrel, sir?': *Romeo and Juliet* as a story of insult 82
   'The degrees of the lie' in *As You Like It* 97
   'Taunt him with the licence of ink': Writing insults in *Twelfth Night* 101

4 Insults as actionable words 111
   Insult and defamation 112
   The stale and the ass: Noting in *Much Ado About Nothing* 117
     Falling 'into a pit of ink' 117
     'Write me down an ass' 120
     Action on the case for words 125
   'Scandalum Magnatum' in *Measure for Measure* 129
     The degrees of insult 130
     Disputes between neighbours 133
     Mitior sensus 136
     'Treasonable abuses' 138

5 Insult and the taming of the tongue 143
   Richard III or the lessons in cursing 144
     'Teach me how to curse' 145

'Blessings for curses' 154
'Curse not thyself' 156
'That was in thy rage' 157
Drowning the exclamations 158
Charming the 'chattering tongue' in *The Taming of the Shrew* 160
  'Of all titles the worst' 161
  'More shrew than she' 168

6 The trauma of insult 173
Words that wound 174
'Half asleep' in *Othello* 179
The 'ancient grudge' in *The Merchant of Venice* 187
Cymbeline and the memory of abuse 196

7 Insult beyond words 207
The insulting gifts of *Henry V* 210
  'This tun of treasure' 211
  'Here is my glove' 215
  'If you can mock a leek …' 224
'Abatement of kindness': The outrages of *King Lear* 227
  Silent abuse 230
  Resistance to abuse 233
  Insult as subtraction 236

Epilogue: Shakespeare's theatre of insult 241
Beyond a cabinet of curiosities 241
Insults and the life of words 243
Lingua, quo tendis? 246

INDEX

absence (of words) 229–31, 233, 235
abundance 12, 21, 24
abuse (definition) 1–3, 5, 22, 53, 134, 183–6, 236, 239, 249n, 253n
abuse/no abuse 1–18, 88, 100, 172, 211, 223, 242, 247–8, 249n
abuser 25, 131, 162, 183–4, 257n
accusation/accused 8–9, 93–4, 102, 117, 125, 163, 179, 180, 182, 185–6, 194, 203, 236
actionable words 111–42, 158, 265n
Adams, Thomas 13, 146, 252n, 269n, 270n
addition 184, 229
affront 4, 210, 228–32, 237–8
afterlife of words 185, 202
Agon 16, 49, 53, 60, 155, 253n, 260n, 261n
Allan, Keith and Burridge, Kate 15, 196, 253n, 261n
ambivalence 3, 11, 13, 27–9, 37–8, 40, 69, 75–6, 80, 144–5, 183, 185, 241, 244, 246, 278n
ambush insult 32, 157
anamnesia (unforgetting) 9, 190, 200

Anderson, Thomas P. 174, 275n
anger 14–15, 20, 57, 88, 116, 125, 137, 148, 152, 158, 194, 243–4, 284n (*see also* choler, rage)
Archilochus 147, 270n, 271n
Auden W. H. 14–15, 253n
Austin, J. L. 6–8, 250n, 276n

babbling 12
back-biting 143
Baker, John H. 126–7, 129, 138, 265n, 267n, 268n, 269n
Bakhtin, Mikhail 3, 23, 27, 250n, 254n, 255n, 256n
ballad 26, 113–16, 266n
banning 42, 44, 143, 151, 245
Barber, C. L. 52–3, 65, 260n, 261n, 271n
Baret, John 194, 278n
base/debase 22, 29, 34, 59, 88, 196–7, 210, 227, 278n
bastinado/bastanado 31, 177
Bawcutt, Priscilla 13, 252n
bawdy 52, 86, 115, 128, 215–16, 256n
BBC 199, 245–6
Beaumatin, Éric and Michel Garcia 40, 259n
belch(ing) 200
Benoit, Jean-Louis (dir. *Henry V*, 1999, Avignon) 210, 215

Billacois, François 82, 218, 262n, 282n
Birney, Alice Lotvin 145, 270n
bitter (*see* sweet/bitter)
blasphemy 46, 88, 112, 143, 161
blot 118–19, 203
blows 31, 33, 83, 84, 87–8, 92, 94, 107, 110, 174, 176–7, 218
boomerang effect 50, 152, 156–7, 197, 226
Boose, Lynda E. 164, 166, 274n
Bourdieu, Pierre 7–8, 251n
box on the ear 91, 177, 217–20, 222
branks 163
brawl 66, 69, 79, 82, 84, 92, 105, 146, 161–2, 165, 168–9, 217, 274n
breath 10–12, 20, 22, 24–5, 44–5, 58, 71, 74–5, 78, 125, 147, 149–51, 153, 157, 189, 196, 202, 280n
bridle 136, 144, 163–5, 167, 273n
Bulwer, John 208, 280n
Butler, Judith 9, 175, 191–3, 251n, 276n, 278n
Butler, Martin 197, 262n, 279n
buzz 174, 190–1

Cahill, Patricia A. 174, 275n
calumny 93, 139, 140, 195, 202–3, 255n
cannibalism (verbal) 26, 39, 49, 54
Carnival 3, 20, 22–4, 28, 68–9, 104, 108, 166, 168, 254n

cart 164–7
cartel 94, 105–6, 108
Castiglione, Baldassare 50, 52, 74, 78, 260n, 262n
catalogue 32–3, 37, 40, 151, 189, 195
Cavell, Stanley 237, 283n
challenge 5, 10, 17, 35, 60, 63, 65, 69, 82, 87, 90–5, 99, 105–9, 119, 216–17, 219, 223
charivari 166, 274n (*see also* rough music)
chatter 159–60, 273n
choler 15, 137, 209, 243 (*see also* anger, rage)
civility 62, 64, 73, 79, 82, 92, 261n, 263n
clamour 12, 146, 159, 169, 229
Clemen, Wolfgang 145, 270n
comparison/comparative 21–5, 29, 30, 38, 57, 58, 159, 197, 202, 272n
competition 15, 16, 25, 52
compliment 28, 55, 62, 70, 76, 139, 140, 129
compound words 25
contract/pact of aggression 14, 16, 17, 58, 220
convicium 111, 134
copia verborum 24, 256n
Cotgrave, Randle 4, 5, 86, 118, 166, 194, 250n, 263n, 282n
courtesy/courtier 49, 51, 60, 61–80, 97, 100, 176, 261n, 276n
coward(ice) 20, 33, 88, 96, 101–5, 108, 119, 140–1, 207

Craik, T. W. 213, 266n, 281n
creative/creativity 19, 25, 38, 242
Cressy, David 141, 162, 269n, 273n
cucking-stool/ducking-stool 115, 164–7, 247n
cuckold 141, 185
curse/cursing 12, 40–1, 44–7, 66, 74, 143–59, 161, 187, 190, 201, 213, 235–6, 243, 245–6, 260n, 270n, 271n, 273n
cynical 29–31, 41

defamation 18, 59, 68, 111, 112–17, 118, 119, 120, 122, 123, 126, 128, 129, 131, 133, 134, 135, 143, 265n, 266n, 267n, 268n, 277n
deflation 35
degree(s) 36–7, 66, 93, 97–8, 101, 111, 129–30, 179, 221, 224
Della Casa, John (Giovanni) 63, 66, 71, 77, 261n, 262n
demythification 34–5
derision 70, 78, 103
detraction 194–5, 204
di Grassi, Giacomo 81, 262n
Dieterle, William and Max Reinhardt (dir. *A Midsummer Night's Dream*, film, 1935) 67
digest(ion) 21, 31, 43, 121, 177, 196, 209, 226
din 12–13, 68, 159, 169, 246
diplomatic insult 211, 215, 227
disdain 51, 55, 57, 61, 70, 77–9, 168, 194

disgrace/disgracing 83, 117, 130–1, 189, 282n
disgust 40, 45, 67, 154, 196, 226, 256n, 282n
Dusinberre, Juliet 98, 264n

echo(ing) 26–7, 35–7, 67, 70, 178–9, 182, 186, 189, 197, 214, 226
effet injure/insulting effet (Larguèche) 2–10, 58–9, 70, 76, 88, 96, 105, 173, 188, 193, 199, 210, 211, 220, 224, 237, 247, 248, 249n, 256n, 271n, 275n, 278n, 283n
efficiency 11–12, 38, 119, 144, 146–8, 237, 168–9, 177
Elam, Keir 15, 20, 253n, 254n
Elliott, Michael (dir. *King Lear*, 1983) 233
Elliott, Robert C. 39, 41, 259n
Emmison, Frederick 113, 115, 128, 265n, 266n, 267n, 274n
emotion 14–15, 60, 173, 180, 189, 208, 243–4, 253n, 259n, 276n
entertaining 30–1, 53, 68–9, 77, 241
envy 33, 38, 41, 243–5, 257n
Erasmus, Desiderius 13, 252n, 284n
esclandre 118
Escolme, Bridget 15, 253n
evacuation 12, 21, 43, 209, 254n
Evans, Robert, C. 174, 274, 275n, 276n
exaggeration 23, 33

excess 15, 17, 19, 21, 23–4, 39–41, 46–7, 70, 84–5, 90, 108, 134, 136, 145, 152, 161, 229, 236, 241, 244–5, 253n
'excitable speech' 9, 175, 192, 251n, 276n, 278n
exclamation 12–13, 15, 33, 96, 144, 146, 150 158–9, 236
excrement 43, 187, 209, 281n
excretum/excretion 40–1, 43, 45, 209, 259n
execration 39–47, 145, 209, 236

face 6, 10, 26, 27–9, 41, 42–3, 51, 68, 71, 72, 89, 116, 118, 138, 150, 168, 176, 178, 192, 198, 200, 207, 208, 218, 219, 228, 232, 238, 243, 245, 247, 251n, 253n, 256n, 257n, 260n, 280n, 283n
fatness/obesity 22–5, 68, 187–8, 247, 255n
Fay Thomas, Miranda 84, 150, 208, 250n, 263n
Felman, Shoshana 175–6, 276n
Fernie, Ewan 237, 283n
festive 2, 3, 17, 19, 20, 27, 52–4, 58, 69, 166, 168, 260n, 261n, 275n
fig (fico) 86, 208, 216, 263n, 280n, 281n, 282n
Fisch, Harold 43, 260n
Fitzpatrick, Joan 225, 282n
flattery 4, 39–43, 149, 201, 229, 258n, 259n
Florio, John 1, 4, 194, 249n, 250n, 273n

Fly, Richard 40, 259n
flyting 13–17, 19–20, 30, 41, 49, 52–3, 56, 67, 69, 241, 252n, 253n, 254n, 261n
Foakes, R. A. 229, 231, 282n
fool 20, 25, 31, 33, 35–7, 41, 42, 57, 59, 79, 84, 102, 114, 121, 140, 141, 149, 189, 192, 193, 200, 216, 232, 236, 239, 257n, 266n
footing 188, 190, 200, 257n
Forker, Charles 217, 281n
frown(ing) 83, 85, 89, 232, 239

gage 216, 217, 221, 281n
Gaignebet, Claude and Marie-Claude Périer 40, 209, 259n
gall 12, 16, 30, 33, 34, 35, 40, 41, 45, 105, 139, 151
Galway, Margaret 14, 67, 252n, 254n, 261n
gargoyle 40, 259n
gaze/eyes 33, 35, 63, 69, 73, 89–90, 116, 118, 168, 192, 200, 218, 236, 237, 238, 245, 257n, 258n
gentle(ness) 17, 61, 64–5, 66, 70–4, 78, 155
gesture 6, 43, 53, 61–2, 84, 86–7, 90–2, 111, 115, 207–9, 215–19, 224, 231, 233, 243, 245, 250n, 260n, 263n, 280n, 281n, 282n
ghost (verbal) 12, 64, 70, 76, 147, 185, 190

Gibbon, Charles 203, 280n
gift 57, 102–3, 110–27, 242
glove 215–24, 225, 227
good name 112, 135, 203–4, 276n, 280n
gormandizing 19–29
Gowing, Laura 112, 115, 265n, 278n
Greek 37
Gross, Kenneth 11, 44, 236, 251n, 260n, 261n, 277n, 282n
grotesque 23, 28–9, 37, 40–1, 62, 256n
grudge 82, 187–95, 200, 235, 257n, 263n, 281n
Guiraud, Pierre 6, 250n

Hall, Peter (*A Midsummer Night's Dream*, film, 1968) 71
hand 89, 98, 103, 105, 146, 151, 158, 160, 192, 208, 215–18, 235, 243, 255n, 280n
hate 40, 43, 47, 56, 67, 149, 155, 178–9, 187–9, 205, 208, 245, 247, 259n, 270n, 273n
Helmholz, R. H. 122–4, 134, 266n, 267n, 268n
historicity (of the name) 191–2
Hoffman, Michael (*A Midsummer Night's Dream*, film, 1998) 71
Holdsworth, W. S. 112, 265n
Honigmann, E. A. J. 180, 277n
horn(ing) 208, 215–16, 280n

Howard, Skyles 58, 261n
Hughes, Geoffrey 16, 86, 253n, 255n, 263n
Huizinga, Johan 14, 53, 253n
humiliation 3, 10, 30, 115–16, 164–5, 167, 226, 246, 274n
Hunter, J. 178, 276n
hyperbole 24, 33, 234

ill name 123, 203–4, 280n
impact 2–3, 8–9, 34, 38, 67, 88, 120, 129, 150, 169, 171, 173–5, 182–4, 185, 214, 218–19, 224, 233, 246–7
impoliteness 87, 276n, 283n
imprecation 34, 38, 40, 43–4, 146–8, 151, 157, 236
inflation 25, 35, 228
Ingram, Martin 161–5, 273n, 274n
injury 1–10, 15, 84–5, 90, 93, 95, 111, 131, 174–6, 185, 193, 209, 224, 233, 236, 239, 247
inner speech 187, 190, 200, 278n
insult (definition) 1–10
insultment 200–1
intention/intentionality 1, 7, 75, 77, 112, 176, 211, 223, 229, 244, 276n
interpretation 3, 17, 56, 60, 79, 87, 92, 111, 133, 138, 211, 229, 239, 245, 265n
invective 13, 20, 40, 67, 83, 128, 143, 149–50, 155, 215, 251n, 257n, 271n

Irvine, William B. 10, 16, 32, 251n, 253n, 257n, 260n, 283n

Jack(anape) 23–4, 42, 109, 161, 221–2
Janoff-Bulman, Ronnie 175, 180, 185, 276n, 277n
Jeanneret, Michel 22, 254n
jest(ing) 30, 50, 58–60, 67, 69, 77, 115, 119, 149, 213–14, 218, 224, 281n
Jew 188, 191–3, 195, 208
joke/joking 58, 60, 69, 77
Jones, Ann Rosalind and Peter Stallybrass 198, 261n, 279n
Jonson, Ben (*The Alchemist*) 81, 262n, 271n
Jowett, John 45, 260n

Kaplan, Lindsay 142, 269n, 270n
Karim-Cooper, Farah 208, 280n
Kermode, Frank 40, 259n
Kerrigan, John 216–17, 224, 227, 281n, 282n
King, Ros 198, 279n
knave 19, 23, 24, 25, 109, 134, 137, 168, 210, 225–6, 231, 246
Krieger, Elliot 64, 261n

lament(ation) 62, 119, 151–2, 200
Laplanche, Jean 153, 271n
Larguèche, Évelyne 2, 6, 28, 173, 187, 195, 237–8, 249n, 250n, 253n, 256n, 275n, 278n, 283n
Lassiter, John C. 129–32, 267n, 268n

laugh(ter) 23, 54, 57, 100, 135, 189, 193, 213, 244, 247
law/legal action 5–6, 83, 90, 107, 110, 111–42, 161–2, 165–6, 193, 220, 222, 265n, 266n, 267n, 268n
leek 21, 224–7, 282n
Lepage, Robert (*A Midsummer Night's Dream*, film, 1992) 71
letter 94, 105–9, 116, 202, 249n
Lewis, C. S. 19, 254n
libel (suits) 113–15, 123–4, 126, 199, 265n
lie/liar/lying 2, 7, 24, 26, 84, 91–9, 105–9, 143, 145, 170, 176–8, 207, 255n, 256n, 258n, 264n
logorrhea 29, 157
Lyly, William 60, 261n

Maclean, Ian 111, 265n
magic (magical power of words) 7–8, 38, 46, 68, 76, 145–6, 150, 192, 259n
Magnusson, Lynne 230, 249n, 282n
malediction 12, 38, 144–53, 156, 189, 251n, 271n, 273n, 276n
manners 61–5, 68, 74, 77, 94, 98–9, 148, 155, 170–1
March, John 133, 136–7, 268n
Marlowe, Christopher (*Tamburlaine*) 145
Mason, Shirley Carr 145, 270n
materiality of words 10–11, 29, 176–7, 184, 189–90, 202, 209, 212

Mazzio, Carla 252n
McAlindon, T. 34, 258n
McDonald, Russ 13, 252n, 256n, 260n
McEachern, Claire 11, 251n, 261n, 266n
McLaverty, J. 2, 249n
Mendes, Sam (dir. *The Tempest*, 1993) 245
metalinguistic 6, 10–11, 21–2, 34, 49, 146
metaphor 9, 11, 22–3, 30, 33, 71, 171, 175, 192, 197, 201, 203, 213, 226, 232, 257n
Milsom, S. F. C. 122, 266n, 268n, 269n
mistaken identity 110, 138, 217, 221
mitior sensus/ in mitiori sensu 136–8, 158
mock(ing)/mockery 11, 25, 31, 53–4, 70, 77–8, 86, 135, 149, 164, 166, 189, 213–14, 224, 226, 243–4, 246
monster/monstrosity 28, 31, 33, 62, 67, 68, 70, 76, 107, 170, 153
moralization (of status words) 19
Morris, Desmond 207, 280n
mortify 3, 10
Moshinsky, Elijah (*Cymbeline*, BBC film, 1982) 199
murmur 82, 185, 187

noise 11–12, 64, 66–7, 78, 80, 159, 161, 167, 229, 236, 251n, 260n, 261n, 277n, 282n

Northbrooke, Thomas 103, 264n
note/noting 117, 203, 229, 266n

oath 23, 28, 70, 114, 209, 216, 218, 220–2, 253n, 255n, 256n, 272n, 281n
offence 1, 4–5, 62, 64, 71, 75, 79, 87, 89, 91, 93, 101, 106, 122, 123, 126, 128, 130, 136, 162, 165, 172, 209, 217, 219, 222–3, 229, 231, 235–6, 276n, 283n
offender 112, 121, 142, 164, 220
offensive 11, 21, 89, 127, 146, 193, 210, 211, 219, 233, 246–7
Olivier, Laurence (as Lear in Elliott's *King Lear*, film, 1983) 233
outrage 2, 5, 10, 70, 85, 87, 210, 218, 227–39, 247
Ovid 151–2, 271n,

pact/contract of aggression 17, 58, 220
Paradin, Claude 3, 176, 249n, 250n, 276n, 284n
paradoxical encomium 228
Parks, Ward 16, 252n, 253n
passion 14–15, 65, 70, 174, 178, 186, 192, 243, 251n, 253n, 259n, 277n, 278n, 280n, 284n
Peltonen, Markku 87, 92, 263n
performance 71, 75, 78, 174, 217, 244–5, 265n, 275n
performative (speech) 7, 9, 192, 251n

physical (injury/harm) 3, 5–6, 9–10, 14, 16, 17, 22, 24, 31, 33, 45, 69, 83, 87, 93, 99, 102, 111, 120, 121, 131–2, 142, 150, 153–4, 163, 171, 173, 176–8, 184, 190, 193, 201, 205, 208, 218, 226, 228–31, 233, 238, 243–5
ping-pong (verbal) 56
playful and serious modes 3, 14, 17, 49, 56, 58–60, 69, 77, 158, 241–2, 244
poison 12, 41, 114, 143, 193
polite(ness)/polish 64, 69, 73–5, 87, 92, 211, 226, 246, 261n, 263n
pragmatic 1–2, 8, 49, 88, 127, 129, 249n, 250n, 252n
praise and abuse 7, 27–8, 55, 70, 74, 78, 104, 154–5, 171, 196, 203–4, 247, 280n
prejudice 190, 192–3
Post-Traumatic Stress Disorder 179, 190, 200
Puttenham, George 1, 22, 34, 44, 151, 249n, 255n, 256n, 258n, 260n, 271n

quarrel(ling) 31, 35, 66–9, 80, 81–110, 135, 165, 216–18, 222–3, 227, 231, 263n, 256n

rage 41, 77, 95, 117, 148, 157–8, 161, 177, 179, 182–3, 186, 195, 228–31, 236 (*see also* anger, choler)

rail(ing) 29–32, 34, 38, 53, 143, 159, 162, 168–9, 257n, 275n
rank (rancid) 29–30, 101, 200–1
rank (social) 101–2, 129, 131, 197, 200, 218
rascal 21, 25, 33, 36, 160, 210, 221–2, 231
rating 194, 220
rebuke/rebuking 13, 120
reception 3, 17, 60, 62, 75, 86, 100, 111, 222, 233, 235, 243
reproach 4, 5, 13, 66, 177, 204
reputation 59, 113, 124–5, 131, 135, 195, 197, 221
resistance to abuse 65, 226, 229, 233–6
reverberation 174, 178–9
Rhodes, Neil 28, 256n
ricochet 228
Riley, Denise 9, 174, 178, 182, 185–6, 189–90, 193, 195, 200, 251n, 275n, 276n, 277n, 278n
rogue 19, 25, 33, 107, 137
Rossiter, A. P. 145, 270n
rough music 115, 161, 165–6, 168 (*see* charivari)
Rowlands, Samuel 148, 263n, 271n
rude(ness) 33, 64, 67, 70, 71, 73, 79, 128, 219, 261n
rumour 113, 131, 139

sarcasm 10–11, 55
satire 29, 35, 39, 100, 115, 116, 256n, 259n, 270n

Saviolo, Vincentio 81, 85–94, 96, 98–102, 105–6, 108, 262n, 263n, 264n
Sawday, Jonathan 34, 256n, 258n
saying and doing/words and deeds 6, 7, 9, 12, 31, 34, 38, 69, 82–3, 91, 102, 110, 136, 146, 156, 188, 242
Scandalum Magnatum 126, 129–42, 276n, 269n
scoff(ing) 77, 115, 143, 208, 243–4
scold(ing) 13, 58, 115, 160–8, 273n, 274n
scorn 4–5, 11, 15, 30, 54, 70, 77–8, 116, 177, 184, 189, 208–9, 213–14, 224
Scot, Reginald 163, 274n
Scott, Tom 13, 252n
Segar, William 81, 91, 262n, 263n
Shakespeare
   Antony and Cleopatra (AC) 11, 115, 160, 164
   All's Well That Ends Well (AW) 102, 114
   As You Like It (AYL) 5, 18, 53, 82, 97–101, 115, 246, 264n
   The Comedy of Errors (CE) 176
   Coriolanus (Cor) 15, 229, 258n, 259n
   Cymbeline (Cym) 18, 101, 117, 174, 195–205, 272n, 279n, 280n
   Hamlet (Ham) 11, 174–6, 207, 275n
   Julius Caesar (JC) 176
   King Henry IV, Part 1 (1H4) 2, 3, 16–17, 19–29, 68, 114, 135, 176, 212, 249n, 254n, 255n
   King Henry IV, Part 2 (2H4) 1–2, 17, 21, 33, 68, 131, 176, 215, 219, 220, 247–8, 249n, 254n, 276n, 282n
   King Henry V (H5) 18, 21, 110, 177–8, 210–27, 246, 248, 276n, 281n, 282n
   King Henry VI, Part 1 (1H6) 153, 177
   King Henry VI, Part 2 (2H6) 153, 218–19, 244–5
   King Henry VI, Part 3 (3H6) 144, 149, 153, 209, 272n
   King John (KJ) 12
   King Lear (KL) 4, 18, 44, 102, 210, 227–39, 242, 246, 260n, 282n, 283n
   King Richard II (R2) 11, 12, 176, 217, 262n, 281n
   King Richard III (R3) 6, 12, 18, 44, 144–59, 163, 208, 246, 270n, 271n
   Love's Labour's Lost (LLL) 11, 67, 110, 209–10, 260n
   Macbeth (Mac) 272n
   Measure for Measure (MM) 18, 113, 129–42, 269n

INDEX

The Merchant of Venice
(MV) 18, 174, 186–205,
208, 245, 247, 278n
The Merry Wives of Windsor
(MW) 21, 108–9, 254n
*A Midsummer Night's
Dream* (MND) 18, 49,
60–80, 110, 261n
Much Ado about Nothing
(MA) 8, 10, 11, 16–18,
49–60, 67, 79, 82, 110,
115–16, 117–29, 155,
199, 203, 242, 246,
251n, 261n, 266n, 280n
Othello (Oth) 18, 117, 135,
160, 174, 179–86, 195,
203, 208, 247, 276n, 277n
Romeo and Juliet (RJ) 5–6,
18, 82–97, 100, 110, 208,
231, 242, 262n, 263n
The Taming of the Shrew
(TS) 13, 18, 144, 159–72,
209, 247, 275n
The Tempest (Tem) 245
Timon of Athens (Tim) 12,
17, 19, 38–47, 251n,
258n, 259n, 260n, 272n
Titus Andronicus (Tit) 173,
177, 275n
Troilus and Cressida (TC)
17, 19, 29–38, 179, 209,
245, 257n, 258n
Twelfth Night (TN) 18, 55,
65, 82, 101–10, 261n
The Winter's Tale (WT) 117,
185, 203, 277n
shame 63–4, 77, 84, 114–15,
118, 148, 165–7, 208,
234, 237–8, 244, 250n,
283n

Sharpe, J. A. 117, 122, 133,
135, 266n, 268n
Sheppard, William 164, 267n,
274n
shield (verbal) 3, 60, 192, 234,
261n
shock 41, 45, 60, 72, 173, 180,
202
shrew 68, 146, 155–6, 159–72,
273n (*see also The
Taming of the Shrew*)
silence 10, 47, 78, 158–9, 176,
203, 229–33, 239, 247
Silver, George 81, 262n
Silverstone, Catherine 174,
275n
simile 21–4, 256n
sins of the tongue 21, 39, 46,
143, 189, 252n, 259n
skimmington ride 165
slander(ing) 7, 11, 18, 30, 57,
59, 112–19, 124, 126–31,
134–6, 138–9, 141–3,
152, 161, 165, 180, 192,
195, 202–4, 246, 265n,
266n, 267n, 269n, 270n,
277n
slanging matches 14
spit(ting) 6, 26, 41–3, 150,
188–90, 198, 204–5,
208–9, 245, 250n, 271n,
278n
spittle 208–9
Spurgeon, Caroline 229, 282n
spurn(ing) 188–90
stain 82, 189, 197, 202–4
stale 8, 117–19, 202, 258n,
266n, 280n
sticks and stones 15, 253n
Stockholm syndrome 183, 186

stocks 164, 228, 230–1, 234–5, 238
strings (of abuse) 19–20, 24–6, 34–5, 44, 67, 156–7, 170, 228, 241
subtraction 229, 236–9
swallow 10, 21, 43, 176–7, 225
swearing 16, 23, 28, 51, 70, 86, 104, 114–15, 141, 143, 154, 216, 234, 243, 253n, 255n, 263n, 271n, 273n
sweet/bitter 8, 11–12, 21, 24, 27, 30, 39–41, 45, 58–9, 61, 66, 70–1, 73–4, 78–80, 119, 147, 153, 155, 181, 200, 212, 214, 222, 239, 244
Swetnam, Joseph 104–5, 264n
sword 71–2, 84, 87, 91, 98, 106, 108, 110, 132, 202, 218
synecdoche 22–3

Tamburlaine (Marlowe) 145
taming of the tongue 13, 18, 143–72, 252n, 270n
taunt(ing) 15, 101, 105, 110, 115, 213
tavern 2, 20–1, 23, 26, 28, 249n
tennis-balls 211–15, 226–7, 281n
Thacker, David (dir. *The Merchant of Venice*, RSC 1993) 245
throat 40, 43, 99, 103, 107, 176–8, 187–8, 196, 200, 202, 207, 226

thumb-biting 6, 83–4, 86, 92, 208, 231, 250n, 262n, 280n
transfer of insult (substitution) 87, 96, 171, 192, 220, 228
transgression 5, 17, 58, 62, 66, 96, 108–9, 148, 228
trauma 173–205, 237, 241, 275n, 276n
tun 211–12

un-sult 16, 241, 253n
Underdown, D. E. 162, 165, 271n, 273n, 274n
unpredictability 2, 176, 247
unruly (tongue) 12, 21, 143, 161, 212, 251n, 252n, 258n, 259n, 268n, 270n, 273n, 278n, 280n
unspeakability 182–5

vanity 1, 11–12, 20, 22–3, 38, 45, 144, 146, 149–50, 154, 184, 214, 236, 264n
venom(ous) 11, 154, 202, 272n, 273n
verbal match 14, 30, 52, 56, 114, 155, 213–14
Vigarello, Georges 23, 255n
villain(y) 8, 19, 23, 25–6, 42, 45, 57, 60, 92, 95–6, 107, 119–20, 140, 156, 186, 191, 204, 207, 210, 221, 242

Warnke, Frank 16, 49, 53, 56, 253n, 260n, 261n
Watson, Lindsay 46, 260n, 271n

Weis, René 82, 262n
Wells Slights, Camille 171, 275n
whore 8, 45, 104, 115, 117, 138, 141, 163, 166, 180, 182–6, 195, 204, 277n
whoreson 20, 32–3, 256n
Willis, Deborah 173, 275n
wind (foul) 10–12, 60, 82, 136, 169

witch 32, 133, 146, 163, 270n
Wither, George 3, 250n
wrangling 13, 164
Wray (Chief Justice) 133, 137
Wright, Thomas 243–4, 284n

Zak, William F. 237, 283n
Zeffirelli, Franco (*The Taming of the Shrew*, film, 1966) 169

www.ingramcontent.com/pod-product-compliance
Lightning Source LLC
Chambersburg PA
CBHW052147300426
44115CB00011B/1559